Stamp Collecting For Dummies

BESTSELLING BOOK SERIES

Where to go for information about your stamps

- Local library
- Specialized philate...s, a... ... available online an... ...elsewhere
- Local stamp clubs
- National stamp organizations, such as the American Philatelic Society and the American Topical Association
- Specialized organization, such as Dogs on Stamps
- Online searches

Choosing an album

- Pre-printed pages or do-it-yourself ...e or both
- Paper quality
- Single country, regional, worldwide, or topical
- What are the provisions for updating?

Where to obtain stamps for your collection

- Local post office
- Local stamp dealers
- Foreign postal administrations or U.S. agents
- Stamp dealers from your own and others' incoming mail
- Swapping

Tool kit ...

- Tongs
- Perforation gauge
- Millimeter measuring device
- Magnifier (one that's at least 5X and perhaps a second at 10X)
- Watermark detector
- Short-wave UV light to determine tagging (if you're collecting a country's stamps where this matters).

Where stamps may differ (varieties)

- Design difference
- Color
- Gum (issued with/without, type of gum, gum/self-stick)
- Perforation measurement
- Configuration (booklet, pane, coil)

Finding a fake

- A narrower stamp
- Uneven perforations

And overprint forgery will have

- Ink of a different color or shade
- Different type or font
- Irregular letter spacing
- Irregular line spacing

For Dummies: Bestselling Book Series for Beginners

Stamp Collecting For Dummies®

Cheat Sheet

Philatelic etiquette basics

- When writing to another collector, or even a dealer, enclose a stamped, self-addressed, return envelope
- When sending anything to another collector, use commemorative stamps that the recipients may soak and save
- Never touch someone's stamps with your bare hands — use tongs

Keep your stamps away from

- Humidity
- Anything liquid other than watermark fluid
- Extreme heat
- Cellophane tape
- Ball-point pens
- Rubber bands
- Paper clips
- Plastic substances you are not certain to be stable and safe (PVC)

References to have on hand

- Your inventory — as much for insurance purposes as for just knowing what you have
- Stamp catalogue or advanced checklist covering your area(s) of interest
- Current subscription to stamp-collecting periodical
- Newsletter or journal of specialty groups to which you belong (save them!)
- URLs of your favorite stamp-collecting Web sites

For Dummies: Bestselling Book Series for Beginners

Praise For Stamp Collecting For Dummies

"Dick Sine has had some of the best writing jobs in stamp collecting, and this book shows why: A thorough knowledge of philately and good writing, mixed with humor and style."

— Lloyd A. de Vrise, The Virtual Stamp Club

"With his deep insight into the 160-year old pastime of stamp collecting, Dick Sine proves that philately is not only the hobby for the 21st century, but one that can be easily and inexpensively enjoyed by everyone! The world's stamps depict life on Planet Earth — from the tiniest microbe to world famous athletes. This book will make understanding and collecting them a joy!"

— Randy L. Neil, author and former President of the American Philatelic Society

"*Stamp Collecting For Dummies* is great for removing so many of the issues a newcomer to our hobby has, allowing instant enjoyment. Stamp collecting can be a complex hobby, and this cuts right through."

— Hugh M. Goldberg, Subway Stamp Shop, Inc.

"This is a long overdue masterpiece, which will surely facilitate the expansion of this royal hobby by allowing everybody the ability to understand the complexities and the beauty of stamp collecting. The breadth of knowledge in this book spans by answering all the initial questions that might arise for the beginner collector, to details for the avid philatelist. A wonderful job by Mr. Sine."

— Chesky Malamud and Eli Popack, Founders of Stampville.com (the online Stamp portal)

"Dick Sine has produced a solid and practical introduction to the world's greatest pastime, stamp collecting. His work is not only invaluable to beginners but also of great value to intermediate collectors, especially with his Internet-savvy advice."

— Gene Mierzejewski, Editor, *The Flint Journal*

Stamp Collecting

FOR

DUMMIES®

Stamp Collecting
FOR
DUMMIES®

by Richard L. Sine

WILEY

Wiley Publishing, Inc.

Stamp Collecting For Dummies®

Published by
Wiley Publishing, Inc.
111 River Street
Hoboken, NJ 07030
www.wiley.com

Library of Congress Cataloging-in-Publication Data:

Library of Congress Control Number: 2001091986

ISBN: 0-7645-5379-8

Manufactured in the United States of America

10 9 8 7 6 5 4 3 2

3B/RV/QR/QU/IN

About the Author

Dick Sine is known in stamp collecting for more than a quarter-century of writing and editing. He is the director of philatelic operations for the Web site www.stampville.com and also assists the noncommercial Web site www.AskPhil.org as Web master. He authored the successful CD-ROM *Encyclopedia of U.S. Postage Stamps* and wrote two correspondence courses on stamp collection for Pennsylvania State University. Former editor of *The American Philatelist* and editorial director at Scott Publishing Co., he also edited the reissue of both the Minkus *Standard Catalog of U.S. Stamps* and the *Sanabria airmail catalog*. He developed and produced the first electronic magazine for stamp collecting, *NetSTAMPS*.

Author's Acknowledgments

Stamp collecting is such a broadly based hobby, both in terms of the spectrum of what is available to become part of your collection and where collectors are located. Even with more than a quarter century as a writer and editor in the hobby, I still did not have enough resources to produce this manuscript without far more help than I thought I would need when I agreed to the project. I am proud to be part of a hobby/industry where no request I made for help in this project was rebuffed. Throughout my career, when bragging about stamp collecting as having the largest body of literature of any hobby, I never calculated how the Internet would so greatly increase the available information.

Fortunately, I was able to seek assistance for this book from long-time friends as well as from some whom I only have known for a short time. I also reviewed the writing of many, many people who have come before me.

Of most help on this project — even though he may not have realized it — is Les Winick, with whom I have plotted on a variety of projects well back into the last century. Also influencing this work are those who helped get the Web site www.AskPhil.org off the ground, as well as the thousands of persons — perhaps you are one of them — who have sent in questions to be answered.

Thanks particularly to those who contributed artwork or other special assistance: Hugh Goldberg of Subway Stamps, Ken Martin and Frank L. Sente at the American Philatelic Society, Dave Cunningham, Joe Luft, Richard Canupp, Eli Popack, and Chesky Malamud.

The people at Hungry Minds are great in a demanding sort of way. I have enjoyed working with Tonya Maddox and Esmeralda St. Clair in particular, but I know there are others there who are part of the team producing this book.

My bride of many decades, Bev, is most understanding of my writing ways and my bounding through the house in search of an idea, a proper word, or a snack.

Publisher's Acknowledgments

We're proud of this book; please send us your comments through our online registration form located at www.dummies.com/register.

Some of the people who helped bring this book to market include the following:

Acquisitions, Editorial, and Media Development

Project Editor: Tonya Maddox

Acquisitions Editor: Michael Cunningham

Copy Editor: Esmeralda St. Clair

Acquisitions Coordinator: Tracy Boggier

Technical Editor: Lester Winick

Editorial Manager: Jennifer Ehrlich

Editorial Assistant: Jennifer Young

Cover Photos: Stephen B. Myers/ International Stock

Production

Project Coordinator: Dale White

Layout and Graphics: Clint Lahen, Jackie Nicholas, Barry Offringa, Brent Savage, Jacque Schneider, Betty Schulte, Brian Torwelle, Jeremey Unger, Erin Zeltner

Proofreaders: Marianne Santy, TECHBOOKS Production Services

Indexer: TECHBOOKS Production Services

Publishing and Editorial for Consumer Dummies

Diane Graves Steele, Vice President and Publisher, Consumer Dummies
Joyce Pepple, Acquisitions Director, Consumer Dummies
Kristin A. Cocks, Product Development Director, Consumer Dummies
Michael Spring, Vice President and Publisher, Travel
Brice Gosnell, Associate Publisher, Travel
Suzanne Jannetta, Editorial Director, Travel

Publishing for Technology Dummies

Richard Swadley, Vice President and Executive Group Publisher
Andy Cummings, Vice President and Publisher

Composition Services

Gerry Fahey, Vice President of Production Services
Debbie Stailey, Director of Composition Services

Contents at a Glance

Cartoons at a Glance

By Rich Tennant

page 161

page 91

page 263

page 49

page 235

page 205

page 7

Cartoon Information:
Fax: 978-546-7747
E-Mail: richtennant@the5thwave.com
World Wide Web: www.the5thwave.com

Table of Contents

Introduction

Welcome to *Stamp Collecting For Dummies*. Use this book as your gateway to a hobby with more than a century and a half of history, customs, and jargon. Postage stamps have evolved mightily since Great Britain's 1840 Penny Black, the world's first adhesive postage stamp, from simple designs featuring the monarch to works of art literally condensed to postage-stamp size.

Hundreds of thousands of different stamps have been issued since 1840, and the great majority remains reasonably priced to the collector. For those that have appreciated in value, their actual market value is determined by factors that you can read about in this book. To preserve that value, you must remember that stamps (with rare exception) are small pieces of paper. If you want to keep those small pieces of paper intact for decades, then you must give your stamps special care.

For many years, in various jobs ranging from editor of *The American Philatelist* to editorial director at Scott Publishing Company to a current slot as Web master at www.askphil.org, I have responded to questions from noncollectors who inherited a collection or accumulation of postage stamps or those who wanted to start a stamp collection for themselves or with their children. These repetitive questions make this book a necessity. Dumb questions about stamp collecting are nonexistent, particularly those from a newcomer to the hobby. After all, prior to thinking of collecting stamps, your only probable association with those little pieces of paper was to affix one to an envelope just before a trip to the closest mailbox.

About This Book

Inheriting a collection of perhaps thousands of stamps can be a daunting experience. Likewise, not knowing what to do after dipping your big toe into the waters of *philately* (the fancy word for stamp collecting) may also cause concern. This book can help you cross the threshold from noncollector to stamp collector because it is based on actual issues raised by people in your same situation rather than merely a series of lectures on the theory of this hobby. Keep that thought in mind and never be afraid to ask questions.

With so many stamps from so many countries, your choice of what to collect is literally without boundaries. This book presents some guidelines to distinguish, outline, and narrow the sometimes overwhelming scope of choices and help you get started, but these are only guidelines. You decide what you want to collect and how.

No matter what interests you have in life, you can parallel them with a stamp collection. You may want to base a collection on your family heritage, your occupation or profession, a favorite vacation trip, your favorite sport, or merely something that attracts your attention. Your collection may consist of stamps from a potential vacation spot that today is but a dream. Or, chronicle the development — through illustrations on postage stamps — of your favorite automobile.

Although I never suggest that your stamp collection may someday be sold for a tidy profit, this book can help you get the most out of your stamp-collecting expenditures.

Why You Need This Book

Unlike other such texts, this one does not dwell on the heavy technical aspects of postage stamps. Certainly, quite a few of them exist that relate to the study of paper, watermarks, printing, inks, and color. You can obtain college credit, and even a degree, in one of the fields of paper and printing. This level of knowledge, however, is not a requirement for enjoyment as a stamp collector. There is plenty of room for you to have a tremendous experience without ever finding out how to distinguish the various types of *rouletting* — a term I leave for Chapter 3.

Much stamp-collecting literature — this hobby has perhaps the largest body of literature of any hobby — is rather formal. Often stamp collecting appears to be somewhat stuffy. Pshaw! A hobby is what you make it, and this book introduces a side of stamp collection that is enjoyable, educational, and actually fun. I may be penalized and suffer loss of my green eyeshade for at least six months as a result of this statement, but I am prepared to stand by my oft-repeated belief that I am involved in stamp collecting because I enjoy it.

After all, how can a hobby be stuffy when countries are issuing stamps that honor and depict the likes of Sammy Davis, Jr., the Marx Brothers, Bing Crosby, and even the World Wrestling Federation?

How This Book Is Organized

This book is organized to provide you with a concise introduction and overview as well as information that has you — in no time — involved in collecting. Only then do you move on to allied areas.

Part I: Getting the Fundamentals Licked

Stamp collecting is not — or at least it is no longer — the domain of near-elderly males. If you fit that stereotype, welcome home! If not, you are still invited to participate as a member of one of the world's oldest hobbies. In Part I you can see when your stamp holdings move from being an accumulation to a collection. There is a difference. You can discover some of the hobby's history that began shortly after the first postage stamp was issued in 1840. From history you move to the anatomy of a stamp, following an introduction to the tools of stamp collection. You need to understand at least a stamp's major body parts. Although the level of detail can become intense, my goal is to offer you only just enough for you to be comfortable. This book provides you the information to purchase wisely and understand philatelic terms and jargon. This way, you can move in any direction that you choose later. Of course, you cannot build a stamp collection if you do not obtain stamps. Your local post office is but one stop on your increasing list of places to shop. Buckle your seat belt, the ride is about to begin.

Part II: Making the Most of Your Moolah

Even if you are beginning your own stamp collection based on the one you inherited, you certainly want some idea of the expenses you face. The value of your material, whether a collection you obtained or one you are building, depends heavily on the grade and condition of the individual items. *Value* is a term with some specific meanings within stamp collection. Knowledge of the concept of value and what sort of questions to ask prior to making a major purchase are important to your long-term return should you ever choose to sell your collection. Everything up to this point in the book applies to whatever you choose to collect, or however you choose to collect.

Part III: Stampeding Is a Group Thing

If you are just beginning a stamp collection, you are in search of a good source of stamps. If you already have a collection underway, you are in search of a good source of stamps to build that collection. There is a pattern here. Not only will you be searching existing sources of stamps, but you can also discover plenty of other possibilities that you have not yet considered. Because stamp collecting is a personal hobby, you may find that involving the whole family increases the enjoyment for everyone. Everyone need not collect the same material, but just enjoying stamp collecting as a family increases everyone's level of knowledge. As you build your collection, you may want to show it off — at a stamp exhibit.

Part IV: Customizing Your Collection

Now comes the time to move beyond stamp-collecting theory. Part IV introduces you to three different general collecting areas. More than three-quarters of all stamp collectors in the United States collect the stamps of the country. That percentage is pretty much mirrored in other countries of the world. Look, then, at a brief introduction to collecting U.S. stamps. You may be able to apply much of what is presented in that chapter to collecting the stamps of any country in which you are living at the time. Because of your heritage, travel, military service abroad, or any other reason(s), you may want to collect the stamps of another country. A different range of challenges faces those who collect stamps from other countries, although the task is far from daunting. Or, you may want to develop a stamp collection that is theme based — thematic or topical — where you collect on the basis of what is shown on the stamp rather than the origin of the stamp. This popular approach to stamp collecting is now the starting point of most new collectors everywhere.

Part V: Protecting Your Collection

Providing a good home for your increasing collection of small paper bits is critical to their preservation. Short of you becoming a neat freak, you should develop an orderly method of handling additions to your holdings. You have the opportunity to choose from many approaches. Having a keen eye for faked material, in case you are offered phony material as *real,* also is a form of protection — protection of your pocketbook. Fortunately, you will not see much chicanery in the hobby of stamp collecting, but a brief introduction to it certainly is in order if only to keep in the back of your mind. Then, again, the darker side of stamps may fascinate you, and you'll want to obtain such material as part of your collection. Properly labeled, spurious material easily fits into a more general collection or even becomes a collection unto itself. In some cases, you cannot be expected to know if an item is real or not, which opens the door to recognized experts who perform verification services in such situations. Unfortunately, this part is that much more important because the fakers do not wear black hats nor do the experts wear white hats.

Part IV: The Parts of Ten

These lists provide specific, hands-on information. First is a listing of items to consider when attempting to identify a stamp, any stamp. You may not need to go through each area every time you want to identify a stamp, but this grouping shows you how complete something as small as a postage stamp is. When you find yourself with stamps to sell or otherwise dispose of, Chapter 17 shows you ten different approaches to consider. Not all approaches work with all stamp material, but at least one can help you each time. And, as much as you need to be grounded in the theory of whatever you do, sometimes not until I see answers to actual questions does the information begin to sink in. So, this part ends with an array of actual questions from beginners or newcomers to stamp collecting.

Part VII: Appendixes

Stamp collecting is one of the few hobbies that you may practice by yourself. It is possible to be a collector for decades with no one around you being the wiser. At the same time, there is much to be gained by sharing your interest with others. Tips on where and how to find other collectors provide you a flying start.

If you cannot find a local stamp club or a specialty group to meet your interests, you can find ample help to start such a group. Internet messaging and chat rooms have stimulated communications among collectors. Stamp shows or bourses are underway every weekend somewhere in this country. Rounding out the section is a rather large glossary of stamp-collecting terms.

Icons Used in This Book

Throughout this book are these handy road signs that point you to valuable advice and away from potential hazards.

The information next to this icon can help you spend wisely and, therefore, have additional pennies (or more) for the stuff you really can use.

An old, old hobby that continues to evolve has developed many shortcuts to help its participants have more fun. This icon highlights some of the most important for you.

This is the type of information you want at your fingertips. Consider marking these pages for quick reference.

Here are terms, used in context, which you will want to know and be able to use in your pursuit of stamp collecting.

No matter how many commercially available stamp-collecting tools you obtain, developing and using your own collection for reference can ease your introduction to stamp collecting early on and enhance your enjoyment down the road.

Part I
Getting the Fundamentals Licked

The 5th Wave   By Rich Tennant

"I'm still feeling nauseous and disoriented all day. I think it's that cheap magnifying glass I bought for examining my stamp collection."

In this part . . .

This part discusses what stamp collecting offers you as a hobby and just what some of the neat things are about it. If you are considering stamp collecting for a hobby, you probably already have an accumulation. You can see tips on how to change your accumulation into a collection.

Postage stamps have a rich history. That history, however, only goes back to 1840. Prior to that time, the recipient paid the postage on a letter. Postage stamps tend to be among the most taken-for-granted items. Discover the various stamps that pay other types of postage. Then, you find out about items that look and feel like postage stamps, but are just not.

Getting physical, you can discover each part of a stamp, so when you hear other collectors talking about measuring perforations, checking watermarks, or if the stamp has gum you can fully understand. Analyzing the physical side of a postage stamp requires at least a minimum set of tools, which are described in detail.

Chapter 1

Uncovering Stamp Collecting's Coolness

Not everyone who is interested in stamp collecting is a collector. Some are pack rats, a cousin of the collector (much as the mouse is a cousin of the rabbit). Still others cannot bear to keep anything that does not have a pragmatic use. You probably are considering stamp collecting for one of three reasons:

- ✔ You inherited a relative's stamp collection.

- ✔ You have a child who needs a hobby quieter than testing the resonance of items struck by a metal object.

- ✔ Upon bringing your firstborn home, you realize that the days of doing anything at the spur of the moment and for sustained periods is gone for the foreseeable future.

If not one of the above, no loss. You are embarking on a hobby that has been with us for more than 150 years and includes people from all walks of life, from all parts of the world, and with amazingly diverse interests. You can set the rules for how you collect: what, when, and to what extent. The freedom is wonderful. And that's a big part of what's so cool about stamp collecting.

It's time to tear down stereotypes and realize just how broad this hobby can be.

Turning Your Accumulation into a Collection

Before you collect, you accumulate. Yes, it is the same concept as crawling before you walk. An accumulation literally may be a pile of stamps, whether loose on a desk, in a drawer, or in a large envelope. You will not be able to find a given item instantly; you will not have any idea of what is included in the pile. A collection has been formed (very often from an accumulation) and has enough of a form that you are able to locate and identify items within it.

Here are a couple of attributes of a stamp *accumulation:*

- Current possessions are in no particular order.
- You don't plan on purchasing any more.

And here are a couple of attributes of a stamp *collection:*

- Orderly storing of items in album, stock book, or individual envelopes
- Purchases made to remain current with new issues and/or fill in previous issues

See the difference? Before you get to the stage of actually calling what you have a *collection,* you need to move beyond buying stamps at the post office and putting them into a drawer. Some basic steps will take you into the collector's arena:

1. **Commit to caring for your stamps and finding a good home for them.**

   If nothing else, leaving those purchases in a drawer is not good for the stamps themselves. They need some sort of a home — an album, a glassine, or at least a box. Part V presents a much more detailed explanation of the various ways to keep your stamp collection healthy and happy.

   In the beginning, you need only to commit to taking care of those little pieces of paper that are subject to all the frailties of any paper. Take care of them and the stamps can be part of your collection for a really long time. See more about this in Chapter 14.

2. **Strategize your purchases.**

   Beyond caring for the stamps, you need to develop some order to your collecting. This may be as simple as being certain you purchase each new stamp available at your post office. More items are available to you if your post office has a philatelic window.

Get your phil at the PO

More items are available to you if your post office has a philatelic window. (*Philatelic* — pronounced "fill-a-*tell*-ic" — is a really fancy way of saying "having to do with stamp collecting." *Philatelist* — pronounced "fill-AT-a-list" — is a really fancy way of saying "someone who collects stamps" — you get the idea.) The catch is that there are only a few hundred philatelic windows across the U.S. This is a quirk that does not sit well among stamp collectors, but it is something that can be overcome with a number of online and mail order services. See more about this in Chapter 7.

3. **Establish a relationship with one or more stamp dealers.**

    This relationship may extend to the point of having them send you material they believe fits your collection. You also may choose to shop from ads in stamp-collecting publications or online offerings, finding all items new to your collection by yourself. You can find out more about strategies in Chapters 7 and 8.

4. **Use a printed catalogue to note the stamps you have and (just as important) those you do not have.**

    The U.S. Postal Service annually publishes a colorful catalogue of U.S. stamps, *The Postal Service Guide to U. S. Stamps,* covering everything from 1847 to the present. A host of private publishers offers a wide range of such catalogues; some are even available on CD-ROMs that provide more detail.

With these basics safely in hand, you can devote your energies to building your collection and seeing where it leads you. Because stamp collectors generally enjoy both the search and research, your collection may easily open up new learning opportunities that extend far beyond stamp collecting. Stamp collecting may inspire you to read new books, travel to new places, try different foods, meet new people — the possibilities are endless! (And that's another really cool thing about stamp collecting.)

Collecting Your Thoughts

Prepare for what is probably the most forceful statement I will make: Stamp collecting has no rules! You are free to collect what and how you want — one more really cool thing about stamp collecting! Of course, before you follow that dictum, you need some idea of just what's available for collecting.

Variety is the fruit of life

For stamp collectors, however, those were fruitful times. Print production was not nearly as advanced as it is today, with many stamp varieties available. Varieties may be in perforation measurement, color, paper type, or definable difference in the actual stamp design (see Chapter 3) from one printing to the next, or there may even be differences among stamps on the same sheet. All these become quite collectible and cause many collectors to salivate while going through mounds of stamps with a magnifying glass and a handful of other tools (see Chapter 3, I tell you!). Thus developed the stereotype of the stamp collector with magnifier and eyeshade . . . with green as the dominant eyeshade color.

Even with the improvements in stamp productions, the "need" for the magnifying glass continues. Changes in production methods brought on new types of varieties. Modern methods may be faster and more colorful, but they do not produce flawless results. Stamp collectors seek those flaws. Life is good for the stamp collector.

For more than the first half-century of postage stamps, first issued in 1840, until about the end of the nineteenth century, commemoratives did not exist. Stamps at that time generally showed a portrait of the monarch, ruler, president, or whoever was leading a country at the time. The same portrait was used for a lengthy set of stamps, each with a different denomination. The same portrait may have been used for more than one set over a period of years or even decades. The stamp designs were rather drab — a single color — although many showed exquisite engraving skills. *Commemoratives* generally are of a more interesting design, and honor a person (other than the heads of government or state), place, thing, or event. Commemoratives generally are on sale for a more limited time and, therefore, are produced in lesser quantities than regular or *definitive* stamps. *Definitives* are often less colorful (although that is changing), produced in far greater quantity, and on sale for a much longer period of time than are commemoratives.

Beginning in the late 1940s, following the end of World War II, postage stamps of the world took on a whole new look. Stamps are now extremely colorful, are able to depict most of the great works of art in postage-stamp size, and offer an array of collecting possibilities. The intervening half-century was one of transition.

From 1840 until now, more than 650 different countries have issued stamps (most are countries that no longer exist in the same form or under the same name). From then until now, something like 450,000 different stamps have been issued. Currently at the rate of more than 12,000 a year! Look at the variety a collector has to choose from. How cool is that?

Your own collection has great opportunity for personalization. You have so many approaches open to you that your collection is "you."

Vegetable, animal, or mineral?

So what does all this mean to you, other than large numbers? In short, no matter what interests you, you can parallel that interest with a collection of postage stamps. You are free to limit or broaden your collection as you like, make those decisions when you want, and literally do your own thing.

In a nutshell, here are the three basic types of postage stamp collections:

- ✔ **Country:** You can create a stamp collection from the stamps available where you live or have visited, the land of your ancestors, or even a travel fantasy. More than 650 countries have issued stamps from 1840 to the present, with many of those countries no longer in existence under the same name and/or government. Currently, more than 260 countries issue postage stamps. Each country's stamps are a possibility for a most interesting collection.

  A very, very high percentage of all stamp collectors collect the stamps of their country of residence. No surprise there. If nothing else, those stamps are the easiest to obtain. The longer you collect stamps, however, the more chance that you will begin one or more additional collections. Your supplementary collections may relate to previous or desired travel, an opportunity to find out about something new, or something as specific as a tribute to an automobile you once owned.

- ✔ **Thematic/topical:** A stamp collection may be based on the design of the stamp rather than what country it was made in. Orangutans depicted on stamps certainly are a possibility, as are spiders. And make your dreams come true with Ferrari racing cars. *Topical* is used in the U.S.; other countries use *thematic*.

- ✔ **Type of mail service:** Airmail, postage due, or one of an array of lesser-known services can also be the basis for a collection. Many countries issue stamps specifically for airmail service. The U.S. still has such stamps in its inventory, although the number is much less now that airmail service is limited to foreign mail. Airmail is no longer a domestic-mail service. The appearance of a postage-due stamp on an envelope you receive denotes that the sender did not pay the full postage cost. U.S. Post Office staff members handstamp or even scrawl with a pen to show postage due, although there have been quite a few postage-due stamps over the years. The situation is somewhat similar with most other countries.

Expanding on your initial collection area

Here is scenario with far more truth than fiction: You visit your local zoo and spend most of your time watching the penguins. You are intrigued by them and decide to collect stamps with penguins as part of the design. After a few years, you find you pretty much have all those stamps. Why stop now? Expand your collection to include what penguins eat, for example. Then, you can consider how else are you able to expand. Use that logic with almost anything, and you have a hobby for life!

Perhaps you would like to begin by collecting the stamps of the land of your ancestors. Depending on their origin, it is very possible such a collection will include the stamps of more than one country, as strife has severely changed country boundaries over the years. Or, maybe you want to begin a collection that shows your occupation as depicted on postage stamps. If you are a truck driver, for example, you have a wealth of possibilities from countries all over the globe. Included are stamps that show specific marques and models of trucks, in addition to stamp designs showing the trucks at work.

Perhaps the niece of a former neighbor represented the U.S. in the Olympic games. That is reason enough to begin a collection of stamps depicting the Olympics — quite a popular collecting area. You may want to limit the collection to just the javelin event, which will provide you with enough stamps to keep you interested and cause you to do a little research to make sure you have not missed one.

The variety of collections that you can pursue has no end. Likewise, there are no requirements as to how much time you need to spend with your collection. Spend a couple hours a weekend when you have some time to kill. Or, if you're so inspired, spend several hours a day researching stamps online and going through your annual guides. The key thought to keep with you is that stamp collecting is a hobby, your hobby, and you are free to practice it as you want.

It's not such a small world after all

I have not given much play to the idea of collecting all the stamps of the world. With the 450,000 or so stamps already issued and the total expanding at some 12,000 new stamps a year, this is an area requiring considerable (!) time, storage space, record-keeping, and, of course, expense. One album manufacturer, Scott Publishing Co., of Sidney, Ohio, produces a set of albums that essentially cover the stamps of the world. The first volume includes the stamps from 1840–1940. The second volume covers 1940–1949. More recently, volumes cover but a single year. The annual volumes, which supplement the series and are therefore considered a "supplement," now contain hundreds of album pages that are printed both sides. Alas, one of those supplements itself may represent a collection . . . that is, choose a significant year in your life and collect all stamps issued that year, knowing that you have a preprinted album to help guide you in your shopping. More about albums and supplements in Chapter 14.

Rebel without a stamp

Only once in history — at the beginning of the Civil War to prevent U.S. stamps from being used in the Confederacy — were U.S. stamps demonetized. That is, postal authorities in Washington, D.C., at the beginning of the war, proclaimed that stamps issued before 1861 were not valid for postage. All U.S. postage stamps issued from 1861 through the present may be used on mail.

Unless you plan to collect counterfeits and forgeries, and you already know much about them, stay away from anything you know to be fake. Also, always buy quality items. Purchase the best example of a stamp that you are able to afford. Many collectors believe that leaving a blank space in your album is better than purchasing a damaged stamp just to fill the space. For more information about forgeries, sneak over to Chapter 15.

Moneymaking Venture

Some folks find that they want to move on to other interests. They've collected penguins, what penguins eat, where penguins live, what penguins wear . . . you get the idea. Those flightless birds may be worth a few greenbacks if you can sell them to the right person.

Many hobbies require a great deal of equipment and supplies that are used up or leave you with a resale value substantially less than what you originally paid. Photography and ham radio are two such enjoyable hobbies.

Stamp collecting does not require substantial investment in equipment or supplies, and you *may* be fortunate enough to sell your collection at a profit . . . or at least for an amount near to what you paid. (More about the ins and outs of value in Chapter 6.) Certainly the returns have no guarantees, for many stamps have quite a low resale value. Further, you are dealing with the fragility of paper, which can degrade over time if not properly maintained. More about storing and protecting your stamps in Chapter 14.

One advantage for U.S. residents collecting U.S. stamps is that unused U.S. stamps can always be used for postage. So, at least for all stamps purchased at the post office at face value, you may have years of enjoyment and, if you're unable to sell them for a profit, you may still use them to get your sewage-bill payment to its destination. Yes, a dozen low-value stamps on an envelope is legal; I do it all the time.

Right now your big question may be, "How do I know how much to pay for the stamps I want?" The answer is easy if you buy current stamps from a post office: face value. But what if you're looking at older or foreign stamps? Here's what you do.

As you become more deeply involved in stamp collecting, your purchasing skills will improve. Also improving will be your identification skills; there will come a time when you will identify as a more valuable item, something originally believed to be of minimal value.

Be wary of anyone who offers you stamps or any philatelic material with a guarantee that it will appreciate in one, five, or even ten years. As with most things in life, there are few guarantees!

So, as you can see, stamp collecting is cool. You get to pick what you collect, and how much of it. You can control the amount of money and time that you spend on your collection. And you don't even need to build an extra room onto your house to store them all.

Chapter 2

A Stamp by Any Other Name

. . . .

. . . .

*B*efore postage stamps arrived on the scene in 1840, whoever received mail had to pay for its postage. Think of paying for mail that you receive in today's environment: You would be required to pay the postage on all the junk mail you receive, along with the bills and holiday cards from relatives you don't otherwise see.

Along came Sir Rowland Hill, who convinced the British Post Office to move to prepayment, at a lower rate. For ideas such as that, he was given the reputation of being a reformer. In the more than 160 years since that first British stamp, many other major changes took place in the movement of mail, necessitating changes in postage stamps.

The more changes there were, the more new and different stamps, the more countries that began to utilize postage, and the more curiosity and interest in those little pieces of paper. Then came the new hobbyist: the stamp collector. As collectors' interest in postage stamps grew, so appeared many other items that look like postage stamps. Some stamp look-alikes have meaning and are used to pay various taxes or services; others are just plain fake.

Paying Prepostage versus on Receipt

The first postage stamp, issued on May 6, 1840, in England, was printed in black ink, sported a portrait of Queen Victoria, and included its value (one penny). That stamp has become known as the Penny Black. Thus, a revolution began — the age of postage stamps. The stamp did not include the name of it issuing country, nor have any Great Britain postage stamps since. The world's first postage stamp also produced stamp collecting's first oddity: the only country never to have printed its name on its postage stamps.

The idea of postage prepayment and postage stamps themselves caught on quickly. Not only did prepayment speed up mail delivery — the letter carrier no longer had to hand deliver each item and await payment — it also provided money up front, as well as money for stamps that were never used for postage (look at all those unused stamps still in the hands of stamp collectors). Brazil followed in 1843 with its first postage stamp, and late in the decade as other countries saw merit to the concept, a flurry of activity resulted. The U.S. issued its first postage stamp July 1, 1847. In fact, two different U.S. stamps were issued that day: a five-cent stamp showing Benjamin Franklin and a ten-cent stamp bearing a portrait of George Washington. Canada's first postage stamp was issued in 1851.

Stamp designs in those early years were rather drab by today's standards. The stamps were printed in one color (black or reddish brown), with the design generally portraying the country's leader or another well-known person.

After postage stamps became established, most countries of the world were using them not too many years later. Beyond their use for basic postage, stamps were soon issued for more specific types of postal services, such as newspaper delivery by mail, special delivery, (a little later) airmail, and others that no longer exist.

Enter the stamp collector

Not very long after the Penny Black and its colleagues around the world came an interest in saving those unusually small pieces of paper. Stamp collecting in its beginning did not look a whole lot like what it is today. But, a collector who is in search of something elusive has the same drive to build a collection today, as collectors had in the mid-1800s. For example, a young lady in the 1841 *London Times* advertised for enough stamps to cover her dressing room wall.

Yesterday's collector

In the following year, the British humor magazine *Punch* mentioned the stamp-collecting mania in which local young ladies were engaged. The magazine noted that the women "betray more anxiety to treasure up Queen's heads than Henry VIII did to get rid of them."

And that was just the beginning. The first postage stamp catalogue, listing all known stamps at the time, was published in December 1861. The catalogue reportedly consisted of ten printed pages. Today, Scott Publishing Co., a U.S. firm producing an annual catalogue of the world's stamps, publishes a six-volume series numbering well into the thousands of pages.

Paris boasts the first stamp club, begun in 1865. The second such club was founded in New York City two years later. The first English-language periodical devoted to postage stamp collecting was published in 1862 in England, followed two years later with one in this country. Stamp clubs sprang up all over this country in the late nineteenth century. The American Philatelic Society (Internet: www.aps.org) was founded in 1887, which continues today, with headquarters in State College, Pennsylvania (see Chapter 8).

Early stamp collectors attempted to obtain all the stamps of the world, an approach that continued well into the twentieth century for many collectors. To show how increasingly difficult such a quest is, a French collector in 1870 had a collection of some 10,400 stamps — about 50 less than the total number of stamps in the world. Now, more than 12,000 different postage stamps are issued annually! (See the section on completing your collection in Chapter 4.)

Today's collector

With more stamps available, collectors can pick and choose collecting areas more easily. Although the vast majority of U.S. stamp collectors collect U.S. stamps, each collector does not necessarily collect all stamps of the United States. Some may collect only airmail stamps, others may focus on just commemoratives, and still others may look only for stamps issued through 1947 (the first 100 years of U.S. postage stamps). The U.S. is a melting pot of people from all over the world, with a hefty percentage of stamp collectors in this country also building collections of stamps from the recent foreign homeland of their family.

People entering the hobby new at this time tend to be more interested in beginning a topical, or thematic, collection (see Chapter 13) rather than one that is country based (see Chapters 11 and 12). A "topical collection" is a collection based on the design on a stamp rather than on which country issued a stamp. Topics are chosen for as many reasons as there are choosers. A topical stamp collection easily may reflect the vocational interests of the collector, or the recreational interests, or a social interest such as the Red Cross or Scouting, or a religious interest. At more than 10,000 new stamps a year worldwide, today's collectors have an ample supply of material to fit virtually any type of collection.

Varying Types of Postage Stamps

Most U.S. stamp collectors are familiar with the stamps that have basic purposes: general postage, airmail (see Figure 2-1), postage due (see Figure 2-2), and stamped envelopes and postal cards. With the exception of postage due, these are in frequent use today.

Figure 2-1:
Airmail
stamp.

Figure 2-2:
Postage
due.

Among the more specialized areas of postage for which stamps have been issued are

✔ **Parcel post:** Today, parcel post is broken down into subclasses, such as bound, printed matter, library mail, and media mail. See Figure 2-3.

✔ **Semipostal:** A portion of the stamp sale proceeds, above the cost of postage, goes to a charity. See Figure 2-4.

✔ **Occupation:** Issued by a country occupying another as the result of war.

✔ **Special delivery postage due:** Payment due because original postage on a special delivery parcel was not enough to cover the rate. See Figure 2-5.

Figure 2-3:
Parcel post.

Figure 2-4:
Semipostal.

Figure 2-5:
Special
delivery
postage
due.

War-related stamps — stamps used by one country occupying another, or stamps for use by the military of a country — used during or immediately following World Wars I and II, have no further reason for use (a good thing). In more recent years, the expanded use of postage meters — by individuals and firms, as well as by the post office itself — replaced the need for additional types of stamps. Meters are single color (usually red or blue) stamps generated by a privately owned machine to the specific amount needed for the item being mailed. The expanded use of meters in business and industry has deflated the use of postage stamps. Firms can more easily control the use of meters.

Revised classes of postage now have extensive and complicated rate structures that make it difficult for most people to know the correct postage and, therefore, force them to go to the post office for rate determination. USPS clerks prefer using their own meters, which are attached to electronic scales. With all this automation, USPS meters have pretty much replaced postage stamp use by postal clerks.

Here are two reasons for you to begin to find out about the various types of postal services for which stamps have been issued:

- ✔ Any one of the types may lead to an interesting collection.

- ✔ Pay particular attention to stamps with inscriptions noting specific classes of mail, such as certified mail, registered mail, or anything else you don't instantly recognize. Stamps noting specific classes of mail may not be scarce items, but they certainly are interesting. Stamps for special classes of mail items are not in general use today because automation and more-complex rate structures have reduced the ability of a single-rate, preprinted stamp to handle special mail properly. **Note:** Finding special-class mail stamps that are still on an envelope (cover) or package (wrapper) adds to the interest. Because material like this is not in current use, the supply continues to age and becomes more difficult to obtain.

Posing As Stamps

Generally, a *postage stamp* is considered a device issued by a legitimate government that maintains a postal service. Such postage stamps are accepted for use in the international mail.

The United States, then, issues postage stamps that easily meet this definition. You will see, however, some items that have the appearance of a postage stamp but are not stamps. Many of these items are valid for other forms of government service. Others, unfortunately, are produced purely for stamp collectors and are guised as postage stamps without the backing of an actual country.

So let's pick on a state. The state of Iowa cannot issue postage stamps. Anything Iowa may issue purporting to prepay postage would be considered a *label* rather than a stamp, because the state does not maintain a recognized postal service. There are some gray areas, to be sure. Hawaii at one time was independent and issued its own stamps. In fact, Hawaii's earliest stamps are among the most valuable known. Issues for Hawaii through the end of its period of independence are postage tamps.

Today's stamp market has a type of label "issued" by owners of privately held islands. These labels have all the physical attributes of postage stamps, except they cannot be used to move the mail. Therefore, the labels are not as highly considered as postage stamps by most stamp collectors. At the same time, the island labels normally are quite attractive and many people do collect them for what they are — colorful labels that make an attractive presentation.

Other labels include Christmas and charity seals, as well as trading stamps such as those produced by Sperry and Hutchinson. More contemporary are the various types of stickers available in most any toy store, complete with their own albums.

With the rapid movement among many postal administrations around the world toward self-stick postage stamps, having a common child's sticker mistaken for such a stamp is quite easy. Many countries depict cartoon characters on postage stamps that look very much like stickers or labels purchased at a department store children's section. As a result, the department store stickers may well pass through the postal system. Such nonpostage labels have made it through the mail, but I certainly do not advocate testing the system. The USPS takes an extremely dim view of such attempts.

Other forms of stamp-like items with no postal validity are labels issued for nonexistent countries. Either the labels are produced by governments in exile or separatists who realize the public-relations value of such labels showing up on mail, or by entrepreneurs who realize the potential financial return of producing relatively low-cost labels and selling them at "face values" of amazing proportion. Some of the better known fictitious countries are Occusi-Ambeno (based on disputed territory in East Timor, although the stamps never saw that part of the world), Nagaland (of which nagahide is not the principal export), Atlantis, and Manumbaland.

In my own collection is a letter received through the mail with postage "paid" by labels from a fictitious country in the Australia-New Zealand area. To the best of my research ability, I have determined that the letter entered the international mail stream in London, England, and never made it south of the equator. The envelope has very little value, other than that of being able to write about it here.

Fun stuff aside, a dark side also exists. Included are fakes and forgeries sometimes so good that experts are stumped for decades. Forgers fall into two basic classes:

- ✔ **Postal forgeries:** Stamps are forged in quantity specifically to be used as postage for purposes of defrauding a government. Although stamp collectors — those exchanging their green eyeshade for a white hat — have initially detected such forgeries, postal inspectors carry out the investigation in the U.S. Generally, postal forgeries are of the smaller, definitive stamps that are in much greater supply than commemoratives. Only stamp collectors tend to look closely at the more common stamps, always in search of the error, flaw, or, in this case, forgery (see Chapter 15).

- ✔ **Philatelic forgeries:** Stamps of this type are faked in far lesser quantities solely to defraud stamp collectors. Normally, philatelic forgeries begin as lower-value items that are made to look like more valuable items by:

  adding an *overprint* (one or more lines of type, or even a simple graphic, applied to a stamp after it has been printed)

  adjusting the perforations by adding them to a side of a stamp where none were previously (reperfing), or removing them by slicing them away

  chemically removing a color to produce a "color-missing" error

  removing a cancellation and adding gum, making a used stamp appear to be mint

Many, many fakes and forgeries exist, but not in a large enough quantity that the beginning collector need lose sleep over the possibility of being duped by one. Part II provides tips on protecting yourself from such fakery; Chapter 15 specifically addresses fakes.

No matter what item I discuss, the item not only may become an area of stamp collecting, but it also probably already is.

As you progress in stamp collecting and your tastes become more specialized, you will be introduced to those areas more rife with fakes. Those specialty areas that have been particularly victimized over the years now include mechanisms within their specialty organizations to inform members of spurious items (see Chapter 15) — dueling magnifying glasses, so to speak.

It is the rare collector, after a few years, who does not come upon at least one questionable item. If nothing else, mounting a fake in your album alongside the good stamp makes for a great talking point when showing off the collection.

Fake stamps, real irony

Stamp collecting has known some very talented forgers over the years. Jean de Sperati may be the most notorious. He worked in Italy, and later in France, and is credited with producing philatelic forgeries of more than 500 classic postage stamps from more than 100 countries. Closer to home was the Mexican forger Raoul de Thuin, whose work was the subject of a very thick book published by the American Philatelic Society. Because fakes and forgeries have become a collecting area of their own, various examples of forgeries by specific forgers may be worth more today than legitimate copies of the stamps that the forgers were faking. Go figure!

Collecting philatelic forgers can be difficult. Many collectors and dealers do not like to admit to having such items, and they are not generally advertised. Many collectors are concerned that a forgery will be purchased as a forgery and then resold, without the caveat, to an unknowing person. That is fraud. Forgeries can be dangerous.

Chapter 3

Dissecting Your Stamp's Anatomy

● ●

● ●

Sometimes even the smallest thing makes the biggest difference in identifying a stamp. Two recent U.S. Christmas stamps, showing Santa Claus on a roof, are different only because of a single small vertical line forming another brick in the chimney. This chapter introduces you to the key body parts of a stamp where such differences generally appear. Although making a find of such magnitude that will even take on your name is unlikely, the chance always is there.

Just as a person's height, weight, skin color, hair color, eye color, face shape, and so on, all go to identify the person, a stamp's color, design, gum, paper type, perforation measurement, and watermark identify the stamp. A subset of this information can also be used to categorize. With so many situations where a difference in a stamp's physical attributes is the difference between two totally different issues, knowledge of these distinctions becomes quite important. Although an attribute difference between two stamps may be the determining factor between an inexpensive and a valuable stamp, more importantly it's the *difference* that counts and not the value. That is, you are not able to determine the value without first precisely identifying the stamp. A stamp's value may increase or decrease, but its physical attributes remain the same. As you begin your stamp-collecting quest, whatever it turns out to be, you'll be applying your knowledge of these attributes constantly.

The stamp-collecting tools section, coming up later in this chapter, introduces you to a variety of items commonly used in the hobby. They're generally inexpensive and rather easy to manipulate, although you may pick up little things along the way to make that usage easier. Before you do anything you believe may, in any way, be harmful to a stamp, practice on a damaged item or at least a very inexpensive one. Never lose sight of the fact that stamps are paper, and once a stamp is damaged, it can't be "undamaged."

The section in this chapter on watermarks may never apply to you and your collection. The importance of watermarks depends on which country's stamps you collect, which time period the stamps are from, and whether you're collecting by country or by topic. Depending on the specific stamp issue you're checking, finding an elusive watermark may be difficult. The basics of how to find a watermark are presented in this chapter. Beyond the basics, however, you may need to get creative. Unusual situations lend themselves to getting help from fellow stamp club members or others who specialize in the same material that you're interested in.

If you're a little shaky with tongs or a magnifying glass, you may need to have a desk mount for the glass and only use the tongs to move a stamp from one place on your desktop to another. Speed is not an issue when it comes to working with stamps. So be comfortable, and by all means, be certain that the stamps are comfortable.

Gumming Right Up

Stamp collectors refer to the adhesive substance on the back of a stamp, which traditionally had to be moistened to stick to an envelope, as *gum*. The term is taken from gum arabic, a derivative of the acacia tree found in Africa. Before the advent of the increasingly popular self-adhesive stamps, additional forms of gum had come into use in stamp production. Dextrine, made from starch and known also as *British gum*, achieved some popularity. A more popular modern gum, introduced on British stamps in the late 1960s, has the less-classic name *polyvinyl alcohol* (normally referred to as PVA, its acronym). There is also a synthetic gum that is so invisible, it is virtually impossible to tell if the gum is still there or has been washed away. This statement comes from experience!

More and more stamps of the world are self-adhesive, particularly those of the U.S. Stamp collectors sometimes have difficulty, however, handling self-adhesive stamps after they have been used. Still, self-adhesive stamps have achieved tremendous popularity among those folks who still purchase postage stamps to mail things; so much so, that self-adhesives have moved well beyond use on the smaller, definitive stamps to colorful commemoratives (see Chapter 1) and even *coil* stamps (those available in roll versus sheet format).

Self-adhesive stamps are still evolving in their technology, and no firm practice, as of yet, has evolved relative to how to keep them. Some stamp collectors believe that self-adhesive stamps should be saved mint, still attached to their original backing paper — although the U.S. has produced a "linerless"

It all hinges on the gum

A hinge's gum is designed to be peel-able. Today's hinges, across the board, are not — and that is a problem. But the industry has been told that a "better" hinge (such as those of old) is coming. This has a Holy Grail-like aura to it, to be sure.

coil where the backing paper is actually another stamp — and used stamps should be saved still attached to the envelope. Other collectors, remembering how badly the gum on early self-adhesives aged, recommend soaking the stamps to remove all the gum. Mixed into the diverse opinions are the differences in gums on the self-adhesive stamps of various countries — just as there are differences in traditional "lick-and-stick" gums.

Play it safe and protect yourself through redundancy. That is, where possible, save used self-adhesive stamps that are both attached and unattached to the original backing. If in the future the gum turns out to be destructive, the soaked examples you have will remain fresh. Or, if the gum remains stable and stamp value is keyed to those items that still have gum, you will have them also. What are a few more stamps to a stamp collector?

Gum presents quite a paradox to stamp collectors. On the one hand, the pressure to collect only *mint, never hinged* (MNH) stamps is tremendous, unless you prefer used stamps. MNH means that the reverse side of the stamp has positively no marks that disrupt the gum's appearance, such as that caused by the stamp hinge. (MH stands for mint, hinged, which isn't used nearly as often as MNH.) A *hinge* is a specialized piece of paper, separate from the stamp, folded and treated with its own adhesive for affixing both to the stamp itself and an album page (see Figure 3-1). Sticking the hinge to the back of the stamp, no matter how special and how easy to peel the hinge may be, still leaves a permanent mark on the gum side of the stamp. The greater the general value of an unused stamp, the greater the difference in value between a mint, never hinged stamp and a stamp of equal quality possessing a hinge mark.

Figure 3-1:
Stamp
hinge;
useful, but
possibly at a
price.

Getting rid of the gum is possible, but not yet recommended. This is one of the many "unspoken" and still-debated topics of stamp collecting. It has been mostly agreed on that gum does not age nearly as well as the actual stamp paper. Climate is a major factor here. At the same time, unfortunately, the value of many older mint stamps may be based on the percentage of gum remaining. To tell you to remove the gum is to tell you to devalue (currently) some of your material. Throughout this presentation, you're going to come upon — and I hope challenge — a lot of illogical approaches that give stamp collecting much of the charm it has.

Understanding how to care for stamps, as noted in Part V, is critical to your collection's long-term health. Without wanting to inject a feeling of fear here, suffice to note up front that most safe-storing tips are common sense.

Wrapping Up with Paper

Paper comes in so many different types that you need a couple of days just to list them. A decent understanding of the basics, however, will go a very long way. Paper identification can be critical if you collect early issues of any one of many countries.

All stamp paper begins as a near-liquid substance made from wood pulp, which can easily be mistaken for thin oatmeal were it not for the odor (and that your Grandmother would never make a batch of hot cereal that large). From there, paper is machine or handmade.

- Machine-made paper is run over a bed of wire mesh, becoming one of two types of paper:

  - **Wove:** Formed when the wire mesh is uniform, similar to window screening.

  - **Laid:** Formed if there are thicker wires parallel in only one direction, spaced farther apart than the mesh. Lines appear in the paper.

- Handmade paper is generally thicker and not as uniform in thickness as machine-made paper.

Wove and laid are two key types of paper. Talking about them is one thing; seeing them is something else. So, look through your desk for a box of stationery, or check at the local office supply store. Obtain a sheet of wove paper and a sheet of laid paper to use as a guide. Save these items, for not only will the paper sheets help you with paper identification, the samples also are the first two items in a reference collection that you will continue to expand as you go through the various chapters of this book.

Paper minutiae

Differentiating among types of paper used for stamp printing may require some specialized tools, such as a *micrometer*. This specialized tool measures thickness to a fraction of a millimeter. I own one, a throwback to my own background in the printing industry, and have not used it in at least the last decade. But if I need it, I know where it is! Paper descriptions used in postage stamp catalogues, or in articles or monographs dealing with a specific stamp or issue, are not normally as detailed and technical as those expected of a paper expert writing in a technical journal for the paper industry. You can find terms such as "thick," "thicker," and "thin," as well as other terms that provide yet another reason for you to have your own reference collection of paper. If you need to identify a specific paper used with a stamp issue, try to have on hand examples of other papers used with that issue so your identification process will include a direct physical comparison, as well as a determination based solely on the written description.

Understanding the difference between wove and laid paper is key. Machine-made paper may pick up foreign substances as the material moves along the belt and begins to dry. The foreign items will stick to the paper and then drop off late in the process, leaving defects in the form of random thin spots.

Also, you will want to be able to tell the difference between handmade and machine-made paper, particularly if you plan to collect early issue from some foreign countries. Thus, if you believe you have a stamp printed on handmade paper, more than one thickness measurement should be made on the same stamp.

The micrometer I own (and have shelved for the past decade) was reasonably priced and has a set of instructions. It is no more difficult to test paper thickness — which certainly does have a learning curve — than it is to find and identify watermarks.

Treading Watermarks

Laid paper comes to be via larger, parallel wires that form a design, which, in theory, is a *watermark* — an intentionally thin area in the finished paper. To put it another way, a watermark is something that *isn't*, rather than something that *is*. Holding the sheet of paper or postage stamp to the light, or using some other device to make the watermark visible, will identify the "missing" paper (see Figure 3-2).

Within stamp collecting, a watermark is such a process produced in the form of a design. Hundreds of watermarks are recorded on the postage stamps of the world, ranging from elephants to pineapples to letters of various alphabets of the world.

Privater Nachdruck ———————— Watermark

Figure 3-2:
A watermark shows up on the back of this stamp.

It is rare to find a stamp that is known with and without a watermark. Therefore, it is not practical to collect only one way. Rather, look at watermarks in the same manner as perforations: They have a reason for existence to the issuing country, and a different reason for existence to the stamp collector.

If stamp collectors had only blank pieces of paper to check for watermarks, the task would be easy. Add to the identification the printing on the stamp, cancellations of various densities, and the watermark's density, and the task becomes more difficult. Spirited discussions have occurred as to whether a watermark actually is present on a given stamp, or as to which watermark is there. That is the stamp-collecting equivalent to whether the point guard was fouled driving for a winning basket or whether the running back's knee was actually on the turf before the football squirted out for a fumble. Fortunately, stamp collecting has instant replay, and a prized stamp may be taken from expert to expert to get a decision.

See more later in this chapter on how to identify a watermark.

Separating with Perforations

The most common method of separating one stamp from another historically was to tear them apart at their *perforations*. Stamp users, who use the perforations without thinking, have a tendency is to take perforations for granted. After the next few paragraphs, you will begin to think before you separate.

The first postage stamps of the world were printed on a sheet without any easy way to separate stamp from stamp. Knives and scissors were used for the job most often, unless some office had a well-trained rodent with extremely sharp front teeth. Too many stamps were ruined in the separating phase and postal customers began expressing their disdain to postal authorities.

Mother Necessity went into the inventing mode and out popped the perforation, a way of removing bits of paper where two stamps meet (see Figure 3-3). Folding the paper at the perforation would weaken the paper and allow the stamps to be removed from the sheet, or each other, with a minimum of trouble. Simple enough.

Figure 3-3:
Close-up of
perforated
stamp edge.

With a head start on postage stamp production in general, England was the first to produce perforated stamps. The first, from about 1854, were "perforated 16," which is a method of measuring perforation by counting the number of perforations per two centimeters.

Perforating versus rouletting

The word "perforation" has one meaning within the commercial printing industry and a different meaning within stamp collecting. Further, the word "roulette" is used in stamp collecting in the same manner that "perforation" is used within commercial printing. Confused? Well, if you aren't, you should be. In the world of printing, perforating means to apply a die to the finished piece for the purpose of making enough slits between two items to permit ease of separation while allowing enough of the two items to remain attached in order to keep them from falling apart unintentionally. When you remove a return postcard from a piece of advertising (junk) mail, you separate the card along the row of perforations. Check the next dozen or so of these that you come upon, and you'll note that no paper is actually removed from the printed piece, only slits are made. This is known as a *perforation* in printing and as *roulette* when it's done to allow two postage stamps to be separated. Only when tiny pieces of paper are actually removed, leaving holes, is the process considered "perforation" in stamp collecting. Both rouletting and perforating were used early in the history of postage stamps because of the difficulty in separating two stamps by cutting or tearing each time you wanted to use one.

Over the years, perforating has become the accepted practice. And, over even more years, the manner in which stamps are perforated has evolved (along with other aspects of the production process).

A gauge of "perf 16" (the manner in which such measurements are reported) turned out to be too flimsy for the stamps to remain attached while one was being removed. That is, the result weakened the connection between the two stamps, causing the stamps to separate when touched. Countries tried various gauges until each country settled on a range that allowed ease of separation while maintaining the physical integrity of the remaining stamps that make up the sheet. What worked best in each case was a combination of the paper itself and the perforation gauge.

Gauging size

Collectors need to measure a stamp for the same reason they need to find a possible watermark: for identification. Stamps with the same design have been produced with two or more different perforation measurements; the generally accepted practice is that a difference in perforation measurement is the difference between two major varieties. It is the same with which watermark is used, if one is used at all. If the actual perforation is 12 per 2 centimeters, the gauge is 12 or, in vernacular, perf 12.

Gauging the United States

Gauges used in the United States are not constant, and are based mostly on who is doing the production. Of late, the measurements (gauges) have been at or close to 11 — some have been 10.8, some 11.1 or 11.2. All this is a bit of a change from earlier methods, when measurements were only to the closest ¼ of a perforation. Now one must measure correct to the nearest ¹⁄₁₀ because of more subtle differences.

Perforation measurements need not be the same on each of the four sides of the stamp. Overwhelmingly, perforated stamps have all four sides the same or two parallel sides matching. Different perforations on a single stamp are known as *compound perforations.*

✔ **Identical measurements on all four sides:** Only one measurement is noted. A stamp with a measurement of perf 12 on all four sides is simply noted as being "perf 12."

✔ **Parallel-matching measurements:** Two measurements are noted. If the top and bottom are perf 11 and the left and right sides are perf 10½, the stamp is said to be "perf 11 x 10½." Horizontal measurements (across the top and bottom) are given first, and then the vertical.

✔ **Compound perforations:** A shorthand method measures the horizontal row of perforations across the top of the stamp, followed by the vertical measurement along the right side, followed by the horizontal measurement across the bottom, and followed by the vertical measurement along the left side.

Only in extremely rare cases do all four sides have a different number of perforations. Even if two sides are the same and two others are different, the items would be considered, say, "perf 12 x 11 x 12 x 10½," beginning with the measurement across the top of the stamp and then proceeding clockwise. This last one may not be much of a shorthand, but it certainly is more concise that going through the complete explanation. Fortunately, you will see this so seldom that there is absolutely no reason to do more than read it now and respond with, "Gosh!"

Rather than physically count the number of perforations in two centimeters, stamp collectors today rely on an inexpensive tool, the perforation gauge (described later in this chapter).

If you have difficulty measuring perforations of stamps in a particular set, or from a span of years of a single country, find examples of damaged stamps whose perforation measurements are without question. Cut each of the sample stamps diagonally so that you are able to line them up easily with the stamp you are checking. As long as you know the measurement of the item from your reference collection, you can verify the measurement of the unknown item. Store each of the sample stamps individually in a small envelope marked with the catalogue number and perforation measurement.

Gauging anomalies

Sometimes stamps have perforations that extend beyond the kind already explained.

✔ **Coil stamps:** These stamps are generally perforated only on one set of parallel sides (see Figure 3-4). The shorthand would be "perf 11 horizontally" when the top and bottom are perforated and the left and right sides have no perforations. Some countries issue coil stamps that have perforations on all four sides, which becomes confusing — but our old standby, the perforation measurement, is used.

Figure 3-4:
Coil stamp.

✔ **Booklet stamps:** These stamps generally have straight edges on one or two sides (see Figure 3-5). Corner stamps have two sides with perforations and two sides without perforations. Older U.S. stamps, in particular, were printed on sheets with straight edges, producing stamps with a single, straight edge (two if the stamp is at a corner). You need to know the specific stamp issue to determine whether a straightedge stamp comes from a book or from a sheet with no perforations on the outer edge.

With the popular growth of self-adhesive stamps has come a new form of stamp separation: *die-cut*. Self-adhesive stamps are produced in two principal layers — the stamp with a sticky adhesive and its backing paper. Following the printing process for a self-adhesive stamp, a steel die is pressed to a predetermined depth, on the sheet, that is just deep enough to cut through the stamp and not enough to cut through the backing paper. Many collectors save them with the protective backing paper still attached.

Figure 3-5:
Booklet
stamp.

In commercial printing this can be done to produce very decorative results, such as note pads in the shape of a firm's logo. In the case of self-adhesive stamps, die cutting permits a printing image that is much larger than a single stamp, without having the design disrupted by pesky perforations and while still permitting ease of stamp removal from their protective backing.

Coloring Your Collection

Until you are searching for varieties of a specific stamp, probably one from the early years, you will not become too involved in color differences. On the other hand, some general information will help overcome what otherwise may become confusion.

Precise, accepted color definitions (such as red brown, yellow orange, and blue black) do not exist and are not used across stamp collecting worldwide. Fortunately, only when you get to the nit-picking stage of your stamp-collecting life — some of us strive for that transcendence, others avoid it like the plague — will my pronouncement make a difference.

A cheaper solution

Color is the most difficult attribute to nail down. Colors not only fade from light, but they also may be affected by proximity to specific chemicals (that is, chemicals specific to the particular ink used on a particular stamp). Ten years ago, when I was actively involved with the only color study group I know of that actually knew anything about the subject, the determination was that a stamp collector needed at least $1,500 in equipment, and the training to use it properly, to do any sort of solid color identification. Expertizing services have such equipment, as probably do a very few wealthy collectors. These experts, including one who was both a collector and a color researcher, concluded that a reference collection was the only way to determine color accurately without getting into the equipment. This was one of the principal reasons why I became such a strong advocate of personal reference collections.

Color guides that you find for stamps are keyed to a specific stamp catalogue, or they endeavor to build their own dictionary of color names or numerical designations. Because each major catalogue publisher has its own naming conventions, such guides are useful only if they are keyed to the catalogue you use. England's *Stanley Gibbons* and Germany's *Michel* have produced color guides; America's *Scott Standard Postage Stamp Catalogue* has not produced color guides in recent decades. Color inks are so sensitive over time that color identification guides used in the commercial printing industry are replaced on a regular basis with *fresh* versions; the same should apply to guides used for stamp identification.

When is a tool not a tool? When it's part of your reference collection. For stamps known in more than one color — where "light green" is a different color than "green" — it is common for at least one of the colors you are trying to identify to be known on another stamp issue where color identification is not an issue. That is, where one stamp design may be known in the colors of green, light green, and yellow green, another stamp may be known only in green. A second stamp may be known only in light green. And, a third stamp may be known only in yellow green. Different printings at different times, where ink mixing was not precise (or even thought to be a requirement), generate these different colors. Or, in a long run, ink may have been mixed differently when it was added to the press. Remember that stamps were produced for postage, not for collectors to analyze meticulously.

Put on your shopping list damaged stamps of the types known only in one color. After you purchase them, cut them diagonally, so the color is easy to determine, and place them on top of the items to be checked. If the color is the same, voila! — you have achieved identification. A major advantage of using a stamp from the same era is that it has had the same number of years to age. Although others are shunning damaged stamps as having no value, you are finding more and more uses for them.

Coloring books

Color is not debatable among the more recent stamps, generally those of the past 40 years or so. Color became an issue much earlier, when clear-cut reference guides and catalogues that a stamp collector could use to recognize color distinctions as a means of stamp identification were nonexistent. Any color printed color guide goes bad in about two years — or at least that's what I discovered when in the printing industry. And, *Stanley Gibbons'* color definitions are not the same as those of *Scott* (America*), Michel* (Germany), or *Yvert & Tellier* (France). For the major colors, they're pretty good, but for the obscure varieties (where color ID is really critical), their naming conventions are unique to their own books. Of the major catalogue publishers, only *Stanley Gibbons* of England has produced a color guide to accompany its catalogue. Just to complicate things more, *Scott* (and perhaps others) is not internally consistent with its assignment of color names.

Denoting a Design Difference

Stamp collecting is a visual hobby first and foremost. Stamp collectors are constantly looking for something different. Such *finds* are the stuff of legends. Although so few stamp collectors will really ever fall on such an opportunity, they still keep their senses sharp by seeking out known differences so they can discover, as well as increase, their collection. Two types of design differences are

- ✔ **Intentional:** On the part of the postal authority issuing the stamps. Perhaps a country noted an error on a first printing and reprinted and reissued the stamps with a correction. The desire to have the person depicted on a stamp look better is enough for an intentional design difference.

- ✔ **Unintentional:** Caused by some circumstance during printing or before that stage as the printing plates were being prepared. Early stamps were hand engraved and hand transferred to the printing plate. As steady as these craftsmen were, variations may be evident. Or, such a difference may be as blatant as a second printing, where part of the design is in a totally different color.

A difference can be anywhere on a stamp: the border (if there is one), a person may have been "shaved" by the engraver, or a queen may have been treated to touch ups of her hair. A denomination may first be without a cents sign, and later with one.

The simple design difference in Figure 3-6 illustrates the infamous Dag Hammarskjold special printing of 1962. The U.S. Post Office quickly reprinted an error version of a stamp honoring the late UN Secretary General — against the strong objections of the stamp-collecting public. The error was an inverted yellow background.

Figure 3-6:
A pair of Hammarsk-jold stamps.

Today, the two Hammarskjold stamps have essentially the same value. The only Hammarskjold items that have increased substantially in value are the very few error stamps used and still on the envelope with accompanying postmark, mailed during the few days between the release of the original stamp and the intentional error. On the release of the intentional error version, which is identical to the actual error stamps, those who held unused copies of the originals wept. Those who happen to have the original error, used and still on the envelope with postmark showing the date before the reprint was issued, continue to smile.

Stamp collectors were furious with the postal service. But the reprint came so quickly that nothing could be done to stop it. Later that same year, the U.S. Postal Service issued a Canal Zone (a U.S. possession whose stamps and postal service were handled by the U.S. Post Office Department) stamp honoring the opening of the Thatcher Ferry Bridge spanning the Panama Canal. The stamp was printed in black and silver, with silver being used for the bridge. Some copies were found with the silver missing, and immediately the stamp collecting community reared up on its hind legs to keep the postal service from repeating the Hammarskjold incident. Stamp dealer H.E. Harris, one of the most prominent in the trade at the time, led the charge and had the reissue stopped through legal action. Today that error is the single most valuable Canal Zone item listed in the *Scott Standard Postage Stamp Catalogue*.

Tooling Around

Stamp-collecting tools may not whir or have flashing lights; however, these tools are still every bit as important to you as a screwdriver and a prayer are to a computer repairman. Of the tools presented here, you may never have need for all (although definitely for tongs). Knowing what is available and how each is used, however, is important. Then, if the situation presents itself, you will know what is available and avoid substituting a device that can cause more damage than good because it is not designed for use with small pieces of fragile paper.

Although many tools range widely in price, beginning modestly is quite possible: a little more than $3 for a good set of tongs, less than $15 for a magnifier, $12 or so for watermark tray and fluid, and $1 or so for a perforation gauge. These prices are the minimum for adequate (or better) items. Stamp-collecting tools are available from most dealers who maintain a storefront business, as well as many other dealers who specialize in accessories. Normally, these items can be found at stamp shows and bourses, as well as through the ads in stamp periodicals and on the Internet. In short, they're easy to find.

Perhaps magnifiers come in the largest variety because of differences in glass size, degree of magnification, and whether the magnifier is hand-held, self-standing, or illuminated. Perforation gauge prices are keyed to whether the measurement is correct to the nearest $\frac{1}{4}$ perforation or to the nearest $\frac{1}{10}$ perforation per two centimeters. Watermark fluid sells in a rather tight price range, and what you pay for tongs is based on your personal preference to length and tip configuration. Because tools are the safe gift, you can quickly amass quite an array of tongs and magnifiers, and no doubt each will prove to be useful at some point in your collecting career.

Stamp tongs

Although tongs look like tweezers, the difference is clearly shown in Figure 3-7. *Stamp tongs* are normally longer than tweezers, and they do not have ridges or sharp edges that may damage a stamp. There is no reason to keep them in a case; dust is not an issue. At stamp shows, many collectors — in true geek fashion — will carry tongs over a pocket flap rather than within a shirt pocket.

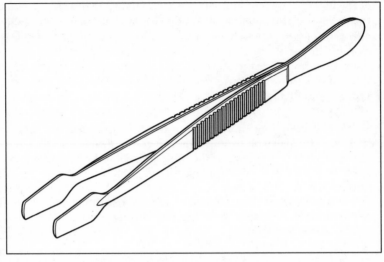

Figure 3-7:
Stamp
tongs.

After you become familiar with them, tongs allow you more dexterity than your fingers, without the danger of rough handling of a stamp or the opportunity for moisture or oil from your fingers to get onto the stamp. Tongs are available in a variety of styles, with lengths ranging from at least 4¼ to 6 inches. Tip designs include pointed, spade, and round. Which length and tip style is your choice? I tend to prefer the spade tip. I have had some bad experiences with pointed tips, having speared more than one stamp.

When attending a stamp show or *bourse* (similar to a stamp show, but without the exhibits), be sure to have a pair of tongs with you to use when inspecting stamps at a dealer's table. This is an easy way to make an instant good impression.

If a single tool exists that is universally important to all stamp collectors, stamp tongs can make that claim. Although you may use any of the other tools listed in this chapter based on your own collecting interests and style, tongs are critical to all collectors.

Perforation gauge

You need a method of measuring perforations (see Figure 3-8). Enter the perforation gauge. As with any specialized tools, perforation gauges are available in quite a few configurations ranging from stamp-dealer giveaways to highly sophisticated devices — you can even find software that can measure a stamp's perforations from a digital scan of the item.

In the end, however, perforation gauges all work the same way. Gauges are designed to count the number of perforations in the linear measurement of two centimeters. Okay, you can do that by hand with little difficulty, as long as the number of perforations is a whole number. But, when the measurement does not come out even, you need something to handle the little extra. Enter the perforation gauge, which historically has been designed to measure correctly to the nearest one-half perforation. Now, some more recent U.S. stamps are measured to the nearest tenth of a perforation. So, you may have to work a little.

Discover how to use the simplest perforation gauge first, the type that measures correctly to the nearest one-half perforation. Look carefully at the gauge illustrated in Figure 3-8. You will see individual lines of simulated perforations, against which you compare the stamp that you are measuring. Some gauges of this type have the perforation lines "raised" for effect; others merely have the lines printed onto the metal. Chances are good that your favorite gauge will be the first type you own.

Notice the perforation lines on the outside border of the gauge. The lines allow you to measure the perforations of a stamp that are still attached to an envelope (*on cover*, to spring another new term on you). Due to the thickness of the metal, measuring an on-cover stamp is sometimes more difficult because of a phenomenon known as *parallax*, the difference in the apparent position of an object when it is viewed from two different points.

Alas, there is a way around that issue. Perforation gauges are also available on a clear plastic base, allowing you to lay the gauge over stamps that are on cover and to measure loose stamps. When purchasing a clear plastic perforation gauge, be certain that the printing is on the bottom of the gauge to eliminate parallax issues when working with on-cover stamps. The printing should be in reverse on one side so it shows through correctly when viewed from the top. You place the gauge over the stamp so the printing (actual measuring mechanism) is literally touching the stamp.

Perforations do not always match up exactly with the markings on the gauge. A variety of factors can cause this situation:

- Not all perforating equipment is calibrated to the nearest one-half perforation.

- More recent U.S. stamps are measured to the nearest $\frac{1}{10}$ of a perforation, making a more sophisticated style of gauge necessary. Although earlier stamps weren't precisely correct to the nearest one-half perforation, the stamps against which they were being compared had perforation measurements far enough away that more precise measurements were not required. That is, you may be trying to determine if a stamp is perf 12 or perf 10½. Now you'll find U.S. stamps of the same design with a possible perforation measurement of 11.2 and 11.3 or 11.3 and 11.5.

✔ Moisture and other conditions can cause individual stamps to shrink or stretch enough to make measurements appear just a little off. Even if the perforations, when applied, were correct to a whole number, post-production changes (such as moisture) can affect the perforation measurement. Fortunately, these changes do not normally affect comparative identification, such as whether the stamp in question is one or the other of two listed stamps. Rather, an inexperienced collector is apt to find such a stamp, which may measure to the nearest one-half perforation off when compared to one of the stamps listed in the catalogue, and believe he has made a major find.

Millimeter ruler

Philatelic linear measurements, as you saw in the section on perforation gauges, are metric. You will see stamp designs listed in millimeters, as well as overall stamp measurements and overprints. Therefore, consider getting a millimeter ruler (see Figure 3-8) that is easy to read, capable of setting up parallax issues, and stable enough not to be affected by heat or cold.

You will find a variety of millimeter rulers, particularly at office supply stores. Consider those with enough bulk to be useful as a straightedge and still help out as a bookmark. I am a strong believer in conservation of effort; your tools are there to help you. Many perforation gauges have millimeter markings along one edge.

Magnifying glass

If any stereotyped tool can be attributed to stamp collecting, a magnifying glass is it. In every sense, stamp collectors are interacting with items that are truly in postage-stamp size. Whether you choose a pocket-sized magnifier, the Sherlock Holmes model, one that is self-standing, or even one that is mounted to your desk or table and surrounded by a fluorescent lamp, you will need at least one. See the example in Figure 3-9. When it comes to selecting magnifying glasses, level of magnification and quality are more important than what style you choose.

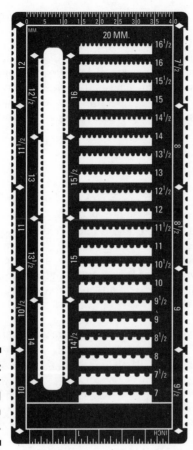

Figure 3-8:
Millimeter
ruler and
perforation
gauge.

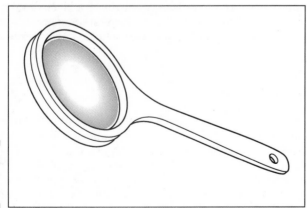

Figure 3-9:
A magni-
fying glass.

Buy absolutely the best quality magnifying glass you can afford. You want one that is sharp from edge to edge, with no edge drop-off, or fuzziness. In my own case, I have a 5X glass that I use when comparing two stamps at one time. I also have a 10X glass that I use to search for specific printing flaws that are rampant in my collecting area. These two magnification levels are the optimum for normal use. Other magnifying glasses that I have accumulated over the years are rather dusty now. Some collectors have much more powerful microscopes and comparators; I've never found the need for one of these.

Watermark fluid

Some watermarks are visible to the naked eye merely by turning the stamp facedown. Some will appear only when the stamp is viewed facedown on a very dark surface. And then there are the difficult ones. A few decades or so ago, chemicals no longer available across the counter were used to detect the more difficult-to-discern watermarks. The chemical was poured over an upside-down stamp resting in a watermark tray, a special glass tray, an ashtray, or a candy dish of a dark solid color. Skip ahead to Figure 3-10 to see an example.

New stamp collectors use *watermark fluid,* which does the same things as its foul-smelling predecessors without the danger of causing permanent damage to the collector.

Even with proclamations of safety, do not use the current watermark fluid in an unventilated area, such as a closet, interior storeroom, or small walk-in safe. Who knows what will be said about this liquid some 30 years from now?

To locate the watermark, all you do is pour enough of the liquid into the tray to cover the stamp and then wait a few seconds until the stamp is saturated. Ideally, the watermark pops out before your eyes as a black design on a white background. Sometimes, "popping out" is an overstatement. This process must be done with dispatch, for the watermark fluid evaporates in a hurry.

Glassine envelopes

Glassine is a thin, dense, transparent or semitransparent paper highly resistant to the passage of air and grease. It is used extensively in the construction of envelopes to hold collectibles. Their very construction makes them a very safe place to store stamps. My whole collection currently resides in glassine envelopes until I can come to some decision — now more than ten years in the making — as to what sort of permanent home I want for it. Because they come in a variety of sizes, there is little in your collection that will not fit snugly in one. Figure 3-11 shows you what a glassine looks like.

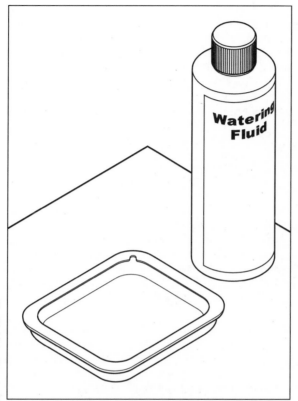

Figure 3-10:
Watermark
tray and
bottle of
fluid.

You are able to write on glassine with pencil, pen, or marker, making the envelopes excellent sorting bins. Make certain that the glassine envelope is empty before writing on it so that your inscription is not imprinted on the cover or the stamp inside. Glassines are generally available in boxes of 1,000 (of a single size), but some stamp-accessory shops offer them in smaller quantities — often by lots of 100. Price is based on the envelope size, with the No. 1 (1¾ x 2⅞ inches) available at about $18 per 1,000; a mid-size No. 5 (3½ x 6 inches) is available at a little more than $40 per 1,000; and a large size No. 10 (4⅛ x 9½ inches) at about $110 per 1,000.

Over the years you will gradually begin to collect glassine envelopes. Virtually all the stamps that you purchase from a dealer are placed in glassine envelopes for transit: for mailing, or for keeping safe until you get home from a bourse or stamp show. At some point, you'll probably purchase some glassine envelopes — the plastic sandwich bags of stamp collecting.

Although I have seen glassine envelopes that show signs of old age, generally speaking, they have quite a long life.

Figure 3-11:
A couple of
glassine
envelopes.
Oddly
enough,
there's no
glass.

Keeping Stamps High and Dry

Never lose sight of the fact that the stamps in your collection are nothing more than very small, fragile pieces of paper. In many cases, the stamps are older than the paper in any magazine in your home. And, unless you also collect rare books, you will have stamps older than paper in any book in your home. Here are some everyday items around your home that should be kept away from your stamp collection:

- ✔ **Clear plastic tape:** Removing clear plastic tape without leaving a residue is impossible. The residue renders a stamp valueless. Perhaps a case can be made for *removable* tape, but I prefer to class them all together to keep from causing any sort of long-term problem.

- ✔ **Photo albums:** The pages are sticky. Again, a residue on the stamp is probable, causing the stamp's value to deteriorate.

- ✔ **Food or liquid:** Don't keep these things on the desk where you work with your stamps. I love coffee, and I normally have a carafe of hot coffee in my home office. But I keep the carafe and my cup on a separate table from where I am working. I know I have klutzlike qualities, and I don't want a recurrence of such tendencies to stain any stamps I have on the desk.

Part II
Making the Most of Your Moolah

The 5th Wave   By Rich Tennant

VINTAGE COLLECTIBLE STAMPS

"Sure it's mint. Taste it."

In this part . . .

The chapters in this part all relate to the financial side of stamp collecting. Whether you complete your collection, or are even able to, is one factor. Also, you can understand a little about how postage stamps are priced by dealers, particularly the least expensive ones. If you choose to specialize in an area of stamp collecting, how does that differ from just diversifying.

While most people expect that a stamp's retail price is only keyed to how rare it may be, Chapter 5 brings you up to speed on perhaps the greater criteria in pricing all but the most rare stamps in the world: a stamp's grade and its condition. Also, you see the difference between the two terms, grade and condition, which are confused all too often and interchanged improperly.

When you see the word *value,* you go to a dictionary for a definition. When you see the word *value* within stamp collecting you understand that it has at least three definitions depending on how it's used. Understanding the differences directly affect your stamp finances. One way to have funds to purchase more stamps is to sell some you already own, and the last chapter in this part provides selling advice.

Chapter 4

Raising Their Green Heads: Finances

• •

In This Chapter

▶ Controlling your expenses

▶ Completeness is a fleeting concept

▶ Selling a stamp: Vast variations in pricing

▶ Collecting for the sake of competition versus investment

• •

*E*very hobby is an expense. But so are food, clothing, and shelter. With a hobby, however, you have a little more control over what you will spend, unless you are one of the very few who jump in with both feet, a checkbook, and absolutely no common sense. Stamp collecting offers you the opportunity to choose a course of action in the beginning that will drive your expenses. Your initial approach to stamp collecting, whether deliberate or subconscious, should require you to proceed with some caution until you get some understanding of your options. After you are involved, you have a number of forks in the collecting road. The next level is to understand pricing. Finally, there is *specializing*. What is it and do you want to do it?

Collecting Perspectives: The "Why" Equals How Much

You're considering collecting stamps; certainly, this is a personal thing. With a hobby so large, diverse, and flexible, there are many people — *many* people — who have taken a personal interest in stamp collecting. And although I cannot necessarily categorize all the individual reasons for getting involved in stamp collecting, generally they fall into some basic categories. Among the considerations, at least in many of the cases, is that of financial requirements. I'm preparing you positively for what you may expect down the road, rather than attempting to erect roadblocks. By all means, welcome. You don't even have to fasten your seat belts. Here are some of the reasons I've heard from stamp collectors:

- My collection is purely for recreation.
- You say "speculation," I say "investment."
- My family and I like to do something fun together.
- I'm a little competitive.
- I'm on a quest to build something significant.

Re-creating recreation

No matter how much we look at stamp collection as a research or educational endeavor, a way to find out about history and geography, or some form of investment vehicle, stamp collecting is still a hobby. That is how stamp collecting began some 150 years ago. Pure recreation is the reason most people enter the hobby. After the proverbial hard day, you are able to sink into such pleasingly mundane tasks as sorting stamps, identifying stamps, mounting stamps in your album, and so on.

I write from experience that these basic tasks provide a great calming influence. From an expense standpoint, you are able to get by easily with a very basic stamp album, a large packet of different stamps or a large stamp mixture, and a way to affix the stamps to the album pages. Thus for less than $50, you can take on all the trappings of stamp collectors, particularly that of having fun with the stamps themselves.

And, if you choose to begin as a wastebasket diver — an enthusiastic stamp collector who would eagerly search through the contents of a wastebasket or their elderly Aunt Mathilda's pile of family correspondence and other papers (or a junk heap) to find a quality stamp — your cost will be even less. The point here is that you really can begin to have plenty of enjoyment playing with postage stamps as a collectible for very little money. In many respects, if you are at all patient, this is an ideal way to begin. In effect, you are able to serve a bit as an apprentice to see in what direction you want to go, and, of course, to see if you want to move forward at all.

Looking for the big return

You want to buy low and sell high? This has been a situation in many collectibles areas, although I am not aware of much success along those lines within stamp collecting. Personal observations aside, you need to prepare differently if you plan this approach. That is, you will need to have resources from the beginning that permit you to properly identify and closely inspect every stamp you purchase.

Because high prices are reserved only for the best examples of individual stamps, you need to be absolutely certain that you are not purchasing material with any flaws, whether visible to the naked eye or on closer inspection. Further, because higher values are often assigned to varieties of issued stamps, you need to be absolutely positive that any such item you purchase is what you believe it to be. That is, you need to feel comfortable that any items you purchase are sound, properly described, and identified. If you have any questions, know before closing a deal with a stamp dealer what your return rights are should you discover that an item is damaged or misidentified.

For example, the U.S. one-cent stamp of 1851 that features a right-facing portrait of Benjamin Franklin has quite a few varieties (see Figure 4-1). Setting aside for the moment the variety with a catalogue value above $170,000, there are other varieties with a mint (unused as the stamp came from the post office) catalogue value ranging from $1,100 to $35,000. Although this may not be the level at which you plan to leap into stamp collecting, it's a level for some stamp collectors. All varieties have identifiable characteristics, which is what leads to each being considered a *variety*. Having to depend on a true expert for formal identification and certification of the more esoteric varieties is entirely possible. However, you can develop the skills to identify common varieties and begin the process of identifying the others. The more identification work that you're able to perform yourself, the less it will cost you in the long run.

Figure 4-1:
U.S. 1851
one-cent
Benjamin
Franklin.

If you want the big bucks, then you've got to follow some rules:

✔ Purchase as many printed references as you're able to locate. Stamp catalogues should be as recent as you can afford. Timeless references can probably only be found used, where prices are keyed to rarity/demand and condition (just like stamps).

✔ You need reliable magnification and measuring devices. If you know you'll be using a magnifier with some frequency, purchase a better-quality device and more than one magnification level. Also, if you plan to work with a magnifier for extended periods, then look at desk models rather than the hand-held types. At this stage in your philatelic involvement, tools cease to be purely for the purposes of enjoying a hobby — industrial-strength equipment is required. Plan to spend upwards of $50 each for a magnifier.

✔ Find a work area that guarantees you the ability to keep your prized paper pieces safe.

✔ Store your high-end stamps so they're not subject to fire, flood, extreme humidity, or theft. At the very least, keep the material away from normal dust. Then, consider a fireproof safe (as compared to a fire-resistant safe) and a bank safety deposit box.

You have all this to do before you ever purchase your first stamp!

Of course, you may choose to totally trust those who sell you the stamps that you'll use for investment purposes. That is your call. If you are that trusting, and you ever choose to collect bridges, I know one connecting two of the boroughs making up New York City that I would have available for you.

Gathering together family and stamps

Stamp collecting is a great family hobby, truly magnificent. Stamp collecting not only provides a wonderful way to become more aware of history, geography, and much more, but stamp collecting also goes a long way toward instilling a sense of responsibility and even building perseverance. Perhaps the only downside to a family-wide interest in stamps is that in the beginning you will need to have some throwaway stamps for the children to work through until they become proficient with the tools. You may need some self-training also. If more than one member of your family begins to collect stamps, you have some economy of scale. Some of the tools may be shared. At the same time, fun begins to leave the experience when there's bickering over whose turn it is to use the tongs or perforation gauge. Have enough of the less-expensive tools at hand.

Each family member needs a personal album, unless a prior agreement has been established that all will share in a single collection. In the early stages, you may find that getting children interested in the stamps of Mexico is difficult after they see some of the colorful modern stamps depicting a favorite sport or celebrity. A child's collection and what the collection consists of should not be nearly as important as the fact that the child is interested enough to pursue a stamp collection in the first place. If your little darling dislikes broccoli at the dinner table, then requiring a collection of broccoli on stamps may be a bit much.

Childrens' stamp albums may differ from the adults' albums. Children may prefer a free-form album, and dislike the structured, preprinted albums. Today, stamp collections that feature giraffes may be arranged on the basis of the country of issue. But, tomorrow, the arrangement can change to reflect the background color of the stamp design. The following day, an important rearrangement may be based on the shape of the stamps — whether triangular, vertical, horizontal rectangle, or whatever. So, a plentiful stock of paper to be used for personal albums is a way to encourage the creativity.

Collecting to compete

If you must have a defined challenge for everything you do, I have something for you: *competitive stamp exhibits.* With these, stamp collectors who love competition can have at it with their peers.

Such exhibits are contested at the local-club level, regional level, at national competitions, and even at the international level. Prizes, awards dinners, opportunities to discuss your winning collection publicly, and all the trappings of a celebrity are available provided that you are able to follow the rules for the events in a wide variety of categories (see Figure 4-2).

Before the stars in your eyes cloud your view of reality, don't expect to begin collecting stamps next Wednesday and then in a month have your first certificate of victory. You have much work ahead, work that will require more expenditure than you would have if you entered stamp collecting purely for recreation. This expenditure can be monetary — the amount tied directly to the type of collection you are building — or the excess expenditure may involve additional research and preparation. Some long-time stamp collectors believe that money is the primary way to make competitive exhibits a success. Yet, too many times I have seen proper material carry the day in a competitive exhibit because of the winning collector's research and skill versus those who prefer to base a competitive exhibit purely on the exhibit's total value.

Figure 4-2:
Rows of
stamp
exhibition
frames.

Just as the investment-oriented collector needs a stable of reference material and precise tools, so does the competitor. Perhaps a difference between the two is that the competitor need not seek out material to hold only for resale at a profit. Rather, competitors are looking for material that allows them to develop the story that they tell through their competitive exhibit. The investor seeks only key items; the competitor also seeks the mortar between the bricks.

The investor may be pleased with a collection that consists of as few as a dozen items that were purchased with the belief that each will appreciate in value with time. The investor is thus able to sell the item(s) later at a profit. The general collector, however, pays little, albeit some, attention to the value of the material purchased. The collector is far more interested in collecting toward some form of completeness, which may be self-defined. The collector's criteria means collecting inexpensive as well as expensive items to fill his album spaces. The competitive exhibitor, on the other hand, builds a presentation — a story — and must then be certain to make the presentation with the best examples possible. Rare, obscure, or previously misidentified items may add to the competition value without regard to the monetary value.

No matter how lofty your goals, begin small. Find out how to interpret the rules of the competitive exhibiting game. If you do want to move up, you only will be able to do it within the regulations. Almost forgot: Among your expenses will be tickets to awards banquets and additional shelving for the various items you win. Think positive! And, see Chapter 10.

Building something substantial

The rare person does not enjoy the limelight for something achieved, whether it is with attribution — it is hard to lead the National Football League in passing yardage anonymously — or quietly through work you have done. To a very large extent, you are able to build a stamp collection that achieves. I do not expect that examples I present here are all-inclusive, and I offer them solely to stimulate your thinking.

If you are able to build a competitive collection that wins a major national or even international prize, you have achieved (skip ahead to Figure 4-3). That is the easy example and a very difficult goal to meet. Nevertheless, it definitely is worth consideration.

Figure 4-3:
Medal awarded for competition.

You also may elect to complete the collection of a country or a range of years of a single country's stamp issues. If you limit yourself to the Christmas issues of 1999, you certainly may want to take pride in obtaining all of those items, however few or many there may be. There are countries whose total numbers of stamp issues and their cost is within the range of most. Although these may not be countries in which you have some interest, you still are able to meet a goal by collecting all its stamps.

Trying to collect all the stamps of a country with a much richer stamp-issuing heritage may be more costly than you initially expect. You can find — for a price — a high percentage of the number of stamps issued by Great Britain. At some point, however, you'll begin to note those with a price tag with more digits than you have on one hand. Thus, a limiting factor has reared its ugly head. Even though you may come across items that are beyond your financial reach, you can obtain some solace as your own study and research allows you to include items that are out of the mainstream and are just plain neat in your collection. You can get *very* close to a complete collection. But *complete* is a fleeting concept. As you begin to approach completion, your own definition expands and takes your quest with it.

If monument building continues as your goal, here is another approach. Do you live in a community with a rich history of logging, mining, or textile manufacture, or even a bedroom community known more for its commuters than anything? If your community has a mining history, as does my own boyhood home, you can derive tremendous enjoyment building a stamp collection showing the historical and technological development of mining. After your collection is complete — not from the standpoint of number of stamps, but more importantly from the standpoint of telling your town's whole mining story — your collection will be in demand for display at local and area museums and libraries, and you will be in demand to trade your knowledge for many a luncheon.

But what of the bedroom community, you ask. Why not develop a collection showing the commuter: what is faced, highway development, various commuter-friendly vehicles from around the world, and even traffic signs. Your completed collection may not make you the same talk of the town as our mining historian, but you nevertheless will have something of significance and — with proper tongue-in-cheek — still may be traded for a chance to be a featured speaker at the meeting of a local organization or two.

Such topical collections, where the intent is to inform and to enjoy, well may have the most modest expense of all. You are not obliged to include any specific (high-priced) stamp, both single stamps and multiples, or whatever else. Rather, you are building this collection purely for the education and enjoyment factors, which is where this chapter began.

Is Completing Possible?

If you have plans to start a stamp collection with the specific intent of obtaining all the items necessary to complete that collection, then you will need to define precisely what you will include. Such a precaution is critical because of the vastness of stamp collecting, the continuing surprises you will encounter, and even that wonderful pettiness that makes stamp collecting what it is. Take a second to scratch your head.

If it is your goal to collect all the stamps issued by the country of Fiji — pretty stamps and a nice place to vacation, I am told — your concept of what you will be collecting may be different than my concept.

For example, the principal postage stamp catalogue used in the U.S. shows about 875 regular Fiji postage stamps issued over the years, along with about 31 stamps of other types, postage due, and so on. That catalogue's competitors, published in France, Germany, and Great Britain, will show about the same number — with the difference only in how each determines what is a variety. You may then believe that you will be looking for a little more than 900 stamps for your Fiji collection, plus whatever new issues come about during the time you are building your collection. Fine. That will provide you with a very nice collection and one that you will not be completing in a short time. Most of the stamps are inexpensive, but some are not.

The 900 number of stamps noted previously is made up of what is generally considered to be major varieties, such as those stamps that have some design differences, a different perforation measurement, or some other major difference. Many of the earlier Fiji stamps, and some of the later ones, have minor varieties, which may come about because of a small difference in an overprint; a single letter may be inverted, the space between the first and second line of type may be wider or narrower than the norm, or the watermark on one stamp in a set is shown upside down, as well as in the proper orientation. Yes, these are different enough to be included by collectors in their collection. With the addition of the minor varieties, your initial goal of 900 stamps has been increased by perhaps as much as 20 percent.

At the same time, the thrill of the search has been increased by even more, because now you are looking at many of the stamps much more closely than you otherwise might. Look, dear, I'm a collector! I now have reason to use my magnifying glass.

But you are not done yet; you have other directions to go in. Do you want to collect only single stamps, or do blocks of four stamps appeal more to you? Instead of, or in addition to, just used stamps, how about used stamps *on cover,* still on the envelope. You won't find them all, but at least some of them will make an attractive addition to your collection that, by now, will have outgrown the album you intended for it. Oh yes, wanna have some *real* fun? Find covers (envelopes) canceled from each of the Fiji post offices. I don't even know if that is possible, but the quest will provide you with plenty of experience in research.

Apply this whole approach to any other country. Collecting examples of cancellations for a single county can present a pretty fair challenge. Such a collection may represent each city, each city in a state or province, only commemorative cancellations that may complement a topical stamp collection, and on and on.

 If you are a topical collector, rather than a country collector, you have every bit as much breadth. You have decided to collect aardvarks depicted on stamps. Are you looking for stamps where the aardvark is the only thing depicted, where one aardvark is the major design element, or where aardvarks are small enough to be recognized but may require your trusty magnifying glass to confirm your suspicion? Then you can add a section on the aardvark's cuisine and where the aardvark family sets up housekeeping.

Completeness is in the eye of the beholder. Or, to use another perspective, completeness is an ever-moving target.

Explaining supply and demand (almost)

The real answer to the question is, "because a formal market for postage stamps does not exist." Getting from the question to the real answer is not as direct as you might expect. Without risking embarrassment at any attempt to explain myself in economics, I merely will note that postage stamps seek their own value level. The law of supply and demand — and occasionally the law of the jungle — rules.

Most stamps pretty much seek their own level and don't change much. Some increase over the years, but most do not.

Postage-stamp catalogues assign a minimum value to each stamp. Because each of the major catalogues has its own criteria for valuing stamps, you will not find any direct correlation among the publishers. Most stamp dealers set a minimum value for anything they sell. Because each dealer's personal pricing criteria is based on his own business situation, in general, for most items selling for less than one dollar, and perhaps even a little more, what you pay a dealer for the stamp pretty much is his/her overhead. Therefore, it's not surprising that stamps increasing in value in the stamp catalogues normally are those above the level where the price is pure dealer overhead, although that is not a hard rule.

If the one stamp costs you 25¢, that cost is to cover all the handling from the time the dealer purchased the item, sorted it, identified it, packaged it, and got it ready to sell to you. Normally, for low-value stamps, dealers will have multiples and will be able to identify the items on sight. As those envelopes fill up with stamps that are quite plentiful, the dealer is able to offer a quantity of them at what appears to be a bargain price. How? When a dealer purchases a collection or other holdings from a collector, only the *better* material is figured into the purchase price. The low-end material tags along.

If the low-value material begins to back up, then the dealer's option is to sell it or watch it begin to clutter up the office area. At the same time, you can always find collectors who want a large quantity of the same stamp for purposes of searching for varieties — another use for your magnifying glass. In case you already have your calculator at the ready, do not expect to purchase one stamp for $25 and 100 of the same stamp for $300.

Burrowing in or spreading your wings?

Chances are close to zero that you will continue your current approach to stamp collecting. After you have become immersed in the hobby and begin to understand what is available to you, your interests will direct you to a different approach. Perhaps you will want to narrow your collecting area, perhaps you will want to broaden it, or perhaps you will want break off what you are doing now and move to a whole different stamp collecting area. Let's look at the implications of each, presuming that you have begun by saving current stamps of your country and any earlier ones you have been able to obtain easily.

Narrowing your focus

Stamp collectors refer to this as *specializing*. Now you're grabbing onto your country's stamps and perhaps already have a stamp album for them. Great. Many people spend a great deal of quality time doing just that, and have no thoughts of changing their approach.

If you want to specialize a bit, then just concentrate on commemoratives. That still leaves you with many stamps to complete your quest. So, perhaps you may narrow things a little more. You can limit your collection to your nation's commemoratives, from their beginning through to the end of the century or any other date that may be significant to you or the nation's history.

Or, you can build a nice collection of stamps from a certain time span, such as a World War, combined with cancellations in use at the time. Of course, when you begin to specialize to that level, you also begin to look more closely for varieties. As you begin to specialize, your horizons expand to include additions formats, such as blocks and the stamps used on cover. See Figure 4-4 just ahead. With commercial covers, you seek *covers* (envelopes) with markings that signify a stamp's first day of issue or — particularly in the case of airmail stamps — the first flight of a particular airmail route, known as *first-flight covers*. Take a gander at Figure 4-5 for a peek at a first-flight cover. As you can see, the number of items you seek when you begin to specialize does not necessarily decrease. What increases, however, is your expertise in a tighter area.

How you choose to specialize is totally your decision. A story within stamp collecting circles tells of a lady prior to World War II who only collected purple U.S. stamps. That is, she only was interested in single-color, purple-ink stamps — pretty much all that was available then.

Figure 4-4:
Plate block.

Figure 4-5:
First-flight
cover.

Broadening your approach

Although specializing is the more traditional direction for a stamp collector to go, sometimes you choose to spread your wings a bit. You now may be collecting only new issues you get at the post office. Then you discover that your post office does not get examples of all new issues. Now you want to expand to include all current issues and perhaps stamps for the past ten years.

Along other lines, perhaps your family emigrated from Panama and you have begun a collection of stamps of that nation. But, given the history of the area, you begin to collect stamps issued by the Canal Zone, a U.S. possession, and perhaps even Colombia. Or, you may be interested in Hawaii and begin a topical collection of anything having to do with the island group. Hawaiian stamps issued before and during the period that Hawaii became a U.S. possession are natural additions.

You are never locked into a collection. With so much material out there for you, even if your first choice is not something you want to pursue for an extended period, you have plenty of wiggle room. Enjoy it.

Chapter 5

Getting a Grip on Grade and Condition

*M*ost postage stamps are nothing more than small pieces of paper. I cannot emphasize the fragile nature of stamps enough. Although stamps are virtually always printed on a high-quality paper that will last for a long time, longevity may be cut short by bad care. After a stamp leaves a post office's control, it can only be reduced in quality — never improved.

Unlike some other hobbies, stamp collecting does not accept restoration as a legitimate effort. Stamps marked *restored* are significantly discounted in the marketplace; restored stamps in the marketplace without such identification are considered fraudulent. See Chapter 15 for more on philatelic fraud. Before any in-depth discussion of value, *grade* and *condition* must be well-understood terms. And, as you begin understanding the terms, you will develop a better understanding of how to treat your prized paper scraps.

Keeping Collectibles Straight

You need to have the following two terms firmly understood and not interchange them.

Grade: The centering of a stamp's design on the actual piece of paper that is considered the stamp.

Condition: An array of situations that degrade stamp value. For more on value, see Chapter 6.

For the most part, grade is a function of the production process. Factors affecting condition come about after the stamp has been produced. Exceptions exist, but generally the theory holds. Grade is a sliding scale that affects value, and condition is an all-or-nothing situation that affects value. All the aspects of condition must be positive, or a stamp is severely devalued. Grade is essentially keyed to the centering of the design on the stamp. Catalogue value is keyed to a specific grade (currently very fine), and market value will increase or decrease based on the stamp being of a greater or lesser grade than the pricing standard.

When it comes to centering, you are looking for extremes: The design is perfectly centered — horizontally and vertically — or the centering is so bad that the resulting item is considered a freak. There may be a premium for either extreme, but the more you move away from the extreme, the greater the decrease in value.

Centering, in some cases, can be so critical to the value of a stamp issue (stamps printed at the same time with the same design) that precise tools may be required to accurately measure the centering. (See Chapter 3 for more information about philatelic tools.) Digital scanning and enlarging the image of a stamp may make such measurement easier, if necessary at all. Yes, this may appear a little much, but remember that this is a hobby, and you are having fun. Some stamp issues are not generally known to have good centering, making those individual examples of those stamp issues particularly desirable when found well centered. Some collectors and dealers may reference such issues as "well-centered for the issue," although this concept is not universally accepted. That is, because some stamps are only known with poor centering, some dealers and collectors will refer to better varieties within such a group as "well-centered for the issue." To some, this is a way to rationalize that an item is as good as it can get, but the stamp still looks worse than other items near it in a collection. To others, the bending of definitions is too strong.

For the most part, you can determine the grade (centering) of a stamp with the naked eye. Because the guidelines for centering are generally not presented in any sort of quantitative manner, you will need to develop your own sense of *grade*. If you prefer greater precision, then you may want to use your stronger magnifier and a good measuring device to check the distance, on each of the four sides, from the edge of the stamp design to the edge of the stamp. This can be time-consuming, which is perhaps why the more rapid visual determination is the general practice.

The condition of a stamp is based on such factors as

- The *freshness* of its color
- Whether it has wide margins
- The cancellation (for used stamps)

These factors can be somewhat subjective, particularly the cancellation. If a collection is built of cancellations, then a clear, heavy, and readable cancellation will enhance a stamp's value within that collection. But if you aren't interested in cancellations, that same stamp will be of substantially less value to you. Such cancellation collections may include a calendar of every day of the year on a particular stamp design, or every post office that ever existed within a city or a county, or even every example of a cancellation device used in a city. Thus, one collector may be willing to pay $2 for a stamp that a second collector shuns, all because of the strength of the cancellation on the stamp.

When a stamp comes from the printing press, the stamp normally looks bright and new as it can be. How the stamp is handled and stored over the years affects its overall appearance. If the stamp is subjected to bright light — particularly sunlight — for extended periods, it can begin to fade and lose its "fresh" appearance. Other circumstances may lead to such defacing; anything that affects paper and printing, also. See "Preserving Condition," later in this chapter, for tips on how to help keep your stamps looking their best.

Making the Grad (ing)

Before beginning a discussion of stamp grading, I am compelled to note that there is no formally enforced grading scheme for postage stamps. That is, everything that I note here and that you see elsewhere is a best-effort situation.

Therefore, before you purchase a stamp of any value, you should see the stamp live.

Margin for error

All stamps, at the time of production, are designed to have a specific width of blank area, without print, from the edge of a perforation on one side to the edge on the other, and the same from top to bottom. This linear measurement, the *margin,* is not necessarily the same from stamp issue to stamp issue, but normally it is the same within the same printing of the same stamp.

In the early days of stamp production, when the perforating process was considerably less precise than it is today, the line perforator may have been applied to the pane of stamps it was perforating a little too close to the previous line, or a little too far away. The resulting stamps may then be of a different width and/or length than the "standard" for the issue. Meanwhile, the actual stamp design remains constant. So, you then have stamps that have larger or smaller margins than the norm for the issue. Large-margined stamps are more desirable than stamps with small margins.

Superb is subjective

Buy/sell ads reference quite a few grading levels, ranging from *poor* to *superb*, and everything in between: *fair, good, fine, fine-very fine, very fine, extremely fine, extra fine,* and perhaps some others. What is needed, and which we have, is a reference point for stamp values in this country.

The Scott Publishing Co., producers of an annual set of volumes that catalogues the stamps of the world, bases its values for stamps on the grade level of *very fine.* A stamp with a higher grade is worth more (no set percentage) and a stamp of a lesser grade is worth less. When the standard changed from fine-very fine, there was quite a rumble because the reference point had changed. The impreciseness of the hobby led to a reference-point change that was discomforting, and some dealers began to advertise stamps that had been "fine-very fine" as "very fine." This is not ethical. Fortunately, unlike what has happened in coins over the years, such practices are not nearly widespread enough to require a grading system such as the one found in coins . . . where, unfortunately, one does not buy a coin, but a grade.

The written definition for the *very fine* grade level is, "stamps may be slightly off-center on one side, but the design will be well clear of the edge. The stamp will present a nice, balanced appearance. Imperforate stamps will have three normal-sized margins."

A stamp's grade cannot change, other than through the flowery language of a skilled advertising copywriter. If you see an ad for a stamp that has a grade of average, that stamp is average no matter how eloquently the writer describes the stamp's beauty?

Going Downhill

You are dealing with paper items, which are subject to the same problems that befell Grandma's letter. Her letter was on the mantel for a month before you stained it with your coffee cup. Or, consider your morning paper that the delivery person nearly gets into the proper slot; some of the pages are creased, torn, or scraped. But, I am a little ahead of myself.

Some attributes that affect a stamp's condition are based on situations

✔ During production

✔ Hinging

✔ When the post office cancels the stamp

Further situations relative to condition are considered faults; bad things that happen to a stamp, such as: pen or marker cancellations, pulled or short perforations, and creases, scrapes, or tears. Creases may be difficult to spot (normally spotted on the reverse of the stamp), or they may be as prominent as dog-earing a page of this book. A pulled perf is one that has been removed from the row, leaving a larger gap. A short perf is caused when separating two stamps, with the separation being uneven enough to have one (or more) perfs appear obviously and substantially shorter than the others. Remember, particularly with older stamps, their purchasers didn't consider them as collector's items, but rather as tools to help move the mail. Scraping a stamp is similar to skinning your knee, but without the blood, tears, and bandage.

Cancels: *You may come to love them*

Many stamp collectors, particularly newer ones, eschew canceled stamps for mint stamps. The latter naturally have not suffered the shock of being sent through the mail, are not defaced by postal markings (cancellations), and generally live up to the definition of mint. However, Postal markings, cancellations in particular, can be extremely interesting and form the basis of many spectacular collections.

Canceled stamp collections may revolve around examples of all the post offices in your county, state/province, or even your city. Some collectors, as a fun sidelight, seek cancellations to form a yearlong calendar, finding month-and-day cancels for every day of the year. Some cancellation calendars formed with cancels on a single, classic issue may not only be difficult to complete, requiring plenty of searching, but may also turn out to have value.

Flag cancellations, where the obliterator is a flag design, are quite popular. Some collections consist of examples of machine cancels made by a particular brand of machine, showing where and when the machine was used. Souvenir cancellations are produced for nearly all major events, from the Olympics to the Super Bowl to coronations to local festivals and fairs.

How you feel about a cancellation on your stamp may be different than what the next philatelist feels. Some collectors are looking for specific postal markings and believe that the prominence of such cancellations on a stamp adds to the stamp's value. Other collectors are not nearly as interested in the cancellation and look poorly on any stamp with a heavy cancel. Therefore, the very same stamp may be appealing and thought to be in great condition by one collector, while another degrades the stamps in his mind because of the prominent cancellation.

Collectors generally consider a heavy, over-inked, ugly cancellation as a negative. Other cancellations, however, affect individual collectors differently. What a cancellation says, how dark it is, and how much of the stamp it covers — some collectors want it to cover very little, others want it all over — drives the collector's interest in a used stamp. If I am seeking a stamp with a cancellation from a certain city or a specific commemorative cancellation, then a cancellation that is ugly to you brings out the glee in me. See several examples of stamp cancellations in Figure 5-1.

Many different types of cancels exist. Here is a listing of the very common types:

- **Bull's-eye:** The complete circular date stamp is contained within the boundaries of the stamp. This is a fun collectible. Some collectors build a calendar of stamps with bull's-eye cancellations, where each stamp's cancellation date represents a day of the year. Skip ahead to Figure 5-2 to see how a bull's-eye cancellation may appear.

- **Slogan:** Used by individual post offices, particularly when a strange juxtaposition of cancellation and stamp design renders a humorous or offbeat result. A slogan cancel that promotes an antismoking campaign and is prominent on a stamp where the design has a person holding a cigarette is worth saving. Many such combinations exist that can brighten up an album page.

- **Machine:** Cancellation applied mechanically or, more recently, by ink jet. Slogan cancels, or merely the common circular date stamp with the city and so on, may be so applied, with an accompanying obliterator for the stamp.

- **Fancy:** A term normally reserved for early cancels that were hand applied and hand carved from cork. More recent cancellations that include some illustration may fall under the slogan or special event categories.

- **Special Event:** These cancellations are used, for a short period of time, to honor an event or other commemoration. Many stamp shows apply for and receive permission for special event cancellations. The Olympic games normally have one for each venue.

Figure 5-2:
Bull's-eye —
socked-on-
the-nose —
cancellation.

Gumming up your goods

Another area with a range of possibilities that affect condition is gum, the adhesive on the reverse of a mint stamp.

- ✔ **Never hinged:** The top of the line. It refers to the back of a mint stamp that has no signs of a *disturbance* to the original gum caused by a stamp hinge.

- ✔ **Lightly hinged:** This suggests a faint impression from a stamp hinge, but it is certainly subjective.

- ✔ **Hinge mark** or **hinge remnant:** A piece of a hinge remains attached to the stamp, or a large and prominent hinge mark is evident; a large part of the back of the stamp with original gum, and the remainder of the gum missing; and, a small part of the original gum in place and the remainder missing.

- ✔ **No gum:** For those stamps originally issued without gum.

Preserving Condition

Although this chapter helps you identify situations already in place that affect condition, here are some suggestions that cannot be repeated too many times. Keep your stamps away from

- ✔ **Moisture:** This may be the most destructive element affecting the paper itself and the gum. Moisture softens the gum and allows one stamp to stick to another. Moisture also promotes the growth of mold and mildew.

✔ **Dust and dirt:** What a stamp can pick up from your desktop can affect it. Cookie or cracker crumbs may cause a stain. Heavy dust may be pressed into the fibers of the stamp paper. Keep your stamp table clean and clear of all foreign objects (unless they are foreign stamps).

✔ **Critters:** This includes insects, many of which look upon a stamp's paper or gum as a tasty bug treat. Unless your be-kind-to-animals instincts include feeding stray creepy-crawlies, be careful and be certain to check your stamps from time to time. If you suspect that your stamp holdings have become critter food, remove your stamps from the area, check them carefully for remaining critters, remove any critters quickly and without squishing them on the stamps, and then treat your stamp desk/storage as you would normally to prevent further damage. Do not return your stamps to the area until the space is clear of critter remnants and any chemicals you used to de-critter the area. What sort of beasties you can expect depends on where you are located: Arctic dwellers have polar bear concerns and collectors in the tropics need to watch out for multilegged creatures.

✔ **Heat:** Whether the source of heat is a furnace duct, stamp pipe, or hot and dry attic, neither moist heat nor dry heat is good for stamps.

✔ **Tape:** Any sort of adhesive tape does not mix positively with postage stamps. In short, keep all tape away from your stamps and albums.

✔ **Office supplies:** Paper clips produce creases. Rubber bands degrade in open air in an amazingly short time and may go through a chemical change that causes the rubber to adhere to the stamp.

✔ **Newspaper:** Stamps are made from excellent, quality paper, which in normal circumstances will not degrade much over the years. Other forms of paper, such as newsprint, will degrade. Keeping a postage stamp on, or even close to, a newspaper clipping relating to the stamp may result in damage to the stamp as the newsprint degrades.

No matter where you live, you need to store your stamps to keep them from your local climate's elements, particularly humidity. Certain parts of the world, however, require specific precautions to safeguard your collection. If you have questions about what you may need to do in your area, check with a local librarian — they have a building full of paper items to keep safe.

To maintain some perspective, if you practice a common-sense approach to maintaining your collection, you will not have any problems, and you won't cause your precious little pieces of paper to degrade before their time. At the same time, a dose of reality will keep you on your toes, which is particularly difficult when comfortably sitting in your chair at the desk or table where you handle your stamps. You are more concerned with the enjoyment you are having at the present than what can happen in the future if you do not take care of the stamps.

Chapter 6

"Appreciating" Value

*P*erhaps the question that noncollectors ask the most in reference to an old postage stamp is, "Is this worth anything?" In every case, the response is, "Yes." All too often the question presumes worth as some astronomical number when compared to what the stamp originally cost. The kicker, however, is just how much the stamp is worth, and in what framework you respond to the question. Rather than provide any sort of answer to that question right now — with or without a hypothetical scenario — first read about the concepts of value and worth from a variety of perspectives. This information enables you to offer a viable response.

Aging: Good for Wine. Good for Stamps?

Is older always better? This is a trick question. The key word in the question is "always," and the answer is, "No." Generally, however, older stamps have more value than newer ones. For example, stamp dealers normally offer less-than-face value for U.S. mint stamps dating back through at least 1950, which can be used for postage (see Figure 6-1), and for some issues dating back even earlier. You are better off using stamps that can still be used for postage to send greeting cards, rather than selling the stamps to dealers who pay less.

Figure 6-1: The Washington /Franklin one-cent stamp, over 80 years old, is still valid postage.

Dealers offer less-than-face value for material dating back to at least 1950 because it's offered to them so often. People purchase stamps from the post office in anticipation of a value increase over the years, only to realize their plan has bombed, and then they try to unload their surplus. Those who offer this material to stamp collectors and dealers often have hundreds or thousands of dollars in postage and seek whatever they can get for it. Further, because the stamps are decades old, the stamp denomination is not high enough to cover first class mail, so the stamps are not as valuable to businesses for their current mailing needs. Essentially, you are seeing a bad investment.

The dealer pulls off some (or sometimes all) of the plate blocks for his stock or for a quick resale. The remainder of the material — known as "scrap" — is sold to individuals for postage at less-than-face value. I cannot remember purchasing U.S. stamps at face value for my own mail in the last 20 years! The supply, however, is drying up a bit. As the rate for a one-ounce letter at the first-class rate continues to increase, more and more three-cent stamps are needed for each envelope. I know because I am still licking them!

When you buy a postage stamp, put it into your album or shoe box, and refrain from using it to mail a letter. The postal service gets the profit from the stamp's sale without giving any service. The USPS calls this *retention*.

A 50-year-old U.S. postage stamp was produced during the beginning of the period when postal services around the world were realizing the sales potential to stamp collectors. So, more stamps were issued. When you find a few 50-year-old U.S. stamps in a drawer of a piece of bedroom furniture that you bought at an estate auction — like so many people that ask me questions have — chances are high that the stamps you found are worth little more than face value.

Age itself does not determine the value of a postage stamp.

Value = x + y

The first U.S. commemorative stamp was the Columbian Exposition Issue of 1893. For the most part, as you would expect, the market value of the stamps in this set increases as the stamp denomination (its assigned postal value) increases. There are exceptions, however, with the two-cent stamp showing a catalogue value less than the one-cent stamp and the eight-cent stamp with a lesser catalogue value than the six-cent stamp. Thus, age by itself does not rule. Eight cents, at the time, covered a specific, pop-

ular postage rate; therefore, the single stamp of that denomination was more in demand at the time than some of the lesser denominations.

Perhaps more important to this discussion is that every one of the second set of U.S. commemoratives — the 1898 Trans-Mississippi Exposition Issue — has a greater catalogue value than two of the initial sets of commemoratives issued five years prior.

More difficult than merely finding early stamps at a reasonable price is to find them at a grade level that you find acceptable. Chapter 5 gives you the scoop on grading and condition. Print quality improved dramatically during the twentieth century.

Reaching Maturity

As a stamp appreciates in value when the demand exceeds supply, the stamp-collecting industry realizes the fact and an adjustment is made. For the most part, this happens for some stamps that are traded regularly. Of the approximately 750,000 different postage stamps issued since 1840, most have a value that has stuck rather close to where they started.

The anomalies easily give pause to the whole value-and-appreciation scenario. These are the many stamps from countries around the world with a value of, say, 25¢, which pretty much sets them in the low-value and easy-to-obtain categories. In reality, however, because there is little active demand for these stamps, the fact that they are in short supply has not been realized.

Because stamp collecting does not have a formal market where prices are established and monitored — except for the stamps of their home country, catalogue publishers do not review their values more often than annually — some stamps may easily hide below the value radar.

Generally, within each country, key items drive the overall value of that country's stamps. Or, at least, the key items set the tone for the country's stamps of a specific era. That is, a dealer looks at the material you offer, while seeking specific stamps or sets. If you have them, the dealer evaluates your material pretty much only on the basis of the grade and condition of those items that he is looking for, and then he adds a little for the remainder of the material. This is not a process set in stone, and some dealers may look for different items than others do. The items the dealer seeks are those that he knows he is able to sell — to a collector or another dealer — quickly. This approach to evaluating a collection offered for sale is a major reason why a dealer is able to come up with an offer so quickly: He is not evaluating each item, but only certain stamps that interest him. Here is a major reason why you want at least two offers from various dealers before you sell: Each dealer may be looking for different items and base a purchase offer on separate material from the same collection.

If you are offering a collection of old material, where nearly all of it is of moderate to high value, the dealer is certain to spend more time per item than if you are offering a collection of commemorative stamps from 1950 to the present.

Appreciation of a stamp's value is not an automatic, nor is appreciation based solely on age, on the number issued, on what has happened to the country in the meantime, or on any other single factor. Rather, there is a combination of factors — perhaps *mishmash* is a better term — that sets the value. Weird as this approach may appear, it works beautifully now, as it has for decades.

Varying Values

Yes, there is more than one varied value. And, you'll notice major differences among them. When considering value, you to need to understand

- ✔ Catalogue value
- ✔ Market value
- ✔ Resale value

The three separate kinds of value do not represent a good/bad situation. Rather, they are three different approaches to figuring value based on your situation. You want to understand each and when to apply it. Knowing when to figure catalogue value is important. But, if you are calculating on the basis of catalogue value when you should be using market value, you can probably come up with a different (and incorrect-for-the-situation) total.

Scanning through your catalogue

A postage-stamp catalogue normally is a reference work that has all stamps of a country, region, or even the whole world listed in a consistent fashion. Catalogue information can enable you to determine exactly which items you do and do not possess and into which sets or categories individual items fall. Stamp catalogues can generally provide a foundation on which to organize your collection.

The first catalogue goes back to the nineteenth century — it and was more of a price list of available material from dealers. Current catalogues, which come in all sizes, shapes, levels of detail, and flavors, are reference works rather than price lists (see Figure 6-2). Although some are still price lists, that fact itself is not a determining factor in the usefulness of the work itself.

Figure 6-2: Stamp catalogue listings.

Among the data presented for each stamp is a *catalogue value*. Well, to be more precise, two catalogue values: one for the stamp as mint and the other for a used version. If you have three catalogues before you, each listing the same material, you will probably have three different catalogue values for the item you are checking. So, what is presented as being an explanation suddenly becomes more confusing, but not really. Each catalogue sets its parameters for how it arrives at its catalogue value. Therefore, you need to read that information before using the catalogue.

The most widely used catalogue in the U.S. is the *Scott Standard Postage Stamp Catalogue*. Each of the six annual volumes has an extensive introductory section, which opens with this definition of catalogue value: "The Scott Catalogue value is a retail value; that is, an amount you could expect to pay for a stamp in the grade of Very Fine with no faults. Any exceptions to the grade valued will be noted in the text." It goes on to state, "The value listed for any given stamp is a reference that reflects recent actual dealer selling prices for that item." In essence, Scott's interpretation of catalogue value is a retail value for a stamp when that stamp is purchased singly from a dealer. Also, Scott has established a minimum value that it will assign to a stamp, which it maintains accounts for dealer overhead in handling an individual low-valued stamp, preparing it for sale. The current minimum value is 20 cents.

Thus, if you calculate the catalogue value of your collection, you are adding up individual values as if you were purchasing those items one at a time. Given that many of the items in a stamp collection were purchased as part of some grouping, the total catalogue value will naturally be a high total. At the same time, if other collectors are also determining the catalogue value, there is a common ground on which to compare. Also, there is a common ground on which to swap material, which is a very common way to build a collection.

Catalogue value is also important when noting the sales price of any item. That is, a dealer may advertise a sale item at some percentage of catalogue value, or an auction firm may boast that a stamp or set sold at auction for some multiple of the catalogue value. Catalogue value becomes the standard.

Here are two scenarios that show how you can take advantage of catalogue value:

- ✓ You are trying to sell 1,000 stamps, each of which is listed at minimum catalogue value of 20¢. You have a grouping with a total catalogue value of $200, but not a grouping with a *worth* of $200. Thus, if you have a collection with 80 percent of the stamps at minimum value (which is not unreasonable, particularly in the early stages of your collecting), you cannot total the catalogue value and proclaim it as the *worth* of your 77 collection.

- ✓ A grouping of stamps at a total catalogue value of $500 is advertised without illustrations and without any descriptions of grade or condition. A less-than-scrupulous person may merely note the catalogue number of each item and assign a catalogue value to it without regard to the grade (of Very Fine) or condition (no faults). Although this is not a common situation, it does occur more often than common decency would dictate.

All this discussion is keyed to the *Scott Standard Postage Stamp Catalogue* and its definition. In other parts of the world, other major catalogues are dominant, each with its own concepts. No right or wrong way exists. Rather, you need to understand what the publishers mean and adjust your approach to buying and selling stamps to those meanings.

Taking note of the marketplace

Where catalogue value represents the theoretical approach to the worth of an item based on research and calculations, market value is the reality of the situation. *Market value* is the amount that you pay a dealer for a stamp, set, lot, collection, or whatever.

Unlike catalogue value, which is respected wherever the specific catalogue is used, market value may be more localized. For example, if you are at a local stamp show, and one of the six dealers there has an item that you desire, what you pay for the item is the market value. The price you pay may be the same, more, or less than the quoted catalogue value. That fact may be relevant to how that item is faring in the marketplace relative to catalogue value. But if you see a few dealers all selling an item at about the same price, and the price is nearly the same as current catalogue value, while other items are selling at below catalogue value, then the item is probably increasing in value. Watch for the next edition of the same catalogue to see if the catalogue value of the item has increased.

A specific item may have a different price from one dealer to another, or even from the same dealer from the one time that you see him or her to the next. The flux in pricing may occur for any number of many reasons. But perhaps the most basic reason for the difference is the lack of a formal stamp market. Therefore, each dealer buys items at the best price and sets a sale price to accommodate a fair markup, while not losing sight of the current catalogue value (see Figure 6-3).

You, as the consumer, may find the same item for sale at a local stamp show for $35, advertised in one of the stamp periodicals for $28, offered for sale on the Internet for $26.50, and recently sold at auction for $45. Why the range of sale prices?

- ✔ The local price of $35 is from a local dealer who takes the time to talk with you, answer your questions, provide advice, and help you even when it will not lead to another sale. You are paying for the stamp and for service.

- ✔ The $28 price is through a media ad, possibly from a dealer who is selling items from behind a PO Box, who is known for his low prices. The quality of this item may be great, but the dealer himself is not available for anything other than selling stamps. No service, no advice.

- ✔ The $26.50 price, through the Internet, is from a dealer similar to the dealer advertising in the print media, but the Internet "ad" was not as expensive — if it cost anything at all. He, too, does not offer any service after the sale. Neither this dealer nor the other is the least bit disreputable; they merely sell on the basis of price rather than service.

US Price List

All stamps are mint (never hinged).

Catalogue Number	Price	Catalogue Number	Price	Catalogue Number	Price
704-15	16.75	1909a	55.00	C7	3.00
730	21.00	2002b	22.50	C8	3.00
731	20.00	2122	16.00	C9	9.00
735	12.00	2122a	49.50	C10	7.75
740-49	7.00	2123-36	2.80	C11	3.85
750	24.00	2168-96	23.95	C12	9.00
751	13.00	2216-19	12.00	C16	5.00
756.65	12.00	2252-66	3.25	C20	1.00
785-94	1.95	2335a	39.50	C21	7.00
803-32	32.00	2419	3.65	C22	6.75
833	19.00	2433	15.00	C24	6.75
834	75.00	2438	4.75	C46	4.00
839-51	22.00	2539	1.60	C91-92	1.00
909-21	1.60	2540	4.50	C93-94	1.00
1030-52	12.95	2541	13.50	C95-96	1.60
1053	65.00	2542	19.00	C100-04	2.25
1254a-57a	5.00	2543	4.00	C105-08	3.45
1612	7.00	2544	4.25	C109-12	3.60
1613-25	2.45	2590	1.75	C122-25	4.00
1633-82	12.00	2592	8.00	C126	5.75
1686-89	14.50	2624-29	29.50	O133	8.00
1757	1.50	2696a	29.95		
1844-69	8.25	2837	2.00		
1897-08	2.60	2840	3.00		
1909	18.00	2842	13.50		
		2975	15.00		

Figure 6-3:
Price list.

✔ The auction lot, selling for $45, may have one of two — or both — reasons for its high price. First, the item may be an exquisite copy, and the winning bidder may have attended the auction and had the opportunity to inspect the item personally. Or, two collectors wanted the item and did not allow market price, catalogue price, or anything but their quest to win get in their way.

Each of the prices in the preceding scenarios may be considered a market value, even the auction realization. What prompted the lot's bidders to that *hammer price* (the price for which an item was sold, such as the price at which the auctioneer's hammer was used to emphasize the great auction term: *sold*) probably will not be known, nor discussed. (It may have been emotion, knowledge of the market, an itchy nose that prompted the price.) The cause of the price may not be known because the final amount was low in contrast to other lots and because the amount was not dramatically above any of the other market prices. And, catalogue editors consider all four of the prices when contemplating the catalogue value for its next edition.

The *market value,* then, is what you pay for an item. That price may be above or below catalogue value, particularly if the grade is higher than that called for by the catalogue. How much below is purely a market situation. If a dealer has quite a stock of the same item, then holding out for a high price as opposed to selling one or more stamps from his plentiful supply is not a good business decision. So, the price is lowered. Or, if a dealer at a stamp show purchases some material early in the show and is able to sell that purchase later the same day, the price may be lower because he has had no "handling" or storage expense. All sorts of reasons come into play.

Some dealers pride themselves on being able to sell at a percentage of catalogue value. That is the basis for media ads for stamps at "50 percent or *Scott"* or sometimes even less. Other dealers restrict their inventory to better material in better grades. Therefore, their prices may well be above catalogue value.

Finding buyers to whom you'll sell

In a best-case scenario, what you are offering for sale to a dealer is something the dealer wants to purchase. Because the supply of most low-valued material is great (of course, that's why it's low valued), the situation is not uncommon where a dealer will pass on your offer to sell rather than even offer you something obscenely low for the material. After all, after purchasing material from you at any price, the dealer must still get the material into his inventory or just lay the purchase aside to be looked at later. If the latter, then what he paid you is an investment that does him no good in the short term.

Efficiency sales

Three different advertised prices — spotted while I am writing this paragraph — offer 2,000 different worldwide stamps for $17.95, 5,000 different worldwide stamps for $80, and 10,000 different stamps for $212. Taking the middle road, you can add 5,000 stamps to your collection and increase its *worth* to $1,000 using catalogue value — and it only costs you $80. What's wrong with this picture? You get the bragging potential, but you'll have a difficult time justifying the catalogue value as worth. In fact, this is one of the most important aspects that you can discover about catalogue values — it's the value of a stamp purchased singly. The 20-cent minimum value, as noted in the previous section, is pretty much a dealer's overhead cost of preparing that stamp for sale. Other than the glassine envelope into which the dealer will place the stamps for resale, the dealer is investing time, which certainly has a value. Preparing 1,000 stamps for individual sale is — if my calculations are accurate — more time-consuming than putting 1,000 stamps into a single envelope and writing the sale price on the outside.

Purchase those 5,000 stamps from a dealer one at a time and — if the dealer has not threatened your very existence in the meantime — you naturally will pay quite a bit more than you would for one package with all 5,000 inside.

It is seldom that a dealer offers you what you are expecting. The dealer's role in the transaction is to obtain material for resale at the best possible price. Your role is to get the best possible price. Unless you have underestimated the value of the material or the dealer has overestimated, his offer will be below your asking price. So, you now have the option of accepting the offer, haggling, or going off to seek something better. For many collectors, this is the fun part.

How do you know when you have the best offer you can get? Although the answer to that varies based on who you ask, my own experience is that if I knew the absolute right answer to that question, I would move on to correctly picking the state lottery number about once a month. Some hints:

- ✔ If you need money right away, take the best offer you can get quickly.

- ✔ If you are convinced that you are being offered too little, excuse yourself to seek out another dealer.

- ✔ If there are no veins popping on the dealer's neck yet, perhaps you can press your luck and try for a better price. If, however, the dealer turns very red in the face and keels over, you know you should have taken the last offer.

Knowing what your collection is worth

It is time to get right down to the messy part: What is your collection worth? The term *worth* is relative. Here are some approaches to defining the term as it applies to your collection.

> ✔ Tally the individual catalogue values of each of the stamps in your collection.
>
> You want to take this approach if you are the boastful type; you will want the highest possible value for bragging purposes. With the presumption that, as a newer collector, a rather high percentage of the items in your collection are listed in the catalogue at minimum value — now at 20 cents — you have many items at five-for-a-buck, one hundred for $20, or one thousand for $200. Sort of makes you want to run out and purchase material in bulk to increase the value and size of your collection.
>
> ✔ Calculate the replacement cost.
>
> Simply, *replacement cost* is what you would have to spend to replace the material in your collection in one effort. Replacement cost is what at least one major stamp insurance provider requires of its customers.
>
> At the same time, replacement cost requires you to understand your collection to the point of knowing how to factor grade and condition into value of individual items. If you are one who will only purchase the best available examples of a stamp, your replacement value will be more than one who accepts the *Scott Standard Postage Stamp Catalogue* standard of Very Fine grade.
>
> ✔ Calculate the resale value.
>
> *Resale value* is the amount you accept when selling your collection to a dealer. How a dealer reaches that amount can often be attributed to voodoo (or something like it), which is why you should get offers from at least two dealers.

A stamp dealer must buy and sell stamps to stay in business. Or, to be more positive, how well a dealer buys and sells stamps directly affects the success of his business. A generalized belief is that the price a dealer offers you for material relates to how quickly the dealer believes he will be able to sell the same material. Although there may be some truth to that belief, it is a bit simplistic.

Certainly dealers need to purchase material so there is inventory to sell. Some dealers have customers with standing *want lists* (lists of material they seek). When they come across wanted items, dealers are quick to buy.

Another more specific reason to make a purchase is to restock the stamps the dealer generally sells over time. Also, the dealer may have dealer friends who are looking for certain types of material; the dealer is purchasing for someone else's inventory. No matter what the specific reason is, it is far from unusual for dealers to purchase only the items they require — and a purchase includes plenty of lower-value items.

When a dealer looks at what you are offering, particularly when you are offering a collection, a single album, or more than just a few stamps, the price the dealer quotes you is pretty much based only on the key items. Thus, if you have an album of U.S. stamps, the dealer pages through the album and spots specific items. If the items that the dealer is seeking are present, the dealer notes the condition and begins a tally. The lower-value material is essentially disregarded and just goes along for the ride.

Dealers strip the material they really want from the rest of what they just purchased when they arrive back at home. Then the remainder may be resold to another dealer or collector, or perhaps just stored. Over time, the dealer amasses quite a bit of the low-value material. The dealer sells the low-value material to a wholesaler, or the dealer makes up his own packets for sale. This is how a dealer can offer 5,000 different stamps for $80 and not lose money.

The difference between catalogue value and resale value can be grand. Although not attempting to defend what may appear to be a low offer from a dealer for material you want to sell, dealers should know what the market situation is for material they are attempting to purchase. If the dealer is wrong, you compensate by having that second — or third — offer. And, if the dealer is wrong too many times, he may want to start looking for a good bankruptcy attorney.

Selling Your Stash

Certainly you may sell your stamps whenever you want. If you wake up tomorrow morning with the urge to leave stamp collecting and sell all your stamps, you can do that. Selling your current collection with the hope of changing stamp-collecting directions is possible, too.

Clunk. That is the sound of the other shoe dropping. Wanting to sell part or all your collection quickly and obtaining the best possible price are not necessarily mutually inclusive. If you are fortunate enough to locate a dealer looking for the type of material that you have for sale right away, everyone is ecstatic. Because stamp collecting is generally made up of small businesses, you need to find a small-business dealer right away — who is interested in purchasing what you have for sale — or work with a larger firm that is always purchasing material to replenish a large inventory. The former requires good fortune; the latter takes time.

Selling directly to a dealer is not your only option. Depending on the anticipated value of what you are selling, you have other options.

- ✔ **Public auction:** Selling at this venue is better for high-value items or collections that have at least some *better* pieces. Public auctions may require months from the time that arrangements are completed until the sale and final payment.

- ✔ **Auctions online:** All you need to do is follow the instructions and place anything up for sale on the Internet that you want. Online auctions are time-consuming because you must prepare and list each lot and follow through with the fulfillment after it sells . . . presuming it does sell. For more information on this subject, consult *Internet Auctions For Dummies* by Greg Holder (Hungry Minds, Inc.).

- ✔ **Local club:** Take what you want to sell to the next club meeting and hope you find someone interested in it. You may be pleasantly surprised.

    You then may be faced with the decision of selling quickly for whatever you can get or shopping around for the best price.

When you sell to dealers, tell them where you bought your material. For the same material offered, why does one dealer offer you an amount that can be less than, or even half of, another dealer's offer? Remember that an evaluation of what you are offering is subjective. Some, and only some, of the reasons why there may be a differential between offers may be that a dealer

- ✔ Misses a key stamp or set when quickly going through your material.

- ✔ Over grades the material. Or maybe the other dealer under graded the material. Remember that a stamp's grade drives its value.

- ✔ Has an immediate buyer for enough of the material that you are selling. Therefore, the dealer can offer you a high amount just to get the sale — the immediate turnaround.

- ✔ Purchases only for stock. Material may not be expected to sell for weeks, months, or perhaps longer.

- ✔ Senses that you are in a hurry to sell and willing consider any reasonable offer.

If stamp collecting's secondary market — the buying and selling after the material is purchased from the post office — was considerably larger, a more formal market and more consistent prices might be in place. But such a situation would add sterility and remove some of the charm. As it is, this buy/sell environment allows you to discover and meet more people in the hobby. Hermits have the option of conducting all their buying and selling by mail.

If there is any advice to offer you from all this, it is "do not sell on impulse." Plan what you want to cut from your holdings and spend some time finding the best way to do so. Selling stamps is as much a learning experience for you as purchasing is.

Investing in Stamps

I have seen people enter stamp collecting primarily to buy and sell stamps as an investment vehicle. I cannot remember any of them being successful. Also, I have seen people profit by building a collection over time and selling their collection for more than they paid. In effect, they showed that, at least in their circumstance, the whole was greater than the parts. And, of course, those fortunate few can find something valuable and then profit from the find. Such finds, however, may be pure luck — such as purchasing a stamp with a printing error at the local post office — or the result of years of philatelic study.

Over the years, collectors have stocked up on U.S. plate blocks, and even full panes (see the Glossary for definitions) of stamps, with the belief that they would appreciate in value. A major reason as to why I am able to purchase quantities of U.S. mint stamps from stamp dealers at below face value to use as postage is because their hoards have surfaced and been sold to stamp dealers. Individuals develop on their own, or hear by way of rumor mills, the idea that specific stamps will be worth considerably more in five years or so and act on their hunches. At the five-year mark, they discover that the stamps are worth exactly the same as they were when purchased. Result: A disgruntled collector sells at a loss.

One observation drives the discussion: The lower the value of a stamp, the less chance it has to increase in value. So, a postage stamp that is issued and listed in major catalogues at a like value to all others of the same country and time period probably will not increase in value in your lifetime. Most of those of the same time period that do appreciate are varieties that are not nearly as widely circulated.

Remember, too, that postage stamps themselves have little face value. So, if you purchase a plate block of a stamp with a face value of 25 cents, you have *invested* one dollar. If that stamp doubles in value in three years, you have a paper profit of one dollar. Although the optimist within you notes that you have doubled your money, the realist reminds you that you have to have many plate blocks before the actual return is meaningful. And, the more of the same item you have, the less chance you have to sell them when you

Stamp coup

A knowledgeable philatelist can recognize a valuable item that is on sale for far less than its true worth, buy it, and make a killing in profit. The ethics of such situations aside, it does happen and it shows what knowledge can do for you.

I remember walking through the rows of dealer tables at a major New York City stamp show some years ago with a friend quite knowledgeable in the postal issues of an Asian country. At one table, she spotted a postal card priced at $1. She made sure that $1 was all the dealer wanted, and then she made the purchase. The next stop was a dealer specializing in that country, who confirmed my friend's belief that the card had a market value of $1,000! It happens. But this one required someone with knowledge to pick it out.

want. Or, numerically, if you have 1,000 of those plate blocks that have doubled in value, you have a paper profit of $1,000. But, to convert that potential profit to an actual one, you need to have somewhere to sell those 1,000 plate blocks. In your travels as a stamp collector, try to find someplace where 1,000 of anything are for sale to you.

Also, I am not aware of any stamps increasing wildly in value solely because of what is depicted on them. That is, a stamp with a celebrity's photo is not apt to jump in value 100 times just because of the stamp design. If there is any great interest in that celebrity's likeness on a stamp, it will be shown at the time the stamp is issued, which is why the U.S. Elvis Presley stamps sold at the time of issue like they were the antidotes to the common cold. Today the catalogue value of the Elvis Presley stamps is the same catalogue value as other stamps from the same time period. But, the U.S. Postal Service sold *considerably* more Elvis Presley stamps than any other U.S. commemorative stamp.

Great American pastime

U.S. stamps with a baseball theme generally have a market value of two or three times that of similar stamps of their time. Even then, the market value is not particularly high, just higher than those issued at about the same time.

As your collection grows and you are no longer purchasing only those stamps that have a minimum catalogue value, you will find that the resale value of your collection is growing. Unlike with other hobbies, whose paraphernalia decrease in value faster than a new automobile just off the dealer's lot, you can have a reasonable expectation of getting some (or much, or perhaps even all) of your money back from stamp collecting in time. Meanwhile, you are able to enjoy the stamps. If nothing else, compare the hourly cost of collecting stamps to playing golf, racing go-carts, or photography. Only do that calculation once, however, for it takes too much time away from the fun of stamp collecting.

Insuring Your Booty

Stamp collecting is a hobby that appreciates. That is, if you purchase wisely and increase the size of your collection, your collection will grow in value. Whether or not you are looking at your collection as some sort of investment, it does not take much time before it becomes a measurable asset worth being protected. Insurance is the next logical step. Because of the specialized nature of a stamp collection, it is possible that the insurance you already have is not doing what you believe it to.

If you have homeowners' or renters' insurance, you have coverage for your stamp collection. That stated, the question really is, "how much coverage?" That question sets the stage for this whole discussion.

Just as your homeowners' policy (for our purposes here, homeowners' and renters' policies will be considered as the same) covers everything at your residence except that which may be specifically excluded, your stamp collection is included. You need to know several things:

- What are the limits of your coverage?
- What is the maximum amount of loss the policy will cover? Without trying to estimate the loss level that your current policy will cover, my own experience is that you don't have to collect stamps long before you approach or exceed it.

    As you approach the limits of your policy, your insurer may have a special *rider* (additional coverage for a specific item with coverage listed at the item's value) that specifically covers your collection. Of course, as expected, you pay extra for the rider. The rider may have its own requirements for record-keeping. At this level of insurance, you will probably be required to keep a current inventory on file with the insurer, where *current* means a specified time or period from any changes.

✔ What information must you provide to the insurance agent? As for what information you need to provide the insurer, that may be a complete inventory with values. You will be given specific instructions about keeping that inventory up-to-date. Or, for the basic policy, there are no such requirements.

✔ At what point should the information be required?

There is nothing unusual in all this. The basic policy considers stamps the same as anything else in the residence. The policy does not anticipate any expertise about stamps, and bases any required record-keeping on a lack of expertise. Everything is clean and neat.

Enter stamp insurance — a specialized insurance in the same manner as classic-automobile insurance or ham-radio-equipment insurance: The provisions of each of the policy types are extremely specific to the type of material covered. Before you add a rider to your homeowners' insurance to cover your stamp collection — no matter what you decide — at least investigate separate stamp insurance.

Who knows your stamp collection? What it contains? The condition of the stamps? What the cost has been so far? Where it is kept? And a lot more other details? There is but one logical answer, "You." You are the one who has nurtured every one of those little pieces of paper, identified them, and placed them in the proper spot.

Stamp insurance not only recognizes that you are the world's foremost expert on your collection, but it takes advantage of it.

Part III
Stampeding Is a Group Thing

The 5th Wave   By Rich Tennant

"In the future, stamp collectors are said to be pursuing philatelic interests, not 'going postal'."

In this part . . .

Many stamp collectors believe that their hobby is better practiced in a group mode, or, at least, where you can share your experiences and questions with a group. Even before that, however, you can find a constant supply of material new to your collection whether or not the stamps themselves are new. Your procurement options range from your local post office to stamp dealers in far-off lands to an auction house. Further, how you communicate with your stamp sources has undergone some real changes in the past few years.

While in search of stamps, you may also be looking for others nearby who share your love of postage stamps. Local stamps clubs are a great gathering place but how to find one near you? If you choose to narrow your collecting interest and *specialize,* then you can find a specialty group from among the hundreds around the world. Beyond those traditional areas is the more rapid means of telecommunication with other stamp collectors: the Internet. What you can expect and how you can take advantage awaits you.

Being part of a stamp club — whether local, a specialty group, or a national organization — can be a positive experience. Making stamp collecting a family affair has even greater possibilities, particularly if the younger members of the family can improve their understanding of history and geography merely because of their association with stamps from all over the world, each with its own story. And, as you grow with the hobby, look for various ways of expressing yourself. One of the approaches to self-expression is the competitive exhibition, which is part of nearly every stamp show. First, find out how to appreciate the exhibits before you even consider participating.

Chapter 7

Leaving No Stone Unturned: Finding Stamps

A particular axiom — perhaps coined right here — claims that to begin a stamp collection you need stamps. In this chapter, I present not only the traditional and expected sources for stamps, but perhaps some that do not quickly come to mind. Enough sources exist that you can ignore, at least for the short term, any means of stamp collection that isn't comfortable for you, and still have many opportunities to obtain stamps for your collection.

Although the concept of rarity normally refers to value, you may look on a rare stamp as any stamp that you want but don't yet possess. (See Chapter 6 for more information about value.) So, clear away some space in your stamp-collecting room and prepare to pile up your quest results.

Discovering Who Your Friends Are

Every day the letter carrier delivers envelopes and parcels to your home, to the homes of your neighbors and friends, and to your place of employment. Even with the increase in metered mail, a fair percentage of the mail you receive is franked by postage stamps. Gather in as many of these as you can, and you are off and running.

- ✔ **Relatives:** You want all their envelopes. Unless there is reason to keep a return address, ask that the stamps not be torn away. The uninitiated tend to damage stamps that way.

- ✔ **Neighbors:** Ditto. This is not necessarily the best opening when greeting a newcomer to the neighborhood. But if you have friendly neighbors, they can be a good source. If you have neighbors from another country, so much the better.

- ✔ **Your church:** A fair amount of mailed-in donations, as well as business correspondence, should come to your church.

- ✔ **Charities with local mail-processing capability:** Offer to remove the used envelopes. You may also want to make a donation in exchange for the one you are receiving.

- ✔ **Small businesses where you know the owner/manager:** Because of increased security concerns of late, many businesses may be hesitant to give up incoming envelopes. You need to assure your friends that the stamp is your only interest, and that you will destroy the remaining envelopes.

- ✔ **Utilities and larger businesses:** If you have the opportunity, seize it. Security issues are more prevalent here. And, if successful, you may find that you are overwhelmed with material. You may want to make this a last stop.

Some people may hesitate to give you their envelopes for reasons of security or modesty. In that case, ask that they merely tear off the corner of the envelope where the stamp is, allowing ample room around the stamp to avoid damaging it.

Looking through your donated stamps

You can get an abundance of material this way, although the number of different stamps may be low. From this bulk, however, you can

- ✔ Choose from the most attractive examples of each stamp.

- ✔ Look for design differences.

- ✔ Find interesting postmarks or anything else that may prompt you to put the whole envelope aside rather than remove the stamp. Check Chapter 5 for cancellation information.

Soaking your stamp

With the bulk of envelopes that you may accumulate in your neighborhood quest, now is a good time to show you how to remove stamps from envelopes or package wrappers. Whether a stamp is self-adhesive or has traditional gum determines the manner in which you soak the stamp free from the cover. Before attempting to soak your stamp, separate the self-adhesives from the gummed.

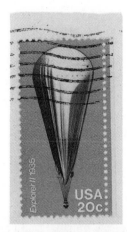

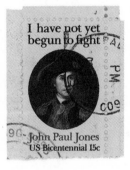

Figure 7-1:
Stamps
ready for
the bath of
their life.

Stamps with traditional gum

You can tell that a stamp is self-adhesive in two ways:

- By the stamp design
- By the perforation (self-stick perfs have rounded edges)

You can follow these numbered steps to soak stamps with traditional gum free from their envelopes or package paper:

1. Using scissors, trim the envelope paper close to the stamp without damaging any part of the stamp. (See how a closely trimmed stamp may appear in the preceding Figure 7-1.)

2. Fill a shallow bowl or sink (drain closed) with several inches of luke-warm tap water.

   Do not use hot water, which may affect the ink on some stamps.

   Also, change the water for the next batch.

3. Float the envelope corner face up, with the gummed side of the stamp below the water level. Do not attempt to soak too many items — at least at the beginning of the process. If the envelope corner sinks, fear not.

4. Leave the item in the water until it soaks through the backing paper and loosens the gum. Test carefully so that you do not tear the stamp. First see if the stamp slides away from the envelope paper.

5. Allow the stamp to float until the envelope paper easily slides away. If, after you have retrieved all the stamps that have fallen off in the water and those that slid away from the envelope paper, some stamps remain, then work with each individually. You may need to carefully peel the stamp away from the envelope paper. The stamp may not budge, because the stamp was applied to the envelope paper with some form of glue rather than its own gum, or because the stamp is from a country using a rather stubborn gum. Your options, based on how important the stamp is to you, are to

   • Work with the stamp some more.

   • Give up and throw it away.

   • Stop the process and allow the stamp/envelope paper to dry and then cut around it. This situation is so unusual that you may never experience it.

6. Rinse the stamps in fresh lukewarm water to make sure all the glue and envelope paper are removed.

Self-adhesive stamps

Self-adhesive stamps present a different set of circumstances. All are not created equally. Not all, then, can be soaked from the envelope or wrapper. There are two approaches:

   ✔ **Clipping:** Neatly clip away the envelope from around the stamp and save it that way. This is your safest approach.

   ✔ **Soaking:** Self-adhesives require more time to soak free from envelopes. Soaking curls self-adhesive stamps more easily than traditional stamps.

   Current U.S. self-adhesive stamps have an extra layer of paper between the adhesive and the paper on which the stamp is printed. So, you can soak the stamp off from the paper in a manner similar to soaking the paper off from stamps that are not self-adhesive, which is explained earlier in this chapter. You want to test first, so only begin the process with self-adhesive stamps of which you have multiple copies.

The principal reason to soak the adhesive away from the stamp is to prevent eventual accelerated deterioration. Although this is but an opinion of some who collect self-adhesives, it needs to be considered; after deterioration begins, it probably cannot be reversed. The first U.S. self-adhesives, the 1974 Christmas issue, have shown ugly discoloration over the years. Prudence strongly suggests, where possible, that you soak one stamp for each stamp still on the envelope. Early self-adhesive stamps from Tonga and Sierra Leone did not exhibit these problems.

Venturing Beyond Your Neighborhood

Now the fun really begins. You have quite a few opportunities to procure material for your growing stamp collection right within your community.

- ✔ **Postal clerk:** Certainly, if you are a U.S. resident collecting U.S. stamps, you will want to befriend at least one, and perhaps more than one, postal clerk. Because each clerk keeps his/her own supply of stamps, it is always possible that one clerk will have an issue that another does not. If you are collecting the stamps of your country and you are outside of the U.S., the best way to obtain current stamps in your country may differ.

- ✔ **USPS Philatelic Center:** These special postal counters in some post offices maintain a much more complete stock. If you do not have one locally, ask where you can find the one nearest to you. If you cannot get an answer and you have access to the Internet, point your browser to http://www.askphil.org/b45.htm for a listing. For other countries, you will need to discover the best approach.

- ✔ **Stamp dealers:** Check your telephone book Yellow Pages for the listing *Stamps for Collectors*. (Skip ahead to Figure 7-2.) Although the number of dealers maintaining storefront businesses has declined over the years, many dealers are still around (they are not always in large cities). Even if only a telephone number is given, but no address, at least call and see if the dealer specializes in some area (perhaps something you are considering) or is more general and just chooses not to sell across a counter in favor of other forms of sales.

- ✔ **Local antique stores, second-hand shops, and pawn shops:** Our little town of 6,000 has five antique shops on one block. Stamp collectors make a regular run along Main Street.

- ✔ **Sales:** Yard sales, garage sales, moving sales, or whatever you call selling personal items out of your home, are another occasion to find stamps. If you spot something, and the sale is outdoors, be *very* careful opening an album or box containing the stamps. A gust of wind may force you to arm-wrestle a chipmunk for the return of a stamp or two.

- ✔ **Local auctions — particularly estate auctions:** If an auction contains any philatelic material, do not trust the auctioneer's description. Check the lot yourself. Chances are the auctioneer does not handle much stamp material, and you may find something far more valuable than the lot description proclaims. Auctioned lots are described on the basis of the album. Perhaps the time span, a general range of countries, and some important or important-looking items may be mentioned. A personal inspection can point out less-obvious goodies and give you more reason to become a winning bidder.

✔ **Veterans hospitals and other government or noncommercial-care facilities:** Locations of this sort are often given stamp accumulations or collections as a tax write-off. Many of these facilities use the stamps in their own recreational programming. Some governmental facilities, however, do not use the stamps and build up quite a backlog without much of an idea as to what to do with them.

Approaching Stamp Dealers

Stamp collecting has been appropriately and primarily conducted through the mail. For those collectors with a stamp dealer in their town, purchasing stamps is easier. Even then, only the extremely rare collector does not correspond with other collectors and purchase or trade stamps by mail.

Today, an accurate count of how many stamp dealers live in the U.S. is nonexistent; whether stamp dealers maintain large operations with dozens of employees or are sole proprietors working from the proverbial kitchen table is also unknown. A high percentage of dealers, however, conduct all or part of their business via the mail and are specialists in what they sell. That is, stamp dealers may specialize in one or a few countries, topicals, airmail, buying and selling collections and accumulations, or any number of other possibilities.

Figure 7-2:
Yellow
Pages
listing.

Just as all pet stores do not satisfy the needs of all pet owners by virtue of what they stock and sell or how they sell, such is the situation with retail stamp dealers. Contacting these folks is really no different than phoning a plumber or a wallpaper store. Here is a listing of various approaches to stamp dealing, followed by a brief description of each:

✔ **Approvals/automatic:** Approvals, a common way of purchasing stamps, have been around for a long time. Automatic approvals may best be equated with a book or CD-ROM "club" that sends you material through the mail along with an invoice. Keeping the material you want and sending the dealer payment for what you kept, along with the material you chose not to purchase, is your option. Often you have little or no control over the type of material that you are sent; in some cases you do. To begin the service, merely respond to an ad in a stamp periodical or even a general-interest periodical, such as *Boy's Life, Popular Mechanics,* or even your Sunday newspaper.

✔ **Approvals/penny:** Penny approvals are perhaps misnamed in today's economy, but they do represent a selection of inexpensive material sent through the mail to you by a dealer. You keep what you want and return the remainder along with payment. This is an excellent method for you to fill in the many holes in your collection with material that you have been able to inspect prior to purchase. This type of approval dealer advertises in a stamp periodical.

✔ **Approvals/requested:** *Requested approvals* may not be a proper term, although it does represent a situation where you ask a dealer for a chance to look at specific stamps with the understanding that you are not obliged to purchase any or all. These approvals differ from the automatic- and penny-type approvals in that

   • You can request specific types of material versus the automatic dealer, who controls the sending totally.

   • The material ranges in value upward from moderate.

Some dealers do not use this approach unless you are an established customer whose purchasing — and payment — tendencies are known. Other dealers may suggest this from the beginning. A great deal of approval buying is conducted through the mail. I hope you are getting the picture that relationships between buyer and seller in the area of stamp collecting may become personal quickly. These buyer/seller relationships are also based on the type of material a dealer has for sale and the specific material a collector wants.

✔ **Collections:** Different from an accumulation, a *collection* is normally sold on album pages, although some of the better material may have been removed. That is, that dealer (or another) might have purchased the collection from a collector, removed the better material that would be more in demand, and then offered the remainder as a single unit.

Collecting, accumulating, gathering, hoarding . . .

I tend to like accumulations for my primary collection, for I then obtain a quantity of low-value material — which normally is what is duplicated — to go through patiently in search of varieties and that elusive item that will guarantee my retirement income. I am sure I will find something soon! Although I have not hit the big one as of yet, I have found items in collections that I have purchased valued at more than I expected to find.

✔ **Accumulations:** Different from a collection, an *accumulation* is a logical grouping of stamps — by country or topic, for example — but with duplication.

Collections and accumulations are methods of obtaining low-value material without having to pay for it on a per-stamp basis. Although these lots normally have been "cherry-picked" for better material, you always have the possibility of finding something of value. Chances of finding high-value material in a collection or accumulation are quite slim, but the chance still exists. I have had considerable luck with this type of material over the years, although statistically, most of what I have purchased has been worth just what I paid for it. The quest itself, however, is a major part of the fun.

✔ **Mixtures:** This is a stamp-collecting term for plenty of different stamps. You may find a variety of countries included, both mint and used stamps (unless specifically noted otherwise), sometimes a fair number of damaged stamps, and certainly the opportunity for duplication. Mixtures offer you an excellent exercise in sorting, which can be enjoyable, particularly if you are not seeking something special. Some dealers will salt their mixtures with the occasional better item. Mixtures are particularly good if you have a worldwide album and you want to begin to fill the spaces.

✔ **Packets:** A counted, unduplicated grouping of a single country, region, or topic. You may see a listing for "100 Dogs," or "500 Czechoslovakia," or "30,000 Worldwide," which are great collection starters and a wonderful gift to accompany an album for a new collector. View a stamp packet in Figure 7-3.

Figure 7-3:
Marked
stamp
packet.

✔ **Price lists:** Prepared and distributed by the dealer, price lists may be sent by mail, fax, or e-mail, or posted on the dealer's Web site (see Figure 7-4). They may or may not be illustrated. You order from the price list and, barring a misidentified damaged stamp, the sale is final. The procedure is no different than ordering auto parts or office supplies by mail. It is an efficient approach, based on the dealer's ability to deliver the item as described, and it is particularly good for collectors who are not near a retail stamp store or any stamp shows.

✔ **Want lists:** Price lists in reverse. The collector sends a list of desired items to a dealer — a blind order. You may not know if the dealer has the requested material. And, in fact, the dealer may not have the material when the want list is received, and may then obtain the desired items from another dealer just to fill the order.

Want-list buying may be in the form of an actual order to be shipped right away, or it may be in the form of "if you see this item in your travels, be advised that I am looking for it." Some collectors may give standing want lists to specialty dealers that are changed as material is obtained and/or when new items are added to the list. It is not unusual for a dealer to remember the "wants" of a favored customer for years and then contact that collector when an elusive item is finally spotted.

US Price List

All stamps are mint (never hinged).

Catalogue Number	Price	Catalogue Number	Price	Catalogue Number	Price
704-15	16.75	1909a	55.00	C7	3.00
730	21.00	2002b	22.50	C8	3.00
731	20.00	2122	16.00	C9	9.00
735	12.00	2122a	49.50	C10	7.75
740-49	7.00	2123-36	2.80	C11	3.85
750	24.00	2168-96	23.95	C12	9.00
751	13.00	2216-19	12.00	C16	5.00
756.65	12.00	2252-66	3.25	C20	1.00
785-94	1.95	2335a	39.50	C21	7.00
803-32	32.00	2419	3.65	C22	6.75
833	19.00	2433	15.00	C24	6.75
834	75.00	2438	4.75	C46	4.00
839-51	22.00	2539	1.60	C91-92	1.00
909-21	1.60	2540	4.50	C93-94	1.00
1030-52	12.95	2541	13.50	C95-96	1.60
1053	65.00	2542	19.00	C100-04	2.25
1254a-57a	5.00	2543	4.00	C105-08	3.45
1612	7.00	2544	4.25	C109-12	3.60
1613-25	2.45	2590	1.75	C122-25	4.00
1633-82	12.00	2592	8.00	C126	5.75
1686-89	14.50	2624-29	29.50	O133	8.00
1757	1.50	2696a	29.95		
1844-69	8.25	2837	2.00		
1897-08	2.60	2840	3.00		
1909	18.00	2842	13.50		
		2975	15.00		

Figure 7-4:
Price list.

Going . . . going . . . MINE!

Auctions are a fun way to add to your collection . . . unless your emotions get the best of you, and you bid beyond your means. Nothing is worse than going to a stamp show, which has a public auction as one of its events, with perhaps $30 cash in your pocket. You park your vehicle in the parking garage, enter the show/auction, and immediately a stamp with an estimated value of $5 takes you. There is someone else in the room that also likes the same item. Your macho side takes hold, and you are determined to win the *lot* . . . but so is someone else. You finally win, at a bid of $22.50. Your parking charge will be $7. Now you need to find some old friend at the stamp show who will offer to buy your lunch, or else you will be a happy bidder with a growling stomach. This is not a fictional situation.

At an auction, you purchase a *lot*, which is normally numbered to allow the auction firm to keep track of the material for the purposes of crediting what you pay as a purchaser to the proper original owner. Although many auctions are made up of consigned material, some stamp auction firms purchase material for resale and are actually selling their own material.

Auctions represent a tremendous method of obtaining material for your collection. You may purchase individual items, larger lots, or just about anything in between. Be neither timid nor too aggressive. Find your own comfort level.

The most important rule of auction buying: Read the terms of sale carefully and understand what you are reading. Auction bids are increased in increments based on the bid level, which is normally a rule within the terms. Although a standardized set of terms for all stamp auction firms would be desirable, such is not the case. Thus, given the chance for differences among the terms of the various auction firms, you will know the terms in advance after reading them. If you do not like or agree with the terms of a given firm or sale, you can move on.

Attending your first auction?

If you have never attended a public auction — where the bidding is done right there, before your very eyes and ears — do not jump into a postage stamp auction as a bidder without first getting a solid feel for what is going on around you. If possible, attend a stamp auction as an observer before you attend as a potential bidder. If you do not have stamp auctions near you on a regular basis, at least attend some form of auction sale. You may notice strange — to you — happenings at an auction, and you do need to get a feel for the flow.

In the U.S., an auctioneer needs to be licensed by the state in which the sale takes place. Normally, the auctioneer and some paperwork handlers staff a public stamp auction. Because stamp auctions may have upwards of several hundred lots to be handled in a matter of a few hours, speed and efficiency are of the essence.

Almost always, stamp auction lots are available for inspection at an announced location and for a specified period of time. This allows you to look at lots, up close, that you have spotted in the printed catalogue. Catalogue descriptions may be well done and lengthy, but the description cannot replace actually seeing an item or a group of items with your own eyes.

On arrival, pick up a copy of the auction catalogue, which lists the lots offered in that sale, in the order of their sale. The catalogue also contains the terms of sale, which is the *law* under which the sale is conducted. Normally, by the provisions of the terms, when you first bid on an item, that bid also stipulates that you agree to be bound by the terms of sale. The terms generally provide for how winning lots are paid for by the bidder and shipped by the seller. If you are in attendance and win a lot, you can normally pay right there and take the lot with you.

Bids are placed in specific increments above the previous high bid, and those increments are normally increased as the bidding level increases. That is, an auction firm may state that for bids up to $15 the increment is 25¢, from $15 to $25 the increment is 50¢, from $25-$100 the increment is $1, from $100 to $500 the increment is $2.50, and so on. This approach speeds the actual sale because moving up in 25-cent increments, all the way to $100, is time-consuming. Also, this structure sets off-site bidders on the same bidding plane as those bidding from the auction floor. Because so much bidding is done from afar, many winning bidders submit their bids by mail, fax, telephone, or the Internet.

Normally, a licensed auctioneer *calls* each lot by integrating bids from the audience and the *book* (bids entered by mail, telephone, or electronically, prior to the actual live sale). Although not necessarily as dramatic as movie-based stereotypes of auctioneers, the concept is the same, ergo the term *call*.

If you are a *floor bidder,* and you win, your winning bid is one increment above the second-highest bidder. In other words, when the auctioneer called for a bid at the price where you won, you were the only bidder to respond. If you are submitting a bid by mail, you have no real idea where the bidding will stop. So, your bid should pretty much be the most you are willing to spend on the item. If your mail bid is the highest bid overall, the actual amount you pay for the item is based on the terms of sale. Some terms specify that the winning bid is one increment above the second-highest bid. If your bid is ten increments higher, you will not be charged the amount of your bid, but you will be charged an amount equal to one increment higher than the second highest bidder. Other auction firms may specify that the winning bid is the highest bid overall, without regard to how many increments over the second-highest bidder the bid was.

This is not the place to discuss which of the two approaches — and there may be others — is correct. That is not important. What is key is that you read the terms of sale and know in advance how the bids are handled. Placing a bid confirms that you agree to accept the terms of sale.

Looking for the right things

Look for several potentially sticky points, which may be covered in the terms of sale, before entering an auction. You need to know how a particular auction firm handles these issues before proceeding:

- ✔ **Shipping costs:** Does the auction firm have a standard fee for shipping? Do you have any say as to how an item is shipped?

- ✔ **Whether lots are shipped in advance of payment:** Some firms have strict "payment first, shipping second" policies. Other firms, if you are a known customer, may ship winning lots with an invoice. Firms may also ask you to provide a credit card number in advance, against which the winning lots can be charged (with shipping) to speed up the whole process.

- ✔ **Provisions for having a questionable item evaluated for authenticity:** If you receive an item and believe that it is not what was described in the catalogue — damage was unreported, it was incorrectly identified, or a stamp is some form of fake — are you permitted a grace period to have the item reviewed by an independent expert? If a problem is confirmed, can you return the item? If an independent expert is consulted, who pays the fee? Some auction firms absorb the fee if the item is found to be problematic, while you pick up the fee if the auction firm was correct. Other firms are so confident in their knowledge that they do not pick up an expert's fee under any circumstances. The terms of sale lay out the provisions.

- ✔ If you are bidding at an auction and do not win the lot(s) you want, how far from the winning bid was your bid? If you are in the audience at a public auction, you have little trouble noting the amount. But, you may want to keep track of many lots. Or, you bid by mail or the Internet, and you did not hear the winning amount. Most auction firms publish and distribute the *prices realized,* a listing of lot numbers and the winning bid for each. If you are a bidder, you may be sent the *prices realized* as a way to keep you interested in that auction firm. Some firms require you to request them, others ask patrons for a self-addressed, stamped envelope, and still others post the prices realized on their Web site.

Entering an auction type that you like

Several types of auctions exist, although you should understand that there are a lot a gray areas relative to type. Note that the terms of sale is either in the printed catalogue for a sale or, if the sale is Web based, accessible from an auction firm's Web site's opening page.

Public and mail auction

Generally, each lot is called in less than a minute, unless there is spirited floor bidding or some problem. Before you attend a public auction with the intention of bidding on one lot (or a dozen), get to the auction site in advance of the sale so that you can physically examine any specific lot, in which you are interested, before the auction.

You, the new and prospective bidder, are in competition with everyone else in the room. Your competition may include others in the same situation as you, collectors and dealers with considerable auction-buying experience, and auction agents who are representatives of collectors and dealers. These agents may be bidding on a high percentage of the lots for perhaps dozens of different clients. Plenty goes on at a public stamp auction. Keep your wits about you, physically inspect stamp lots that are of interest to you in advance, and enjoy.

Mail sales are sometimes advertised as *mail auctions*: A mail sale requires you to submit a bid by mail by a given deadline. Again, you need to know the terms of sale. If you ask some firms holding mail bids — during the period when bids are being accepted — what the current high bid is, they may tell you; others do not. Generally, lower-value material is offered via a mail sale when compared to a public auction.

Internet sales

Today, some auction firms that conduct public auctions post their sales on the Internet and accept bids via the Internet (as well as by telephone, fax, and in person). Web sites, such as eBay and its competitors, also offer stamps to bid on. Just as with public and mail auctions, you need to understand the terms of sale, which may be labeled differently on a Web site. The terms of sale is still the document that controls the manner in which the Internet sale is conducted. With these systems, you are not bidding on lots where the bidding closes on all lots at the same time. Rather, the person posting the material for sale through one of these firms is given a set amount of time that the item is made available for bidding. You, as the prospective purchaser, place your bid according to the rules, and when the bidding closes, the high bid wins. In this auction venue, however, bidding often becomes furious in the last hour of the sale period. Some bidders revel in their ability to jump in at literally the last second with the final and winning bid. This is known as *sniping*. Bidders who have been victimized by such an approach abhor sniping; successful snipers point to skill and good timing for their victories. The approach is legal, but only works when a sale ends at a specific time. Some Internet auction software keeps a lot open for a period of time — I have seen ten minutes — following the most recent bid. Thus, two snipers who really want a lot can go at it until one tires or believes the bidding is too high — rather than one of them winning because the time limit expired. Just keep remembering: This is a hobby. To find such sites, use a regular Internet search engine and query on "stamp+auction." Check each site carefully, and watch the action for at least a few days before you dive in.

The popularity of this medium shows that it works. At the same time, there are problems. Always tread carefully, of course. I have used this medium quite a bit. I find the Internet enjoyable and easy to use. In all cases, follow instructions carefully. The systems are automated and do what you instruct them to do rather than what you meant to instruct them to do.

If you are a buyer, you need to be sure that you receive your winning lot within a reasonable time after you have sent payment. Otherwise, contact the firm sponsoring the online auction site. If you are a seller, you not only want payment prior to shipment, but you also need to be sure that, if the payment is in the form of a bank check, the check will clear the bank successfully. Also, sellers may get stuck when a winning bidder never sends payment. Again, contact the host site to have disciplinary action taken against the offender. Such action may not help your specific situation, but may keep the offender from that site again.

Stamp dealer

Some dealers run auctions as an extension of their business, while some stamp firms have their own Internet-based auctions using specialized software. Much smaller versions of the eBay types, these auctions receive fewer bidders, but they may still generate the same spirit level as the others. As a buyer, you are most interested in going where you can find what you seek. Through your normal Web prowling for stamp-related Web sites, you may discover dealers who are offering this approach to purchasing. Because so many of these small auction Web sites are coming and going rather rapidly, check at Joe Luft's Philatelic Resources on the Web (`http://www.execpc.com/~joeluft/resource.html`) for an idea of what is available at one time. This is the most honored and respected general stamp-collecting link site.

Beyond those auction types listed, there are intermediary situations:

✔ Web sites that contract with various public auction firms to serve as a funnel for public auction bids

✔ Mail sales via the Web

✔ Some local stamp clubs conducting *club auctions* as a meeting program

Here the trappings are the same as a public auction, without the professional auctioneer. Not only do you get great experience with your auction emotions, but you also may be able to pick up something you need.

Chapter 8

Getting a Little Help from Your Friends

*A*lthough having a most enjoyable stamp-collecting experience without ever meeting another philatelist or discussing your collection with another stamp collector is possible, such situations are extremely unusual. You need some camaraderie to go with that collection! However, finding fellow collectors — especially those who share your particular collecting interests — may be tough to do. The Internet makes that task easier. For further information on this subject, see *The Internet For Dummies,* 7th Edition, by Levine, Baroudi, and Levine-Young (Hungry Minds, Inc.).

Even if you do not find a stamp club nearby, you can find abundant assistance to help you begin and sustain a stamp club. The same information may also help you start a specialty group, if you so choose.

Stamp collecting has taken to the Internet quite strongly. Swapping, buying and selling, information exchange, and even online club meetings all take place among people from all parts of the world — restricted only by time zones and an individual's sleep patterns. A speedup in communications has led to improvements like speed in record-keeping. If you are regularly sharing information, want lists, or are swapping via the Internet, you'll find that cutting and pasting from a computer-based inventory system is much faster than typing in your information each time. So, name your computer and consider it just another one of your stamp-collecting friends. It will appreciate your bonding efforts.

Collecting Friends

You wake up in the morning and immediately conclude that you want stamp-collecting companionship. You are in search of at least one other stamp collector with whom you may share problems and discoveries, learn together, swap tales, and generally enjoy the hobby. Ideally, a stamp-collecting companion lives right next door. Realistically, you probably won't be that fortunate; you'll need to search a bit to find hobby mates. (Finding a stamp club is an extension of a search for comrades and is treated separately in this chapter.)

Beginning right from your own neighborhood, check out these hot spots:

- **Post office:** If you are not comfortable asking the clerk if he knows any other stamp collectors, at least pay attention to other postal customers and their buying habits. Sometimes being too aggressive in search of other stamp collectors may be misinterpreted, and thus prompt security concerns.

- **Local library:** Some years ago, a study concluded that collectors tend to be higher up the intellect scale than those who do not collect. And, among collectors, stamp collectors were at the top. Although I can pretty much assure you that beginning a stamp collection does not add 50 points to your IQ, I can note from experience that stamp collectors are among the most inquisitive, thoughtful people I know.

- **School library:** You may also find success telling a teacher-friend of your interests with the hope that the news will spread.

A brief word of caution is in order. Use discretion when seeking out fellow stamp collectors, because many people immediately equate a stamp collection with high value. Be sure to have the "word" spread that you are just beginning a stamp collection, or even just considering one. Discretion may keep your home from becoming an unannounced meeting place for the Guild of Home Burglars. Then, after you have established your collection, a major security move is not to brag about the items that you have procured and the value of your collection.

You can make "stamp friends" both locally (if other philatelists are in your community) and with collectors far away. You never know when another collector who is able to help you with a key part of your collection will appear. Likewise, you can meet other collectors who you can help. Collect stamp-collecting friends as you would collect stamps — carefully — and take care of them. Use all possible approaches to find others who share your passion.

Club Hopping

You may have been directed to a local stamp club in your search for stamp-collecting companions. Good for you. If not, let me introduce you to local clubs. To forestall confusion, local stamp clubs — which may be chapters of the American Philatelic Society, American Topical Association, or one of the many specialty groups — run themselves. These sites can give you great, copious lists of clubs:

✔ **The American Philatelic Society** (APS), at P.O. Box 8000, State College, PA, 16803-8000; phone 814-237-3803; Web site www.stamps.org, boasts more than 50,000 members and offers a wide range of services. It has hundreds of chapters, principally in the U.S. By being a chapter, these local clubs are able to take advantage of some specific APS benefits that assist in club operation. The APS maintains a list of its chapters on its Web site (www.stamps.org/directories/dir_LocalClubs.htm) for your reference and access.

✔ **AskPhil**, the stamp-collecting information Web site maintained by the Collectors Club of Chicago (Internet: www.askphil.org), also has an extensive listing of local clubs. This listing numbers more than 1,000 clubs and is not limited to clubs with any specific affiliation (Internet: www.askphil.org/b02.htm).

✔ **The American Topical Association** (ATA) at P.O. Box 50820, Albuquerque, NM 87181-0820; phone 505-323-8595; Web site http://home.prcn.org/~pauld/ata, is the largest organization specifically serving the topical stamp collector. It also has chapters, which are available online at http://home.prcn.org/~pauld/ata/chapters.htm.

✔ **Linn's Stamp News** is the nation's only weekly stamp newspaper (see Figure 8-1). You can find its club listing on the Web at www.linns.com/reference/Clubs/club_a.asp.

Figure 8-1:
Linn keeps it
coming at
you weekly.

Now armed with a listing of about all the large local clubs you can find, you're ready for your first visit. No doubt you want to glance through your album before you leave for the meeting. You arrive promptly, just a few minutes before the stated start time. You walk into the meeting room. Lo and behold, you observe a group of people just like you! Yes, the local stamp club is made up of (hold tight, now) people from your locality. You need not, therefore, feel the least bit out of place.

At least for your first visit to a stamp club, travel light, and bring

- ✔ **Cash:** In the event the dealers do not accept credit cards, you'll need some.
- ✔ **Copies of your want list:** In the event one or more dealers have set up shop, you'll want to give them a copy.
- ✔ **Duplicates:** Perhaps a few in small envelopes, for trading purposes.
- ✔ **Notepad, pen, and paper:** To jot down vital information.

You gain little by showing up with your album and other bulk. Even if you generally have nerdlike qualities, save that impression for another time. If nothing else, stay loose enough to be able to visit with as many people as you can, get to know them a little, and see what others are doing.

A typical stamp club meeting is normally quite simple. For many clubs, before the meeting begins (or after it ends), a period of time is reserved for buying, selling, and swapping and may even include local or regional dealers. As with most organizations, a part of each meeting is dedicated to club business, and the program is normally the highlight of the meeting!

Stamp-club *programs* are normally talks given by individual collectors from the club or from a nearby club, discussing their specialty or favorite items. Other program possibilities are slide slows provided by the APS or other larger organizations. Miniauctions also make good programs. Each club settles in on what's comfortable for that club.

If you are fortunate, you'll hook up with a club that also has refreshments. Some clubs meet informally at an eatery prior to meetings. (You can see what draws my interest.) Just remember to wash your hands after chowing down on the doughnuts — so that you don't glaze anyone's prized stamp.

I have attended stamp club meetings with a half-dozen in attendance, as well as meetings where more than 100 chairs were occupied. Numbers are not important. The opportunity to meet and interact with other collectors is important. I cannot remember attending a local stamp club meeting where anyone else there had the same collecting specialty as mine, but that didn't matter. I was able to step into a three-dimensional stamp-collecting situation for a few hours.

Looking back at your first stamp club meeting, what did you gain?

- ✔ Meeting people just like you who collect stamps for the fun of it
- ✔ Finding out where to obtain stamps locally, if possible
- ✔ Gaining some idea of who the more knowledgeable collectors are, in case you have some questions
- ✔ Knowing you are not alone

Specializing Isn't Just for Surgeons

In most respects, a *specialty stamp-collecting group* (club, association, or society) has but one difference from a local club: Its focus is narrower. A specialty group may be local, national, or even international. All that's really needed for specialty groups to begin to flourish is a small number of individuals who share the same common interest.

Areas of interest are as wide ranging as the hobby itself. Here's a listing of a few areas of special interest followed by an example of a group that shares that interest:

- ✔ Regions of the world (the Latin American Philatelic Society)
- ✔ Single countries (the American Helvetia Philatelic Society)
- ✔ Specific aspects of one country (the Plate Number Coil Collectors Club)
- ✔ Postal history of a single country (the Norwegian Postal History Society)
- ✔ Postal history of a U.S. state (the Pennsylvania Postal Society)
- ✔ Specific type of postal history, which crosses all borders (the Military Postal History Society)
- ✔ Topics (the Lighthouse Stamp Society)

You can read more about U.S. stamps in Chapter 11, more about foreign stamps in Chapter 12, and more about topics (also known as *themes*) in Chapter 13.

Although you may suggest additional categories that I haven't mentioned, you can at least get a feel for the breadth of interests already covered by specialty organizations. AskPhil.org has an online listing of more than 525 specialty groups (see Figure 8-2). New groups form all the time, and from time to time, interest in a given group wanes and that group disbands. The key for you here is that new groups form rather frequently, and all that's required in forming a group is enough people who want to share the information.

Unless based in an area where many members can attend meetings regularly, specialty groups tend to be more newsletter based than meeting based. The specialty club's regular publication — whatever the format or frequency of issue — tends to be the organization's lifeline. Within its pages are member names and addresses, offers to buy, sell, or swap, notices of new finds within that area of interest, news of upcoming stamp shows (often the gathering spot for specialty groups), and perhaps lengthier articles explaining in detail some aspect of that specialty.

Specialty groups come in all sizes, from a handful of members to thousands. Sometimes two different groups are formed to cover the same specialty — whether from lack of knowledge of the other or from a sense of wanting to *do it my way* — and in time they may merge, or not. Bringing a group of collectors together who collect the same stamps is the whole purpose of a specialty group. A local stamp club, on the other hand, brings a group together on the basis of where they live.

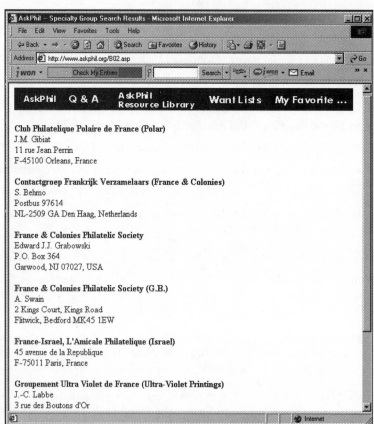

Figure 8-2:
Screen shot
of AskPhil
specialty
group list.

As a result of bringing people with a common interest together, research and information on new discoveries are shared, exhibition ideas are swapped, and the aphorism, "birds of a feather flock together," is put into action, perhaps selfishly. The specialty group newsletter also features information and articles that are considered too unimportant for general stamp-collecting periodicals.

The same resources for finding local stamp clubs, mentioned earlier in this chapter, work for finding specialty groups. At the very least, the resources provide a solid beginning point for you. In addition, as you discover stamp dealers who can provide you with material for your specialty, ask the dealers for information on groups that they know. No matter how rapid communications become within the hobby of stamp collecting, old-fashioned word of mouth remains quite useful.

Making Friends Online

No matter how many local stamp clubs exist or how many people attend the various stamp shows and bourses each weekend, I continue to believe that stamp collecting is a haven for the introverted person, or at least that part of an individual that exhibits tendencies of introversion. Enter online communication. Now, many more stamp collectors begin to interact. While communicating online, collectors don't have to face each other and can remain in seclusion.

Perhaps as long as ten years ago, the first stamp-collecting computer bulletin board came into existence. It was part of the CompuServe network and continues today. Check out *CompuServe 2000 For Dummies* by R. Michele Phillips (Hungry Minds, Inc.) for more on this online source. This stamp-collecting gathering place preceded the Internet and was included in the subscription-based CompuServe system. Much has changed.

Today, philately's electronic side of communications parallels the more traditional mail/personal side:

- ✔ National-level organizations have major Web presence. (Note addresses earlier in this chapter.)
- ✔ Specialty groups use the Web in addition to their traditional means of communication: the printed newsletter or journal.
- ✔ Local clubs have Web sites to inform members and attract all collectors to the stamp shows they sponsor.
- ✔ Stamp dealers use Web sites and e-mail to buy and sell, with some moving exclusively to the Internet because they believe it offers lower operating costs and a wider range of customers.

✔ Commercial stamp publications use Web sites to promote their periodicals and other products, such as handbooks and other references.

✔ Stamp collecting is well represented in the Internet-only phenomenon of subject-specific e-mail lists and chat areas.

Chat rooms

Chat rooms — an interactive part of a Web site that offers messaging between two parties — are a great way to converse with stamp friends as if you were in a room with them. CompuServe and Virtual Stamp Club are two services that have scheduled chat-room activies. Both of those services are reachable through an online search. Because chat rooms allow you to extend your reach in your communication with other collectors, and sometimes dealers, they are a means of sharing information, as well as buying, selling, and swapping material. Not only does each chat room have its own method of registering and logging in, they also tend to be upgraded from time to time, necessitating your relearning the steps. Even with those warts, chat rooms can be a fun way to meet people and share information. I have been involved in one or the other of the two chat rooms that I mentioned for more than ten years. I have met people there who I continue to consider friends — some I have met in person, others I have not. You always have the risk of someone trying to use a chat room for some sort of scam. So, always be careful if someone you have not come to know tries to negotiate something too good to be true . . . it probably is. Until you find out who the regulars are, it is best not to offer any information about yourself that can be used to cause you any sort of harm. Also, do not send off a large quantity of stamps or payment for stamps without more assurance than, "I will send it to you by return mail." Everyone is not as honest as you or me . . . and you can't be *that* sure of me.

Forums and message boards

The Usenet stamp-collecting forums listed here are both very active. Go to the Internet (www.usenet.com) to sign up.

✔ rec.collecting.stamps.discuss
✔ rec.collecting.stamps.marketplace

Although other stamp-collecting related forums come and go, these two have been around for a long time and appear to have staying power. Essentially, the Usenet stamp-collecting forums and message boards are places on the Internet where you can post messages and read the responses from others.

Dealing online

The national-level, specialty, and local stamp organizations are all addressed in this chapter. Their digital presence is an extension of their overall efforts. Stamp dealers may be different. Some dealers operate in the traditional manner only. Other dealers operate in the traditional manner, as well as via the Internet. And now, some stamp dealers choose to do business solely over the Internet.

To find stamp dealers who buy and sell via the Internet — whether by means of a business Web site or only via e-mail communication — you need to check one of many listings. AskPhil.org and the American Philatelic Society are already noted. Members of the American Stamp Dealers

Association (ASDA) may be located through the organization's Web site, www.asdaonline. com. Lists of stamp-collecting links also provide an opening to dealers doing business on the Internet. The oldest stamp-collecting link list is Joseph Luft's Philatelic Resources on the Web, www.execpc.com/~joeluft/resource. html. Other link lists exist; not all are based in the U.S. If you use the Web as the basis for your shopping, you need to become familiar with sites having lengthy lists, as well as querying the basic search engines for *stamp collecting.* Perform search-engine queries no less than every three months, and you will be amazed at how much the listings change.

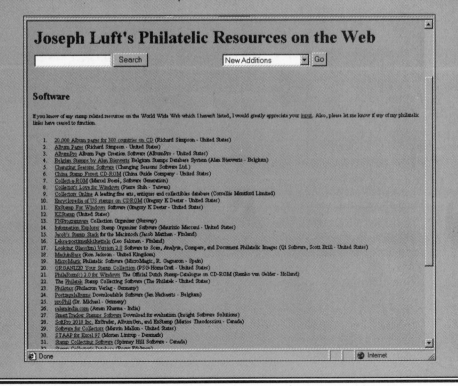

Similar to the e-mail list, the *message board* requires you to log on to a central site to read messages, respond, or post new ones. While the chat rooms operate in real time — you chat with one or more people as long as all of you are connected to the system simultaneously — message boards allow you to upload your message for others to read later.

You can find two basic styles of e-message board: those that are moderated and those that are not. Each type has its strong supporters. Moderated boards have reviewers to be certain that the messages are on topic, that they do not contain any objectionable language, and that they do not appear to be some form of scam. Moderated boards tend to have messages tightly on topic. Unmoderated message boards have no such review. Therefore, you can find more of the occasional joke and political observation, as well as more personal reactions to other messages. Sometimes even stamp collectors overreact in a manner that does not exhibit the restraint I would like to see. Quickly moving on to another message is the best way to react to a message that you don't like.

I take part in both types, the moderated and unmoderated, and find they both work equally well in the long term. The moderated message boards can have stretches of sterility; the unmoderated boards can get out of hand. Whether a message board is moderated or unmoderated is the decision of its owner.

I frequent two general boards for stamp collecting: Stamp Collecting Forum and The Virtual Stamp Club, which also hosts other, more specialized message boards (see Figure 8-3). Both CompuServe's and Virtual Stamp Club's stamp collecting message boards are moderated, which is rather normal for a message board sponsored by a commercial operation.

> ✔ **CompuServe:** `http://go.compuserve.com/collectibles`
> ✔ **Delphi:** `www.virtualstampclub.com`

 Internet-based messages boards and chat areas tend to come and go. I am noting only those with some solid history and reasonable expectation of continuation. There are others in the same category, and many more that are smaller. As you become more adept at cruising the Internet for stamp-collecting areas, you will come upon them.

One other type of online feature is the Question-and-Answer service of AskPhil.org (Internet: `www.askphil.org/a.htm`), where you may submit a stamp-collecting related question and receive a rapid response either posted for all to see (but not respond to) or directed to you. Unlike a message board, AskPhil's Q&A service is not a discussion.

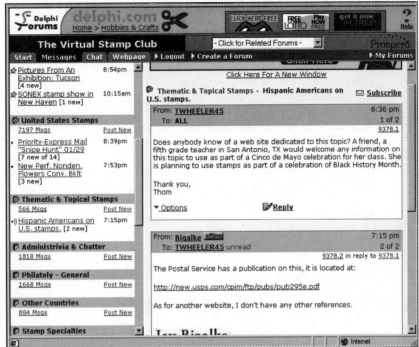

Figure 8-3:
Threads
about
stamps.

An e-mail list is similar to a message board: with the latter, you must go to the message board to read the messages; with the former, messages come to you in the form of e-mail messages and you have a central address to post or respond to messages. E-mail lists have a speckled history within stamp collecting. Because the lists are relatively easy to establish, quite a few have come into existence. Only the strong, however, remain. The largest of the current lot, and (again) one that appears to have lasting power, provides a registration form at the Web site www.philatelic.com. After you register, you receive all messages posted to that list.

As part of registration, for this list and all others, you receive information as to how to post a message, respond to a message, and leave the list (*unsubscribe*). Keep that information! Registration itself is usually pretty simple and should only require you to provide your real name and your e-mail address. I normally shy away from systems that want more information. Sharing the name of my pet iguana is not something I want to do.

Soon after the list manager accepts your registration, you will receive messages. If you like the message content, and the number of messages is not too much for you, just be a part of the action. If you don't like the tone of the messages or if you are receiving too many, use the address provided to you following your registration to leave the list. Ten messages a day may be overwhelming to some, while 40 messages a day may be a light day to someone else. Only you know what is comfortable for you.

One principal caveat to remember: When you post to the list, everyone on the list receives the message. So, if you want to respond privately to one of the messages, using the "reply" button on your e-mail system probably will not do the trick. You need to have the e-mail address of the person you want to reach. Some mail-list systems provide the individual e-mail address with the name of each person posting a message, while others do not. The manner in which stamp collecting has taken to the Internet may well parallel the growth of the Internet. Within stamp collecting itself, where movement is compared to slow glaciers, online growth and interest is nothing less than amazing.

The computer is warm now, so what else will it do?

Coercing with Computers

Stamp collecting, when analyzed from the outside, is little more than a great deal of data — text and illustrations — along with the need for record-keeping, measurements, comparisons, and discussion. Substitute a personal computer for your ballpoint pen, and you have virtually no conversions to make.

Over the past ten years, a number of specialized computer programs have been produced for stamp collectors. These programs (see the following examples) are improved as the PC technology changes and evolves, or as other programs, which fit contemporary operating systems more easily, supersede them.

- ✔ **Album page production:** Computer-generated album pages are an alternative to preprinted album pages.

- ✔ **Checklists:** Normally found for topical areas, checklists may list stamps by country and describe what is on each stamp. I have seen nearly 500 such lists, with more showing up all the time.

- ✔ **Inventory databases:** Most stamp-collecting software helps you keep track of your collection. Some are specialized and others are general (they can be used for any type of collection).

For a more comprehensive listing of stamp-collecting software, check Joseph Luft's Philatelic Resources on the Web, www.execpc.com/~joeluft/resource.html, or the Philatelic Computing Study Group, www.pcsg.org. The former has a more extensive listing of links; the latter has fewer links but offers reviews.

Keeping inventory

No doubt the most-used computer applications in stamp collecting, perhaps other than e-mail, are inventory programs. They come in a variety of forms, but all seek to achieve the same end: Reduce the repetitive bookkeeping that a stamp collector does to keep track of a growing collection. Minimize your record-keeping effort, and you have more time to work with the stamps themselves. Enter the *inventory program,* which is a specialized database for stamp collecting that is generally country based (designed for collectors of a specific country rather than a topic). The developer provides you with a flying start in the form of all the stamp information from a country. As you may already perceive, this is the approach designed to save you the most time and effort. Publishers of such programs provide an annual update that adds the stamps of the preceding year to your database. All you need to do, then, is check off those you own, and your inventory is essentially complete.

An inventory of your stamp collection is little more than an orderly log of key data: catalogue number of the stamp, date of issue, face value, color, brief description, when purchased, purchase price, current value, and as much more as you would like. Keeping track of perhaps thousands of items by hand can be tedious. You need to build and maintain an increasingly large database (an orderly compilation of data). The database may include stamps from a single country or multiple countries.

Inventory programs with accompanying developed and complete databases, as you can guess, are available principally for those countries with the most collectors. You will have a much easier time finding an inventory program instantly suitable for handling your collection of Belgium or Germany (with many collectors each) than for St. Pierre et Miquelon. For those interested in countries without as many collectors, you can find inventory programs in "skeleton" form, which allow you to enter any data you want. The skeleton programs' disadvantage? The data-entry part becomes tedious. The advantages? After it's finished you never have to type the basic information again (big point for the skeletons).

A record rate

Compounding the bookkeeping requirements, if a collector wants to keep an accurate record, are both the normal and rapid increase in the number of items held and the annual issuance of new catalogue values. For most countries, the percentage of items for which catalogue values change each year (with the issuance of the newest catalogue edition) may not be high — perhaps in the 10 to 15 percent range. If you have 5,000 different items in your collection, you have more than 750 values to change each year, and not always the same ones.

The overall advantage of a commercial stamp inventory program is its ability to do the formatting for you and provide you with necessary guidance on how to expand the information.

Prepackaged

So many inventory programs are currently available that listing only a few examples is difficult. New programs are released from time to time, particularly as technology changes and newer features become available at minimal cost. The first inventory programs were purely data. Now, some come with illustrations of stamps; others have stamp identifiers that speed up some of your labor by helping you differentiate look-alikes. Other programs permit you to add your own illustration. Yet, the inventory programs of the very earliest type are still available for those who want only the record-keeping and do not want to be slowed by bells and whistles that will not be used.

Because of the number of available inventory programs and the diversity among them, here are some considerations when shopping for a stamp-collecting inventory package:

✔ **General look-and-feel:** Never purchase an inventory program without first seeing a variety of *screen shots,* which are actual illustrations of various screen views from the program. Seeing a variety of screen shots gives you a solid idea of how you, the collector and user, can interact with the program.

- Does the data-entry approach, no matter how much or how little you need to enter, appear natural to you?

- What is good for you may be terrible for your closest collector friend.

- Are the reports the program generates for you, whether on-screen or printed, what you want and in a format you want?

- If the format is not what you want, are you able to change the look?

✔ **Skeleton or data inclusive:** You have to decide which works best for you. From there, you have to make sure you're getting the best program of whichever kind you chose.

- Is a database included, and how current is the one that comes with the program?

- How often is data updated, and at what cost to you?

- Is the data that's included proper for your collection? That is, if you collect U.S. single stamps, plate block, and first day covers, and a program has no provisions to log first-day covers, you need to know that right away so that you can factor that information into your purchase decision.

- If the program is a skeleton, are you able to enter more than one country and keep the information separate?

- Are you comfortable with the screen layouts? Does information flow easily on the screen? This can be a personal matter. One person's logical layout is another person's travesty.

- Is there adequate help if you have a problem or question? You should see a help feature within the program at the very least. Even smaller software publishers now include both Internet-based and telephone-based provisions, with telephone support sometimes at a fee after a stated grace period.

✔ **Catalogue system referenced:** If you are looking at a program that includes a database, you should know which catalogue system is used.

- If you are collecting U.S. stamps, you may prefer a package using the *Scott Standard Postage Stamp Catalogue* system.

- If you are collecting a country other than the U.S., what system is used, and are you able to enter catalog numbers manually from another system?

- Because catalogue publishers normally do not license use of their systems when the use will be alongside another publisher's system, are there any provisions for you to have more than one catalogue reference and still be within the copyright law?

✔ **Illustrations:** Stamp collecting is a visual hobby. How important is it to you to see things in the program you're using?

- If you are considering a program with a database, are illustrations included?

- How large are they, and will they be helpful for purposes of identification?

✔ **Varieties:** Programs with a built-in database provide listing capability for major varieties, perforation differences, color differences, and so on. Generally, these are listed in catalogues.

- What provisions are available to you for entering minor varieties? This may not be listed in a stamp catalogue, and you, therefore, will need to create your own listing. Perhaps you have a stamp with a plate flaw that you want to list along with the major variety, a block of four, or anything other than the major variety. Are you able to do that at all?

- If you are able to enter minor varieties, how difficult is such a procedure? Take nothing for granted.

In theory, no such creature as a perfect stamp-inventory program exists. You may well find a program that is perfect for you, which is all you can ask. Your colleagues, likewise, may come up with half-a-dozen reasons why the program you love cannot work for them. As you can see, this is a personal thing. When you find a program that you like, spend some time getting acquainted with all of its features. Chances are good that you will be surprised to find something you did not expect. Here are three that are definitely worth looking at for starters:

- ✔ **Stamp Collectors Data Base** (SCDB Software, 8505 River Rock Terr., Suite B, Bethesda, MD 20817; phone 1-800-321-7232; Web site www.scdbsoft.com), is one of the oldest continuously available programs of its type. Stamp Collectors Data Base utilizes the *Scott Standard Postage Stamp Catalogue* system, and accommodates stamps of United States, Canada, United Nations, and Israel. Windows-based only.

- ✔ **EzStamp for Windows** (Softpro 2010, 18 Leverhume Cres., Scarborough, ON, Canada M1E 1K4; phone 416-261-7763; Web site www.members.home.net/mariost), does not use *Scott Standard Postage Stamp Catalogue* system (based on lesser-known/used Minkus system) but otherwise is full-featured. EzStamp for Windows accommodates stamps of United States, Canada and Canadian Provinces, United Nations, Great Britain, Channel Islands, Ireland, Germany and German States, Berlin, Vatican City, Israel, Greece, Greenland, and Netherlands. Windows-based only.

- ✔ **Compu-Quote Stamp Keeper** (6914 Berquist Ave., West Hills, CA 91307; phone 877-462-2980; Web site http://compu-quote.net), after a brief hiatus, offers a new version that continues its long and successful tradition. Compu-Quote Stamp Keeper accommodates U.S. single stamps, U.S. plate blocks, and U.S. first-day covers, as well as stamps of United Nations, Canada/British North America, Great Britain, Germany, East Germany, and Israel. Available for both Windows and Macintosh.

Okay pessimists! What if you can't find what you want? Are you destined to paper and pencil for the remainder of your stamp-collecting life? Absolutely not! The inventory programs discussed previously are specialized databases — whether the actual data is part of the program, or you enter it yourself.

Do it yourself

An option open to you, therefore, is that of developing your own inventory package. If you are comfortable with a spreadsheet program (such as MS Excel for Windows or the Mac) or a database program (such as MS Access for Windows or FileMaker Pro for Windows or the Mac), you have the tools necessary to set up your own program. The sophistication of your project is dependent on your skill with the program and the amount of time you want to spend in development. If you are adept with any of the programming languages, such as Visual Basic, you're probably not even going to continue to reading this, and I will suddenly be alone. However, if you would like more information on the subject, try *Visual Basic 6 For Dummies* by Wallace Wang (Hungry Minds, Inc.).

Your own package has some positives, the greatest of which is that you can build it to your own specifications. You can include just the features you want (or, are able to build) and you can leave out all that you don't want. If meticulously entering the data for all the stamps of the country you are collecting, or at least all stamps that you possess, is onerous to you, then this approach won't work.

Whether you choose a spreadsheet or a database is a personal decision. I have used both, and I'm currently using a spreadsheet. Candidly, and perhaps embarrassingly, I cannot remember my reasons for switching. All I know is that my current system works well for me. Even though I collect the stamps of a country with *many* stamps, I have traded off the time required to prepare my own database with the comfort of knowing I have exactly what I want.

Although your setup will be to your own taste, both on the basis of which types of data you log in and in what order, here are some of the more critical basics:

- **Catalogue number** (perhaps fields for more than one catalogue system, if you are using more than one)
- **Catalogue value**
- **Configuration** (such as single stamp, block of four, first-day cover, or whatever, and perhaps a brief description)
- **Date of issue**
- **Provision to note mint or used**
- **Quantity**

One other spreadsheet feature that I use keeps running totals of the value of my material. Apart from the vanity of knowing that amount — you are invited to my party when the total catalogue value hits one million dollars, but don't reserve your plane tickets yet — I can also use that number as a check against my current insurance coverage.

Checklisting it out

Although available software is skewed heavily toward the country collector, you topicalists (Ah ha! You have a name now!) are not left totally in the cold.

Many, many topical *checklists* — small databases listing stamps associated with a specific topic — are available. The largest source of topical checklists is the American Topical Association, which is mentioned earlier in this chapter.

Its list of checklists, which are available on printed sheets or in MS Excel format, numbers well over 400. Although some of the largest topics, those with the most stamps, may not be available (yet?) and are reserved for the organization's printed handbooks, you have quite a selection from which to choose. Simple in nature, checklists note stamps that apply to the topic (or whatever) along with country of issue, catalogue number, and maybe a brief description.

A postage stamp catalogue serves as a checklist for individual countries. If you are collecting a topic, you need to find out which of the hundreds of thousands of stamps issued fit that topic. You have the option of going through the pages of a stamp catalogue, one by one, and reading individual stamp descriptions. Many of those who do it, relying on a stamp dealer for help, hope to find someone else collecting the same material and use their checklist, or to locate a checklist as described above. In any case, without a catalogue to help you know what stamps have been produced that you may want to add to your collection, you need some sort of checklist as a guide.

The ATA is not the only source for checklists. In my Web prowling, I continue to discover downloadable checklists or checklists that otherwise may be utilized in record keeping. To get to these non-ATA checklists, you need to be lucky or spend a little time perfecting your Web-search techniques. My favorite approach is to use one (or more) of the major search engines and enter a query for "*topic*+stamp," where the word *topic* is replaced by the actual topic name. And I don't use quotation marks for this type of search. Because each of these checklists is a labor of love of the individual who produced it, there is no consistency as to how each is presented. Nor is there necessarily a standard set of codes to make searching easier. A fast method to start this process is to begin with Joe Luft's Philatelic Resources on the Web (www.execpc.com/~joeluft/resource.html).

Topical checklists, whether produced through and offered by the ATA or elsewhere, are subjective. That is, the person developing the lists decides which stamps are to be included. Thus, if the checklist developer decides that anything resembling the topic may be seen on a stamp, that stamp is included in his/her checklist. Another developer may choose only to include those items that occupy perhaps 20 percent or more of the stamp design. No rules exist.

A small, negative aside: Topical checklists not only give you some idea as to the size of the topic in terms of stamp numbers, but they also provide some clues as to which countries are the most prolific when it comes to its designs fitting a specified topical area. Although you're able to guess where to look for many stamps of a given topic, I guarantee you'll be surprised about the stamps of countries other than your own.

Storing at home

Your home computer has the potential of becoming quite important in how you store your stamps. Two types of computer-based packages assist you in developing your own stamp albums (see Chapter 14). One computer program allows you the capability of designing and printing your own pages. This approach is developing quite rapidly now. Later versions contain a database, or attach to a database, which tells the album-development program the size of the stamps. That is, if you want to make a page for a specific set of stamps, the program knows, in advance, the dimensions of the stamps, saving you from having to measure them. Other programs, without that capability, require you to know the measurements.

You may not want to invest in a specialized album-development program, particularly if you already have access to and know how to use a more general drawing program. The specialized programs may allow you to produce finished pages more quickly, particularly if you don't have experience with general graphics packages. The drawing program may provide you with considerably more flexibility. Again, you have all sorts of choices.

A CD-ROM, boasting more than 20,000 album pages for 300 countries, (Internet: www.geocities.com/albumpages) is now available. These are not pages that you are able to modify, but they are an amazing collection of ready-to-print pages.

Newest to the digital scene is EzGrader, a program designed to measure the degree of centering on a stamp (the principal guide to grading a stamp), as well as the stamp's perforation. Both of these measurements can be difficult. The program's Web site (www.members.home.net/ezstamp/grader.htm) allows you to test the program before you buy. That itself is a great feature.

For this program you need a scanner, preferably one with a flat bed, where you lay the stamp or cover down flat and it does not move through the scanner. You probably should be sure that you are adept with a scanner if you plan to do much digitally that is relative to stamp collecting. My best advice for scanner use is to follow the manufacturer's instructions to the letter to get started, before you begin to listen to the many suggestions you receive from fellow stamp collectors. You can get some direction on this subject from *Scanners For Dummies* by Mark L. Chambers (Hungry Minds, Inc.). Or, check out *Teach Yourself VISUALLY Digital Photography* by Elaine Marmel (Hungry Minds, Inc.) for some accessible expert assistance. You must understand how the scanner works in your environment as a base line and then tweak your approach for optimum results.

Chapter 9

"Familializing" Yourself with Stamps

*O*ver the years, much has been said and written about involving youth in stamp collecting. An interest in postage stamps is best developed from within. That is, if a family adds stamp collecting to its quiver of family projects, the actual love of stamp collecting will develop at individual rates — by person — rather than on a schedule dictated by club meeting times or other external factors. The enjoyment of stamp collecting is purely personal. My personal belief is that grandparents and grandchildren often have a "grand" time finding out about stamp collecting together.

If one single approach worked, this chapter would be unnecessary because you would see stamp collecting as a family endeavor all around you in your neighborhood. Rather — because stamp collecting is so personal — what works for your family may be totally unlike anything any other family is doing. Look at what is presented here and see what benefits you and encourages you to begin.

Making It a Family Affair

Consider how you want to approach this family venture. Do you want a family collection or a family collecting? The former is a single collection, all members presumed to be sharing equally, with some form of democratic approach as to how to proceed and what to purchase. The latter is the sharing of stamp-collecting ideals — discovering, developing, enjoying — with each person building an individual collection and then sharing that collection with the other members of the family as it is being developed.

My vote is for a "family collecting," where the enjoyment is that each helps the others with a personal stamp collection by looking out for items that they may need. If Mom is working on a country collection, Dad and each of the children are aware of items that may help that collection. Dad may be building a topical collection of racing cars. The younger child loves to collect flags on stamps — even though he has something like 75 copies of the same flag stamp, it's still a collection that *he* is building. The older child, who loves the family pet, is collecting dogs on stamps.

Each begins at his or her own speed and level of commitment, which cannot be forced. But, in the "family spirit," each member also helps the others build their collections. Each member may have a different approach to an album (see Chapter 14). Each member, no doubt, has a different approach to a collection . . . even if one or more individuals are collecting similar material. For example, father and son may each want to build a collection of U.S. stamps (see Chapter 11), but the father may be looking for commemoratives from the year of his birth to the present and the son may be intrigued by all the stamps with U.S. flags.

With reading skills not yet honed, the children are not ready to research the backgrounds of the stamps in their possession. So, organizing the stamps into some coherent presentation may not yet be within their consideration. As they add stamps to their collection, however, questions may arise — this is the perfect time for parental "influence" to help the child understand what is depicted on each stamp. Before a child can find out about what is depicted on a stamp on his own, parents are able to help. Perhaps the desire to "do it myself" becomes strong enough that stamp collecting becomes a positive factor in reading development.

Baby steps

Many stamp-collecting programs for children have been started, but none continue today on any major scale. Although the various programs — whether at the local-club level or national level, through the American Philatelic Society (APS), American Stamp Dealers Association, or the U.S. Postal Service — have certainly brought to the hobby many who were introduced to stamp collecting through these formal programs, no major long-term positive result is known. Nevertheless, stamp collecting continues to attract new people.

My point is quite simple: There's no reason to push a child into collecting or to micromanage his collection development. Following are some specific suggestions for helping your child develop as a collector:

- **Do** encourage children to add whatever stamps they want to their personal collection. If a stamp really does not *fit* a collection, the child has ample time to reach that realization and find the stamp a new home.

- **Don't** stifle a child's creativity, as may be shown through the child's stamp collection, or the manner in which the child arranges or mounts her stamps. If you're concerned about your young child damaging his stamps, merely be certain that the only stamps he gets are stamps of such low value that their destruction is not a problem.

- **Do** provide each stamp collector in the family with a personal set of tools. Metal stamp tongs with pointed edges aren't the best for seven-year-old collectors, but plastic tongs are safer and work quite well.

- **Don't** overwhelm a young collector with a bunch of stamps at one time. It may even be better to wait until the child mentions that she is out of new stamps to review before loading up.

- **Do** help the child soak any stamps. Here is one situation where family cooperation is important.

- **Don't** insist on doing everything and relegating the kids to watching only.

- **Do** continue to question your child about the stamps:

  > What flag is that?

  > What breed of dog is that?

  > Do you know what country issued that stamp?

  Children who collect stamps tend to be more inquisitive than other children, so some challenging questions that get the child thinking can lead to further development of the stamp collection and (more importantly) of the child.

- **Don't** be judgmental. When all of you are engaged in the hobby, the children are equals. You may be there to provide support, but decisions, such as what to collect, how to arrange, what to exclude, and so on, must be left to the collector.

Growing up

Although children should have the right to play with their stamps, remnants of a jelly sandwich on their hands while they grip their tongs isn't a good idea when playing with someone else's collection.

Strong ground rules need to be established for times when the children are observing or assisting with the parents' collection. (You can find more rules for stamp handling in Chapter 14.) These should be simple rules:

- ✔ Have clean hands.
- ✔ Use tongs to touch the stamps.
- ✔ Don't add or remove anything from an album or envelope without asking.

Guidelines such as these (more of a situation of respect for personal property than stamp rules) can be followed when children are working with their own collection.

When it comes to stamp collecting, the more you look at your child as an equal participant in the hobby — and the child looks to you as an equal within the context of stamp collection — the healthier the development.

A child's question about items in your collection is a great opening for parent/child cooperation. If the answer is easy, provide it. If the answer requires some research, and the child is capable of it, point him in the proper direction and follow up. And, if the question requires you to research the answer, do so quickly to stay within the child's interest span. Admitting that you don't know the answer is not a sign of defeat, merely a challenge to find the answer.

Statistics show that as teens age and move toward other interests, they tend to put aside the stamp album. Then, after teenagers grow up and begin their own family, they tend to return to the hobby. So, if your resident teenager shows less interest in his or her stamp collection in favor of the opposite sex or sports, you are witnessing a natural situation. Keep the album, because chances are very good that it will be used again at a later date.

If you are a member of a local stamp club, take your stamp-collecting children with you to a meeting at least once. Prior to arriving at the meeting site, be sure that the children understand that the experience may be quite boring or rather exciting. No matter which, the child is expected to be patient and polite — just as you had to be on your first trip. After you and yours arrive inside, introduce the children (proudly, of course) as young stamp collectors. Using my own experience as a guide, if you proudly introduce your children to the collectors, you may not see your children the remainder of the meeting. Other collectors adopt them temporarily and question them on their interests. The other collectors will share experiences with your children, too — just like a *real* collector. The object lesson here is that a stamp collector is a stamp collector, no matter what his or her physical size, age, or collecting interest.

Collecting Encourages Discussions: Who Knew?

With the whole family involved in stamp collecting, a host of discussion points among parents and children immediately become available. Under the talking-about-stamps umbrella, abundant stimulation to discovery begins to roll out — discovery for both parent and child. If you believe that you'll have all the answers to your children's questions about stamps, you haven't been paying much attention to how much more quickly children have taken to the computer revolution than have adults.

For those of you who are involved in home schooling, you know how lessons can spill over into family discussions. Parents of children in traditional education environments who take a solid interest in the daily goings-on can also discuss and relate school-time activities with what happens outside of those four walls. Postage stamps allow you to grab onto such discussions and make a quantum leap.

To use U.S. stamps as an example, just about anything presented in a school history lesson is paralleled in the subject of a postage stamp. With more than 3,000 different U.S. stamp designs, and many commemorations quite broad in their scope, you have a pretty good chance of developing the relationship between stamp and school.

When the bright-eyed one comes in from school and mentions that the day's history lesson revolved around the Industrial Revolution or the importance of the railroad to westward expansion, you merely need to reach into your album of tricks (we don't keep postage stamps in a bag) for illustrated examples.

First comes the school lesson. Then comes the at-home discussion. Then the particularly motivated child takes the stamp in question for some further research in an encyclopedia or on the World Wide Web to pin-point just what the stamp was commemorating and to see how close it is to what the teacher was talking about in class. Remember that youths who are interested in stamps and stamp collecting are generally more inquisitive and resourceful than youths who are not interested in stamps. Tap into that vein of inquisitiveness, and the family can have hours of meaningful fun. Oh yes, you will discover something also.

Note that using postage stamps in this manner is not really collecting. Using stamps as a tool to teach your children is, however, a tremendous opportunity to increase philatelic interest and appreciation that may well lead to the development of a collection.

From collecting to a career

With regard to your child's own collection or accumulation of stamps, as well as his or her interest in yours, notice if your child enjoys measuring and categorizing the stamps. Note whether your child's interest in measuring and categorizing is even greater than your interest. Many careers require such a skill set, and you may be observing the early traits that can be honed in the years to come. If you find that your child's measurements lead to accurate results — better than your results — the youthful one may have a major role in helping you with your collection and may love doing it!

Along similar lines, a child's ability to set up a computer database and log in the items in your collection may easily outweigh yours. Again, everyone learns. If such tasks are done eagerly, you can be sure the results will be great. Because children know when they are being given kid things to do, any time that they are able to participate as equals with an adult leads to long attention spans and quality results, as well as the potential for much more development.

If stamp collection does anything for an individual, as well as for a family, it develops patience.

Beyond the classroom is a large world. Apart from building a topical collection on any of these subjects, you and your family can enhance the enjoyment of one of your recreational interests by discovering the background of stamps issued on the subject.

While adult collectors are bitten by the *completeness* bug that drives them toward continually building a collection to a preset (and oft-changed) goal, children are prebitten and will pick up a single stamp and wonder what the stamp's design signifies. The child collector is more interested in the story behind the stamp. Learn from that! Are you able to pick a stamp randomly from your collection and know what that stamp commemorates and why? This is particularly difficult when choosing a single stamp from a set that was probably purchased as a set, without concern for the individual stamps within it.

You can find many stamps that relate to major world events, incidents that come and go, and events that merit headlines on the front page or sports page of the daily newspaper. A volcano blowing its top, or some other problem in a country that you only know through your stamp collecting, can prompt further discussion, and perhaps research, based on a stamp's design. The Olympic games, soccer's World Cup, and rock stars and other pop icons are all subjects that are shown on postage stamps — stamps are no longer purely the head of state's design domain.

Although you may need to take the lead when talking about revolutionary activities in the mountains of a country that your child cannot pronounce, your child can take the lead when bringing you up-to-date on a film or rock star depicted on the new-issue release of another country. Stamp collecting breaks down the adult-youth and parent-child barriers, which can be a very good thing. Those barriers are quickly replaced when it comes to deciding who feeds the family dog.

Trying Some Scenarios

Here are some scenarios, presented in a concise manner, that may help you in your total-family, stamp-collecting involvement. Nothing here is written in stone — not even in soft clay. Rather, these scenarios are offered as beginning points for you to begin tapping additional ways to involve everyone.

Extending the classroom: Today's happenings

The family's younger members return home from school to discuss the day's happenings. Postage-stamp subjects that you are aware of are among the items up for discussion. Use the stamps(s) to prompt your young student(s) to look more deeply into the subject. Discuss the topic under the umbrella of helping to develop the stamp collection rather than of allowing your young student(s) to learn more. Sneaky, huh?

Extending the classroom: Off on a tangent

An in-class study of, say, the French and Indian War is not complete. A young member of your family continues to have an interest in the subject and wishes the class could spend more time on it. Fortunately, you remember that a 1930 U.S. stamp commemorates the Battle of Braddock's Field (Battle of Monongahela) and a 1958 stamp commemorates the British capture of Fort Duquesne (which was renamed Fort Pitt). Both of the commemorated events are very interesting, and they relate to significant parts of the greater development westward of the U.S. A little research, the results of which would be placed, with the stamp, in your child's album, can provide an understanding of why our country expanded in the manner it did. Unless your children are going to school near where I did — where Braddock's Trail just about crossed through the school playground — the significance of the events may not be as great. You, however, may live near the site of another important historical, scientific, or cultural event or two.

Extending the classroom: The project!

What better way to illustrate those school projects than with professionally designed and produced postage stamps? I remember doing a junior high school history paper with stamps as the illustrations. Of course, there was not as much history way back then, and dinosaurs had only recently gone out of vogue as pets.

Not only do stamps provide the illustrations, but by arranging them well, they also help with the outline and flow of the paper itself. For students just starting with school projects and papers, this additional organizational help will be appreciated. Some of the more recent U.S. definitive series, which honor individuals without noting their achievements on the stamps themselves, are excellent prompts for school projects.

Logging family fun

If your family loves to travel for fun, or if an athletic or musical interest has the family visiting other towns frequently, consider logging the trips through postmarks. Prepare postal cards, or even picture postcards, in advance with the date and location of the event, and then drop the card at a post office or into a mailbox in each city that you visit. The cards are returned to your home with the postmark of the city you visited. This makes for an interesting scrapbook of family activities. Add a few photographs and you really have a keeper! And the common postmark is the basis for the whole thing.

Building your reference collection

Throughout this book, I have espoused the importance of a reference collection to help you identify paper, specific colors, overprints, and perforations. Generally, a reference collection is only developed out of necessity. If young family members take on the task of developing the reference material, not only can they grasp the technical side of stamp collection more quickly, but they'll also make a significant contribution to the family enjoyment of the hobby. Your children will need access to duplicate stamps, a good set of measuring devices, and a solid list of what is needed. Children will also need to recommend purchases of inexpensive items to flesh out the reference collection when the pile of duplicates runs short.

And, referring to the "Extending the classroom: The project!" section earlier in this chapter, would not all or part of a completed reference collection be the basis for an excellent science project on color or the application of various types of measurement?

If not first base, perhaps database

Rainy days, particularly those that wash out a youth event, may not normally be a pleasant time for children or their parents. An ongoing project that is not time critical and that does not require much setup or tear-down time is ideal. Add to the mix a computer-literate child, which is not hard to find. Developing or maintaining stamp-collection inventory databases is a great exercise in computer use. The easy way out is to use a commercially available postage-stamp inventory program. The more adventuresome way is to provide the younger members of your family with a list of what's needed for the database and the requisite snacks, and stand back.

You may be surprised at the result. Not only will your needs be met, but chances are good that they can be improved on. If the results are not too sparkling, nothing is lost as long as your children are developing the database from scratch or working with a copy of what already exists. Chances are good that the biggest problem you'll have during this otherwise drab period will be keeping the snack dish supplied. Such a project may well require more than one rainy day. But as long as there is nothing pressing about it, the development time and work are as important as the result.

Make sure any projects are meaningful and not just make-work — children know the difference. The price grows, as does the interest in the stamp collection. You'll love the day that your child comes to borrow a cup of stamp hinges from you for his own collection or project.

Chapter 10

Showing off at Exhibits

• •

In This Chapter

▶ What's in it for me?

▶ Building your exhibit, brick by brick

▶ Using criticism to your future benefit

▶ What are the categories, Alex?

• •

*W*hen building your collection, you develop a fondness for showing it off to fellow collectors, family, or whoever happens to be close at hand. Your creative imagination begins to churn with the thought, "Are there others out there who might like to see the work I have done?" You are proud of what you are doing, and you are beginning to share what you are discovering. You also may be one who enjoys the constructive criticism from others as an effort to improve your work.

Perhaps competitive exhibiting is for you. Rewards may be rich, although not in the form of cash. Rewards come to you in the form of what you discover, the interaction among fellow collectors, perhaps a medal or prize, and an introduction into a whole new part of stamp collecting. If financial return is all you seek, play the lottery.

Exhibiting: So What's the Big Deal?

After you are hooked as a competitor, you can *justify* exhibiting at stamp shows in major cities and resort locations, and even expand your foreign travel a bit. But I am getting ahead of the story. Rather than a formal period of internship as an exhibitor, or any sort of training, what you find are distinct levels of competition:

> ✔ **Local club:** Many collectors are satisfied preparing exhibits for one or more local stamp shows in their area.

✔ **National:** After being bitten by the competitive bug, some collectors seek to be a part of national-level exhibits. Although national-level shows do not have entrance requirements, the show's exhibit committee always has the right to refuse an exhibit, but rarely does so.

✔ **International:** Qualifying for an international show requires that an exhibit has received a *vermeil* (a color that is also known as vermilion) medal in a national-level competition. On a scale of bronze, silver, vermeil, and gold (with some shows adding a silver-bronze and/or a large-gold), vermeil is a well-respected award at a national-level show. That bit of complexity aside, you should not figure that you can qualify for an international show right away.

Only a small percentage of stamp collectors exhibit competitively. Those who do, however, really enjoy it and appear to profit greatly from what they learn from building their exhibit, showing it, and then making improvements on the basis of the post-competition critiques. Stamp collecting is a big, wide hobby with room for many ways to participate.

Building a stamp collection is such a personal experience, particularly when you go beyond the preprinted album pages where you need merely fill in the spaces. Soon you realize that you are off into uncharted territory. Others may have a collection with the same basic title, orientation, or even just about the same material . . . but you added your own touch to your collection. Naturally, extending from that personal touch is the desire to show your material to others. How many people buy a classic automobile and keep it in their garage without showing it to others?

If you volunteer to present a program at your local stamp club, you have an opportunity to share your collection with others; this is a great opportunity for you and your fellow club members. A club presentation can be a great learning experience for you and the audience. Exhibiting at a stamp show allows you the opportunity to show your collection to more people than would normally attend a single stamp club meeting, and you are free to show that collection as often and at as many shows as you want.

Discovering So Many Things

Put together a competitive exhibit and instantly you begin to discover — finding out about exhibiting, discovering how other collectors look at exhibits, finding out more about the material that you are exhibiting, and learning about material, that you do not yet possess, that enhances your exhibit. Take lots of notes.

About exhibiting . . .

Particularly as a beginner, but even after you have been exhibiting competitively for a few years, you come to believe that no one knows all there is to know about this aspect of stamp collecting. You can study *The New Philatelic Exhibitors Handbook* (Randy Neil, Subway Stamp Shop, Inc., 2121 Beale Avenue, Altoona, PA 16601) and read articles and commentary on competitive exhibiting in the various stamp-collecting periodicals (See more on finding resources in Appendix A of this book). Exhibiting is a continuous adventure.

Beginning with your first time as a competitive exhibitor, you will have fellow collectors who view your exhibit and approach you with, "Nice exhibit. I'm sure it'll do really well. But, have you ever considered adding *XYZ* or using a less fancy type style?" In short, everyone is an expert willing to give advice. The judges, however, are the only ones who mete out the awards. As long as you have skin that's thick enough to handle the advice, you are off to a grand set of experiences.

Do not exhibit for the first time without first spending a fair amount of time actually studying other exhibits at a stamp show. If your maiden voyage is in a few months at your club's next show, get yourself to the closest club show as soon as possible. The stamp-collecting periodicals all have listings of upcoming shows, as do many Web sites, such as www.stampshows.com. After you arrive at the show, look at the exhibits carefully and see what there is about each exhibit that you like the most and the least (see Figure 10-1). Your exhibit can be just that: your exhibit. After you make your own first exhibition effort, be prepared for the suggestions and offers of help.

Willingness to share is one of the great benefits of stamp collecting. Do not shy away from telling fellow collectors and exhibitors that you are new to exhibiting. In return, you can hear the experiences of others who have been at it for a long time. About the only downside to this spirit of sharing is that you need to sort out information that can help you from that which will not. Unexpected help may come from stamp dealers who see your exhibit. Some may approach you to ask if you want them to be on the lookout for material that can help build your exhibit. Always say "Yes," but you are free to accept or reject any material offered, as well as enter any further arrangements. That is, you may simply accept such offers in passing and make sure that you are not obligated to anything, or you may encourage one or more dealers to search actively on your behalf.

Be sure of the arrangements that you make with dealers. When a dealer phones you with an offer of a fair amount of material for you — which you are not prepared to purchase at that time — you are under no obligation to buy it. More positively, how great it is to have a personal shopper keeping an eye out for something specific to your needs?

Figure 10-1:
Row on
row of
competitive
exhibits at
a large
international
stamp
show.

About your own exhibit . . .

With your exhibit on display for all to see at the stamp show, you will no doubt spend at least a little time nearby watching the reactions of onlookers. Hovering over the exhibit like a vulture awaiting prey is not recommended, but the occasional walk-by is reasonable. Listen to what others say about it, and watch how other collectors inspect your exhibit.

Do not be shy about identifying yourself as the owner of the exhibit being discussed and joining right in. With nothing more involved here than your pride and ego (and everybody knows how small each of those is), pick up all the information that you can. Direct the discussion, as best you can, toward what can be done to improve the exhibit. Areas of improvement will probably be based on one of the exhibit components to be discussed later in this chapter. You need not be defensive because you prepared the exhibit based on the best available information.

Approach competitive exhibiting with an open mind, and you can reap many rewards. Do not feel badly if, after your first attempt, you feel you have the intelligence of an electric eel with a short circuit. Only the rare first-timer sees — soon after the prized (differentiated from *Prize*) exhibit is mounted into exhibit frames — more than one area where things could have been done differently, better, not at all, or whatever. Stop for a moment: Is this not the same feeling that you had as a second grader when you appeared in your first school play? Butterflies! . . . and you promised yourself never to ingest an insect.

About human nature . . . many, if not most, of the people who make comments to you about your exhibit are positive. You are, of course, a minor celebrity of the moment. You can, of course, be accosted by the rare (in many senses of the word) person who is critical because you should have used a different example for the third item of the seventh page of your exhibit.

Golly! This person has memorized your exhibit better than you have. Perhaps this person is an expert telling you that instead of exhibiting competitively you should be mowing your lawn. But, wait! Don't allow attitude to replace information. Agree to consider the suggestion and then check the suggestion against what you have. Hmmm. Then ask someone more knowledgeable than you. That person agrees with what is in your exhibit and pronounces the suggested change as . . . well . . . as something you should or should not do.

You discovered the subjectivity of stamp collecting and exhibiting firsthand. But don't dismiss all suggestion givers as being overbearing meddlers. The next one may be valuable to you. In the meantime, you have found out how intense some are with regard to the hobby.

REMEMBER

The critique mystique

National-level competitive exhibits and many local-club exhibits set aside time, following the posting of awards, for the exhibitors (and any others who care to attend) to meet with the show judges. Known as *judges' critiques,* these sessions can be tremendously useful. Occasionally they have periods of humor and sometimes even some bruised feelings. Although judges work from exhibiting guidelines, the key is both in their interpretation of the guidelines and how they express their interpretation to the exhibitors.

After you have decided to exhibit competitively, and whether you have an exhibit at a show, be sure to attend the judges' critique. Tell the judges that this is the first time that you have exhibited. If it is the second or third time that you have exhibited the same material, tell the judges of the changes you have made since the last time you showed the material. If you have entered an exhibit, get to the critique session early and hang around afterward to pick up all you can from the collective tree of knowledge.

Here Comes the Judge

A group of philatelic judges, accredited and not accredited, reviews your competitive exhibit at the stamp show.

- ✔ In the U.S., the 35-plus national-level shows are required to use judges accredited by the American Philatelic Society.
- ✔ In Canada, the accrediting group is the Royal Philatelic Society of Canada.
- ✔ The International Federation of Philately (FIP, the acronym is based on the name in French) accredits judges for the jury at international shows for which it gives patronage. Shows sponsored by local clubs may not have a requirement as to who is selected to judge. But, generally, accredited judges are used whenever possible.

When you are new to exhibiting, which group is accrediting the judges at the show where you are exhibiting is not as important as knowing whether or not they are accredited. Accreditation requires apprenticeship under the watchful eye of long-term judges, among a series of other requirements.

1. Judges at a stamp show review each exhibit page by page.

2. Each judge notes his/her opinion of which basic award level each exhibit falls into as well as a choice for any special awards available for presentation. Set levels of awards are available to each judge.

   Basic award levels are normally noted as gold, vermeil (gold plate over silver), silver, and bronze with the possibility of additional levels, such as large-gold, and silver-bronze. Some shows actually award medals; others present certificates with the medal level noted, and ribbons are attached to the exhibit frames to alert show attendees to which exhibit won which prize.

3. The grand and reserve grand (second prize overall) awards are drawn from the gold medal winners.

In other words, the top two awards are selected after the judges pick the gold medal winners. Normally the judges have the freedom to award as many of each prize level as they choose. Therefore, it is possible, although highly improbable, that all the exhibits may win a gold medal or a bronze medal. All national-level shows, and many local shows, require that the judges gather together in a meeting room to take questions from exhibitors about their own or other exhibits. This judges' critique is normally open to the public and is a tremendous learning event for all exhibitors and other show attendees.

Gathering collectors together

Competitive exhibiting may well be the best way, in the world of stamp collecting, to stimulate interaction among collectors. Few collectors begin exhibiting competitively in a vacuum, with no help at all. After your first exhibit, you can share tidbits of information with others just like you. Regarding the judges' critiques, you are part of a group that believes the judges just didn't understand the subtle and not-so-subtle statements of their respective exhibits. (My favorite judges' critique opened with the chief judge of that show pouring glasses of wine for the exhibitors and other visitors. By far that was the most civilized critique I ever attended. After all, who could question the judgment of anyone who would be such a good host?)

You will notice a great sense of camaraderie among exhibitors — particularly at the judges' critiques, where exhibitors in attendance are all searching for that single clue, that little bit of information that will enable them to make their exhibits strong enough to advance to the next medal level in the next competition. That camaraderie has led to an organization for competitive exhibitors — the American Association of Philatelic Exhibitors (P.O. Box 451, Lexington, GA 30648, USA).

Individual relationships, which are more personal than an organization or the public critiques of a show's exhibits, can be developed. You meet others with your stamp-collecting specialty, whether exhibitors or not, who seek your counsel relative to their own collections. After all, if you are exhibiting a collection, you certainly have knowledge of that collecting area. Wait a minute; you are being approached as an expert! Perhaps you need a new wardrobe to accommodate your exalted position. Back to Earth. You begin to realize that if you have prepared a competitive exhibit and have won an award, others collecting the same type of material come to you for information. You have taken an additional step that most stamp collectors don't take. Enjoy it, but don't let it dominate your thinking.

Each award wins only one *level* award. Exhibits not believed strong enough to merit a bronze award normally receive a *Certificate of Participation*. Clubs or regional federations may also sponsor special prizes, which may include the top exhibit entered by an exhibitor under the age of 18, the best exhibit of French stamps, or the top exhibit by a member of the club sponsoring the show. Many shows also award special prizes for an exhibit that stands out for one reason or another, without regard to the medal awarded.

Building a Competitive Exhibit

Presenting the important components of a competitive exhibit is relatively simple. Refining those components, however, to make the exhibit a contender for the top award in any competition is not a textbook situation. But you must start somewhere. Gain an understanding of these components and how they work with each other, and you should be able to put together an exhibit that looks like it belongs with the others. If you really do well in your first competition, by all means, give me the credit. If you don't, chalk it up to a first effort. How can you lose?

The key areas to know are

✔ Design and layout

✔ Equipment

✔ General exhibit write-up

✔ Planning

✔ Title page

✔ Other pages

Although the list may appear somewhat redundant, there is method to this madness — in a competition you are expected to show creativity and uniqueness within a tightly structured environment.

A key concept to keep in mind is that, generally, your personal collection is different from a competitive exhibit based on it. The former has no guidelines — in fact, I am one who strenuously argues against any boundaries as to what or how you collect — and the latter should be constructed within the (sometimes seemingly tight) guidelines on which the judges review your effort.

Finally, before you leap into putting together your first exhibit, know the physical characteristics of where you will be exhibiting: How many pages fit into each exhibition frame (the device in which exhibit pages are placed so they may be seen and not touched by visitors)? What is the maximum number of frames permitted for each show? Although the normal-size frames used at national and international stamp shows accept 16 album pages, local shows may have smaller frames, taking 6, 8, 9, or some other number. You want this information so that you know what your total allowable page count may be and so you come out even at the end of your final frame.

Before you hunker down, write or phone the organizers of the first show that you want to compete in for an exhibit application. Applications are required for each show, and each application is different. See Appendix A for more information on national shows and addresses of periodicals that list the local shows. The application should provide answers to the following key questions:

✔ How many pages does each frame hold?

✔ What is the maximum number of frames allowed for each exhibit?

✔ What time should the exhibit be brought to the show? Or, should the exhibit be mailed in advance of the show? Are there special packing or mailing instructions? To whom and where is the exhibit mailed?

✔ When the show closes, where do you pick up your exhibit? Or, when is it mailed back to you?

✔ What is the day and time of the judges' critique?

If you have your exhibit shipped back to you, be certain to check each page immediately on its arrival. All stamp insurance plans (See Chapter 6) cover your exhibit while you are at home working on it, sending it to or from a show, or while the exhibit is at the show.

Have a plan

At all stages, be aware of the budget for your exhibit. Building your competitive exhibit is great, but it must be kept in perspective. My personal preference is to distinguish the exhibit through the level of research and knowledge involved, rather than how expensive the material is. When planning your exhibit, keep the following factors in mind. They are general by design; being too specific at this stage may force you away from that aspect of uniqueness that you need before you begin to form the exhibit within the accepted judging guidelines. Spending additional time with these items will pay off for you later when you are able to move through the "building" stage much more smoothly.

1. Know what you want to exhibit.

2. Know how to define your exhibit for the judges through the exhibit title and the title (opening) page.

3. Know how large your exhibit should be. The maximum number of pages allowed in the stamp show competition is a limiting factor; you need a solid handle on this, at least at the beginning of your career, before you build your exhibit. Then, get a feel for how much material you have that fits under the umbrella of your exhibit's title.

4. Outline your exhibit. Your exhibit is a logical story that needs to flow like a book. What sort of story are you planning to tell?

   When you are developing your outline, and particularly for a first-time exhibit where you are lacking valuable experience, you may want to begin to lay out your exhibit pages on stock pages, which allow you the flexibility of adding, deleting, and moving the material at will. The old-timers do the same thing, although many may wait until their outline is complete and then see how closely they come to it before adding or deleting material.

5. Be sure that you covered everything included within your exhibit title, and make sure you have not included anything beyond the title's scope. Confused? Let me explain some pitfalls. Perhaps you are interested in the stamps of Bermuda, and you want to build a competitive exhibit based on that interest. The first part of your planning (knowing what you want to exhibit) is under control for the moment. You then set a tentative title: no surprise, *Stamps of Bermuda.* That honest title is your way to explain the contents of your exhibit. To the judges, however, it suggests that you will be showing all the stamps of Bermuda, including the most valuable that may cost more than $100,000 each!

I will wait until your symptoms of hyperventilation subside before continuing. . . . With the need for a better title firmly in mind, you decide on something like *Bermuda's George V Issues,* which is a manageable stamp grouping that provides enough challenge to your pocketbook and allows you to locate what you need without requiring you to strike a vein of gold ore in your backyard.

So, you need a subject that you can develop, preferably without undue expense, and that is titled such that you convey to the judges what they can expect and grade you against.

If the Bermuda commemorative stamps are your exhibit approach, presuming this exhibit is for a local show, you may use each of Bermuda's commemorative set titles for the year span you choose to show as a major heading. Subheadings may be any minor varieties that you have. You may also have provisions for first-day covers or examples of some/many of the stamps that were used and are still on their envelopes.

If you are lost at the point where you're supposed to start telling the stamps' story, then by all means get to a stamp show and review the exhibits. After going through this chapter, match the information presented against what you see on display. Then, you are actually ready for your own outline, which you can convert for use on the exhibit's outline page (described later, in the "Other exhibit pages" section). The outline is subject to change until the time your exhibit is completed (for you always will want to tweak it a little), similar to how something like this book is prepared.

After your outline is complete, investigate other competitive exhibits that may parallel yours. You'll be better off if you do not duplicate someone else's approach. You want to be judged against exhibition guidelines, not merely compared to another exhibit.

Unload the equipment here, fellas

For your first competitive exhibit, you have no need to scour the countryside for any special tools. You probably have all that you need in your stamp-collecting suite of rooms (or wherever you work with your collection) right now. As with anything else that is compulsive (did I say that?), you can find the need for some items beyond the normal stamp-collecting tools (see Chapter 3). Computer-prepared exhibit pages have come on the scene rapidly in the past couple of years. Just as a *stock page* (a manila or plastic page with pockets to hold the stamps) permits easy movement of material to end up with the most attractive and advantageous presentation, current page-layout programs allow the same flexibility on screen. Then, with the click of a digital rodent, you see the printed page just as you want it. Meanwhile, you can store the complete set of exhibit pages for the time — and there *will be* the time — when you want to revise the pages.

As you progress with your exhibiting, and more and more little things begin to make a difference, consider adding these to your toolbox:

- **Kneadable eraser:** This eraser has the look and feel of clay, which allows you to form it for special use. Kneadable erasers are excellent for removing small marks on album pages caused by pencils, dust, or other smudging.

- **Moist hand wipes:** Wipes, such as those provided at a restaurant when you order ribs, come in handy. You do not want to redo an exhibit page because something got transferred to a page from your hands and cannot be removed with the kneadable eraser.

- **Illuminated magnifier:** Get an illuminated magnifier, preferably one that mounts to your desk or worktable. (See Chapter 3.) This device has many uses. A mounted magnifier comes in handy when you spend lengthy periods of time reviewing stamps for proper identification. It can also allow both hands the freedom for more precise cutting of stamp mounts and improve the accuracy of hand-drawn lines on exhibit pages (another reason to use a computer).

- **Transparent ruler:** This should really be a part of your basic, nonexhibit set of tools. I must have three or four different transparent rulers, and I am not even an active exhibitor. Combining a transparent ruler with a desk-mounted magnifier allows you maximum flexibility to position stamps more easily for measurement and, ultimately, proper identification.

- **Paper cutter with wheel blade:** An item that is used to cut stamp mounts more precisely than a pair of scissors or a traditional guillotine. Neatness counts.

The preceding group is rather critical to your page preparation. Randy Neil, in his *The New Philatelic Exhibitors Handbook*, adds a few more items that further aid in the exhibit preparation:

- **Tiny vacuum cleaner:** Normally battery operated, this vacuum can keep your work area dust free. **Note:** Remove all stamps from the area before using this item!

✔ **Additional desktop lighting:** This gives you the capability to direct proper lighting to whatever part of your work area needs it, and not just that section where you do most of your work.

✔ **Cushioned chair on wheels:** Why not? You owe it to yourself.

If a computer does not produce your exhibit pages, you need a decent type-writer with a fresh ribbon. You also need a marking pen for making any lines, because a typewriter does not do lines well. Depending on your own situation, you may come up with many additional items that you cannot do without. As you continue to load up on tools, preface each purchase with the mantra, "Aren't obsessions fun?"

Unlock the designer within you

If you are the type of person who constantly rearranges the furniture in your living room because it just doesn't seem right, then you can never get beyond this section of exhibit preparation. Rather than perhaps half a dozen items in a living room (maybe more, I lead a Spartan life), you may have literally hundreds of stamps and at least 16 (perhaps as many as 160) pages to arrange them on. This is no place for someone who is unable to make a decision.

From the perspective of a long-time observer of stamp shows, exhibits, exhibitors, judges, and judging, I believe that bad *presentation* — jargon for exhibit-page design and layout — is more apt to downgrade your exhibit than a good presentation is to enhance it. That is, the judges are looking for what material you present and how coherently you are presenting it rather than how neat the type style is and if the headline color coordinates well with the color of your text type. In essence, nothing should get in the way of the stamps being exhibited — they must carry the day and tell the story.

Your design needs to be understated and consistent. Be certain that you use the same type style throughout. All the headlines of the same level on your outline should be the same size and style, and the body type should be the same throughout. If you place a border around the stamps on the first seven pages, do the same for the remaining pages.

1. **Using stock pages, place the stamps in the proper order.**

2. **Add small blocks of paper to simulate where the write-up text will be placed.**

3. **On that rough layout, note if there appears to be a good flow.**

4. **Step back to be sure that no page is crowded with too much material, or crowded toward the top, or one side.**

If you are showing a lengthy set of stamps, be certain that the layout is pleasing. Various experts have more specific advice for page layout. For your first effort, I recommend that you use your own common sense, after having seen how others have done it.

The write-up: Don't overdo it

The explanation that surrounds a stamp or a set in your exhibit, and why it is included, is called the *write-up* in the vernacular of competitive stamp exhibiting. Using your daily newspaper as a parallel, the write-up is more closely related to photo captions than to a news article (even small articles). In the early days of electronic communications, people paid for a telegram by the word. For the purposes of your exhibit write-up, think of your explanation as a telegram — with a fee of $5 per word! How much are you willing to pay for your exhibit write-up?

For example, harkening back to the mythical exhibit noted earlier, suppose that your exhibit of Bermuda commemoratives includes the first-day cover of a smaller set, and a principal Bermuda government official autographed the set. Then be certain as to who signed the cover and what the title of his position is. Do not include the circumstances of why he signed the cover or how you came to possess it — neither can impact your exhibit. Bear the following in mind as you create your write-up:

- ✔ Only include information that is necessary.
- ✔ Keep it brief.
- ✔ Be objective.
- ✔ Make it absolutely factual!

Judges have many pages to review at an exhibit. If they become bogged down with an exhibit, it is duly noted in their memories, and perhaps even on their notepads, for the purpose of downgrading.

You never know; one of the competition's judges may possess *real* expertise regarding the material that you are exhibiting and may be able spot write-up errors on sight. Such a situation is costly to the fate of your exhibit in that competition, as well as to your reputation. Write-ups cannot be redundant or unnecessary. If the judge can see something on the page, mentioning it is unnecessary.

After your text is under control, you face the issue of placing it on the page. As long as you are comfortable with the content of the text itself, then the text block should be considered as a component of the finished page and should be treated in the same manner that you treat the stamps. That is, you position the stamps and the text blocks so that they make the most attractive presentation possible. Do not crowd them or try to practice some ultracontemporary design.

If you are using a computer to generate your final pages, be certain that you are using a consistent type font for the text. Be sure that any headlines are also consistent and go well with the text font. If you are using a typewriter, be certain to begin with a fresh ribbon and type carefully. If you handprint the text, use a good pen, black ink, and paper stock, and have all the accessories necessary to allow you to place the text exactly where you want it. Although my high school guidance counselor wanted me to consider medicine purely on the basis of his evaluation of the readability of my handwriting and printing, I have never handprinted an album page.

Neatness counts, no matter how you prepare the pages. There is no room for ink blotches, pages typewritten with dirty keys, or streaks caused by poorly maintained computer printers. Fingerprints, too, are in bad taste.

The title page

The most important page of your exhibit is the title page. It serves many purposes on a single piece of paper, which may be stretched to two if you have plenty to tell:

- ✔ **Precise definition of the exhibit scope:** Don't include *anything* that is not critical to explaining the exhibit.

- ✔ **Significance of the exhibit:** If your research has turned up something important, it needs to be stated here.

- ✔ **Story development:** Explain the flow of the exhibit. Just like a short story in literature, you need a beginning, middle, and end to your exhibit.

- ✔ **Highlighting key items within the exhibit:** Use a scarce item, complete sets, or anything special to draw the attention of the judges.

Judges, with limited time to review all the exhibits, read title pages. The better your title page is in capturing the attention of the judges, the more time the judges will spend with your exhibit and the better the judges will understand your exhibit — what you are trying to say and the significance of the material that you are showing.

Do not use the words "rare" or "scarce." Do not refer to what an item cost you or its current catalogue or market value — all of these are considered to be in bad taste.

You will probably change the title page of your exhibit more often than you will any other page. As you add anything to the exhibit, over time, or as you choose to alter any of your presentation, you need to go back to the title page to be certain that any changes are reflected in the opening statement.

Other exhibit pages

Opinions vary on what is needed for the remainder of the pages (other than for topical/thematic exhibits, where an outline page is required). Because exhibiting and judging guidelines are not specific in this matter, you are free to use what you like. Remember that everything in the exhibit must be designed to enhance the story that you are telling.

- ✔ **Outline page:** If you are exhibiting topical material — a thematic exhibit — you need an outline page as your second page. If you do not exhibit topical material, you still may want to include an outline page. The outline is far more detailed and specific than the title page is able to be.

- ✔ **Section-opening pages:** Section breaks may be inappropriate with smaller exhibits (those with fewer pages). When you are preparing an exhibit that fills ten 16-page frames — 160 album pages — such break pages make much sense. They keep those looking at your exhibit, particularly the judges, on track with where you are in your story.

- ✔ **Synopsis page:** You know the drill — tell them what you are going to say, say it, and then tell them what you said (see Figure 10-2).

When preparing each of your pages, do it with real care. No one well-prepared page is going to win for you, but a poorly prepared page can be the principal reason for a downgrading of your award level. After you are finished with the individual pages, arrange them as they will appear in the exhibit frames to see how they flow from one to another.

I know stamp collectors, who are active exhibitors, who have purchased or made an exhibit frame that holds 16 pages — pretty much the standard. A 16-page frame can handle other configurations, such as 6-, 8-, 9-, or 12-page arrangements. Until you have the need for your own exhibit frame, laying the pages out on a dining room table or on the living room floor with no children or pets present, will fill the bill.

Don't be surprised if you find that the layout in a frame configuration causes you to want to change some, or even many, of the pages. Looking at a set of pages one at a time, as you would in an album, may well provide a different perspective than looking at the pages a group at a time. Oh yes, good luck.

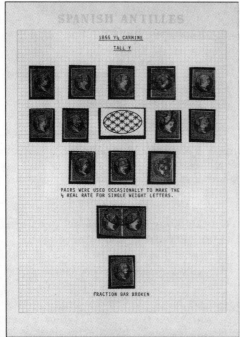

Figure 10-2:
Example of
exhibit page.
Note the
concise
presentation.

Picking Your Exhibiting Category

Competitive exhibiting continues to evolve. A country's national philatelic federation sets the guidelines for shows under its control, and the International Federation of Philately sets the guidelines for shows for which it gives patronage. The national federation in the U.S. is the American Philatelic Society (APS). In Canada, the national federation is the Royal Philatelic Society, Canada (P.O. Box 929, Station Q, Toronto, ON Canada M4T 2P1; Internet: www.rpsc.org).

The most recent set of guidelines from the APS sets down exhibit categories, known as *divisions,* from which exhibitors showing at national shows in the U.S. may choose. Some of the division categories that you may consider as a newcomer to competitive exhibiting are

- ✔ **Traditional Philately:** Includes definitive and commemorative postage stamps, their origin, and their production (see Figure 10-3).
- ✔ **Postal History:** Movement of the mails.
- ✔ **Aerophilately:** Movement of the mails via air.
- ✔ **Astrophilately:** Stamps and covers commemorating launches, recovers, and so on.

✔ **Postal Stationery:** Postal cards, stamped envelopes, and aerogrammes.

✔ **Special Studies:** Research projects in areas, such as perforations and methods of preventing fraud.

✔ **Topical/Thematic:** Where the exhibit's focus is on the stamp's design instead of how it was produced, when issued, and so on.

✔ **Illustrated Mail:** First-day covers, advertising covers (properly used covers with decorative or otherwise significant advertising information printed on them).

✔ **Patriotic Covers:** Covers used during periods of national conflict with preprinted or hand-drawn slogans and/or illustrations.

✔ **Youth:** A category with age restrictions.

✔ **Display:** This is the newest area. It permits nonphilatelic material (known as _collateral_) to a much greater extent than the other divisions. The category may include maps, photos, and drawings. Such collateral cannot dominate the exhibit.

More types of exhibits exist, as do more sections within an exhibit. The divisions and sections noted here are more in line with what first-timers may want to tackle. As you develop more and more experience, not only will you begin to consider other exhibiting divisions, but you may also become part of a group lobbying for yet another revamping of the guidelines.

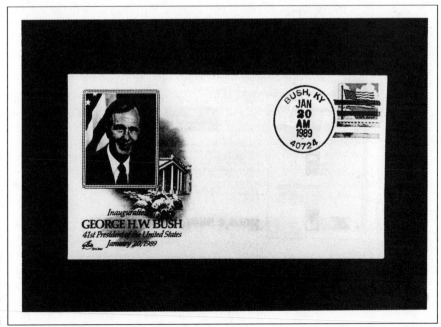

Figure 10-3:
An unusual Inauguration cover, postmarked from Bush, KY the day of George H.W. Bush's inauguration.

Singing the song of tradition

Before reading this chapter, if someone were to have asked you what you would see at a competitive stamp exhibit, your response would probably have been, "Stamps." That is the traditional exhibit. To quote from APS guidelines, this category is for "Material issued, or produced in the preparation for issue, used, or treated as valid by governmental, local or private post agencies, or by other duly commissioned or empowered public or private authorities, as postage for the purposes of transmitting mail or other postal communications, and postmarks, directions and markings required or used by postal agencies."

You have some choices about how to proceed and still stay within this category, such as

- **Broad country exhibit:** This follows the chronology and entire period in a country's postage-stamp history. You cannot go into much depth on any one item because of the expansive nature of the subject. Countries that have issued fewer stamps are good candidates for such an exhibit.

- **Specific date range or specific set of stamps:** This includes the exhibit suggested earlier on the King George V issue of Bermuda. This range of stamps consists of those issued during that king's reign, when his image appeared on all the Bermuda issues. This type of exhibit can include varieties and forerunners of the subject.

- **Single stamp:** This type of exhibit only works with those stamps with many, many varieties and usages. Varieties may include color variations, paper differences, and perforation varieties. Usages may include stamps on regular mail, on airmail from that country's post offices located in another country, on mail that has been censored during wartime, and many other possible situations (see Figure 10-4).

The more detailed your subject, the more you need to know about stamp design, printing, paper, and what causes production flaws. I personally find that sort of information fascinating; others consider it equal in excitement to watching water evaporate from a pothole in the street. This is the type of research that provides you with a steady stream of learning opportunities. And you thought this might be a boring hobby . . . pshaw!

Showing stamps by function

Perhaps because the story is easier to weave, or maybe because it is only cyclical, postal history exhibits appear to be in the majority now. Postal history exhibits try to tell a precise story of how covers or postal markings make their way through the mail. Included in the display are how particular postal markings — not only cancellations — were used, rates between two points, specific mail routes, and specific happenings along the way.

Figure 10-4:
A common stamp on *a very uncommon cover,* postmarked the morning of the Japanese attack on Pearl Harbor, Hawaii, and posted from there. Note the censor mark.

A postal history exhibit is an exhibit of items that have been carried by a postal service, whether official, local, or private. Such exhibits will show routes, rates, and markings, and/or the classification and study of postal markings on covers or stamps applied by those services or institutions, and the marks of obliteration on postal items.

Merely showing items in your postal history exhibit is not enough. You must show what they have done to further your story.

Find out about the various types of postal markings, beyond the traditional circular date stamps, used on the material in your postal history exhibit. Among the items of importance are

- ✔ Any routing notations
- ✔ Back stamps
- ✔ Postage due marks
- ✔ Receiving marks

Postal rates are critical to a postal history exhibit. Before the formation of the Universal Postal Union in 1874, postage rates between nations were negotiated among the individual countries. The rate from Chicago to a city in Switzerland may be based on the route taken and the various borders the letter crossed on its way. Explaining the route and the associated rate may be quite a feat — one that requires a fair amount of study.

Showing the Keystone State

I am interested in how the mail moved during the Pennsylvania oil boom of the mid-1800s. I have quite a few covers in my collection from the many small towns that made up that part of the Keystone State. What I have not done, and a major reason why I have not exhibited the material, is show any sort of relationship among the material.

To carry that a touch farther, I have a few covers from a town that went from an open field, to a population of 15,000, to no population in about three years. In fact, one of my covers is post-marked about 30 years after the town became a ghost town, and I have not researched why there was a post office and no town; that would be the fascinating portion of my exhibit. But, those covers alone don't do much for any *story* I would tell. My limited research has turned up the fact that most people using the post office during the brief boom time stuffed cash into envelopes to send back to their families. That post office did not have money-order capability, necessitating the cash-stuffing practice. I would love to find a cover from that town where the edge of the envelope appears to have been torn off hastily to get to the money. Such a cover normally would be disregarded (and possibly even discarded) because it was damaged. In fact, in this case, the damage would say something important about how the mail service from there was handled.

Serious exhibitors of postal history material develop strong personal libraries. They also tend to have friends who also collect postal history . . . and these friends have libraries. If you like history of any type, postal history begins to grow on you.

Nailing your topic

A topical or thematic competitive exhibit incorporates the understanding of how a stamp is produced with the development of a story based on the stamp designs. Topical/thematic collections are usually devoted to a single subject like ships, soccer, primitive crafts, or music. They work from a single subject — such as penguins — and develop it further with related material on the penguins' habitat, or what they eat, or some other fact relating to their existence. You can read more about topical stamp collecting in Chapter 13.

The stamp's country of origin, date of issue, or purpose of the issue — airmail, special delivery, and so on — are of minimal importance to the topical collec-tor. Unlike most other types of competitive exhibits, the topical/thematic exhibit is judged against a score sheet. At some stamp shows, the composite score sheet, showing the jury's decision, is given to the exhibitor. If you receive one of these, use it as the basis for improving your exhibit for the next outing.

Choosing what to exhibit and titling may be among the more difficult aspects of the project. You want to be precise. If you choose the topic *Birds,* you are being very general and may spend more time merely showing stamps with birds than telling a story. The award you receive will reflect the too-broad subject. If you are too narrow, such as *Birds Native to My Back Porch,* you may only have a handful of stamps that depict the types of birds that you want to show, and your story will be far too brief to fill even one 16-page frame. So, carefully think through just what you want to show and tell.

Your title page and outline (or plan) page are even more critical with a topical exhibit because the score sheet has specific scoring provisions for the introductory material. Originality is another concept specifically noted on the score sheet.

Here is where your nonstamp interest in the selected topic can help you. If you are exhibiting bicycles on stamps, you may have six stamps purporting to show the same bicycle model. Your own experience can differentiate among them by year, accessories, or which were sold in which country. You are using your own originality to set your exhibit apart from another exhibit with the same title.

Originality also includes the theme itself. One of my favorites, as much for what I discovered by looking at the exhibit as anything else, was the exhibit showing graduates of the U.S. Military Academy at West Point, New York, on stamps. Some of the most famous U.S. Army generals in history, whose image appeared on postage stamps, were represented. But, there were many other Americans, and a whole section of men from other countries, who also graduated from that institution. It was one of those exhibits that was the talk of the show. And the audience found out about American military history.

With a topical/thematic exhibit, your only boundaries are essentially the story line you establish and being certain that all the stamps shown pertain to the topic. The situation is a little more complicated, but you have the freedom to express yourself through your display. You need to know what material is available; therefore, a checklist of what stamps have been produced that meet your topic is required.

From the *stamp* side of things, showing your knowledge of stamp collecting by including varieties as much as you can is to your advantage. Rather than show all single mint stamps, you may include — where they are available — strips of coil stamps, booklet panes, pictorial cancellations that apply to the topic, and even freaks, oddities, and errors just to capture attention.

Displaying some class

The display class is the newest exhibit category. It continues to evolve as I write this section. To quote the American Philatelic Society's *Manual of Philatelic Judging*, "The Display Class . . . blends together two distinct aspects into a whole exhibit. First and foremost, exhibits in this class must be a philatelic undertaking. However, a full one-third of the material in the exhibit can be nonphilatelic, but must relate and be relevant to the development of the exhibit. Combining these two aspects gives exhibitors greater latitude in the selection of material and the manner in which it is displayed. Additionally, the values placed on the various aspects of the display class exhibit are such that creativity, ingenuity, and originality are stressed and are rewarded."

In this class, then, you can show the picture side of a picture postcard, the printed message on the reverse of a postal card (such as an advertisement or meeting notice), post office forms, stamp dealer literature, whatever it is that fits into your exhibit story, and other memorabilia.

The reins have been loosened a bit with this class and potential exhibitors — perhaps you — who may shy away from the tight structure can now spread their wings a bit more. The class is definitely not freewheeling, and it is not a dumping ground for those exhibits that just don't fit another class. Rather, the display class opens exhibiting up to more freedom. A score sheet is recommended for all display class exhibits, and it can be used at all national shows in the U.S.

You do have a place in competitive exhibiting, but only you can find it. Visit a stamp show with exhibits, and spend some time looking at each of the exhibits. If there is a judging critique, attend it. Ask someone at a stamp club meeting if they ever exhibited; if they have, ask them if they would mind helping you with your first exhibit. Then spend some time thinking through just what approach you want to take . . . and take it.

Part IV
Customizing Your Collection

The 5th Wave   By Rich Tennant

"Hopefully, after you're done examining the stamps on brochures from London, Moscow, and Beijing, you'll talk to me about actually traveling there."

In this part . . .

This part presents three scenarios about starting a different type of collection. From the perspective of an American living in the United States, the first chapter discusses beginning (or extending) a collection of U.S. stamps. You can find some major advantages to collecting the stamps of the country in which you reside. At the same time, a high percentage of your stamp-collecting friends are doing the same thing. If you want to do something different, then, or perhaps have some other reason, collect the stamps of another country. That chapter points out how you can go about adding to your collection, as well as finding friends to share your interest.

Topical or thematic collecting is a totally different approach to postage stamps than collecting by country. A topical collector has interest in the stamp's design rather than its origin. Your imagination is the only limit to your horizons as a topical collector. You may collect purely on the basis of what you see, such a rose for your collection of roses on stamps. Or, you may become a little more esoteric and choose to collect only those stamps depicting people who have been college presidents, whether that information is noted on the stamp itself. The challenge is yours, totally.

Chapter 11

Uncle Sam's Stamps

• •

• •

Collecting the postage stamps of the country that you reside in is different from collecting stamps of another country. Collecting from "home" literally immerses you in stamps to the point where you may not even realize how many are around you. You can purchase newer issues from the U.S. Postal Service through the mail or at post offices that are perhaps within walking distance from where you live or work. You'll encounter a high percentage of stamp dealers selling older U.S. stamps at stamp shows, bourses, or a nearby retail outlet owned by the stamp dealer. The U.S. Postal Service produces a regular guide, *USA Philatelic*, which shows the products (including stamps) that are currently on sale through the USPS. Note the address near the end of this chapter to obtain this publication.

The real fun kicks in, however, among your own family and friends, and their friends, all of whom have long-term family storage areas — attics, basements, and garages. Correspondence dating back decades, or even well into the last or preceding centuries, may be lurking in those seldom-visited storage areas. If keeping the material is no longer desirable, you may become the high-class equivalent of a trash hauler. Remember that one person's trash may become another person's stamp collection jump-start. Chances are slim that old stamps that have been hidden for years in household storage areas are still post-office fresh, unused examples of the early stamp rarities they once were. What you will see, however, are old letters with their envelopes ("covers" to philatelists). More on what to do with any old letters and envelopes later in this chapter.

While collecting your country's stamps by purchasing a stamp album and filling in the spaces is perfectly all right, you may find that beginning your collection with a little knowledge of postal-service history (since stamps were first used) can make the process more interesting. A knowledge base of postal history may spark you to begin your own research in one of *many* directions. In fact, this chapter kicks off with a historic overview.

The Letter-Carrier Perspective of U.S. History

Collecting stamps as a hobby dates back to the nineteenth century. Prior to 1847, a person receiving mail would pay the postage, not the person sending it. In that year, the first U.S. postage stamp was issued expressly to prepay postage. Through 1851, stamp usage signified prepayment; otherwise, the recipient paid. However, in 1851, postage prepayment was required. Mail was different then; mailings were mostly official, dealing with government matters, or between businessmen. Very little mail at that time was personal. And actually, there was very little mail at all.

Rushing along

Soon, however, America was bursting at its seams. Gold was discovered in California and the rush was on. Families that were once close-knit began to spread across the continent. Settlement in the midlands was also underway. More mail was thus sent back to friends and family to report on conditions from the frontier. The U.S. had come through its painful Civil War by the end of the nineteenth century. Many people continued to settle in those lands that would fill out the country's boundaries, and now they were really digging in to build a nation.

Until this time, U.S. postage stamps bore the images of major figures in the nation's development: George Washington, Benjamin Franklin, Thomas Jefferson, Abraham Lincoln, and Andrew Jackson (see Figure 11-1).

Commemorating the event

A large exposition in Chicago during the years 1892 and 1893 celebrated the 400th anniversary of Christopher Columbus's first voyage to the New World. The celebration provided the basis for the first U.S. commemorative postage stamps: 16 different items telling the Columbus story (see Figure 11-2). From the two beginnings — the first postage stamp in 1847 and the first commemorative stamp in 1893 — has come more than 3,000 *face-different* (visually different from one another) U.S. stamps.

Figure 11-1:
First U.S.
stamp.

Figure 11-2:
Stamp from
the first
commemo-
rative series
(1893).

© 1992 USPS

Commemoratives may be of a person, place, event, concept, or whatever (see Figure 11-3). Each state has been honored specifically no less than twice; some were honored many more times. One pane (an uncut block of stamps) of 50 different stamps shows each state flag arranged on the pane according to each state's date of entry into the Union. Another 50-stamp pane is arranged alphabetically by state, showing the official bird and flower of each.

The U.S. space program has been chronicled on stamps from the early flights, through the first walk in space and the historic first man on the moon, to the more recent space-shuttle missions. Various multiyear series provide introductions to people who may otherwise escape our knowledge. The Black Heritage Series, for example, honors deceased African-Americans.

The Legends of American Music Series presents the variety of music in this country through its commemoration of rock-and-roll stars, country music stars, Broadway musicals, opera singers, composers, conductors, and folk singers. Sports heroes, such as baseball player Roberto Clemente, have been honored on stamps, as have other baseball greats: Babe Ruth, Lou Gehrig, and Jackie Robinson. Other sports legends also appear on commemorative stamps: Knute Rockne, Bobby Jones, Babe Zaharias, and others. Efforts of the U.S. Olympic teams are regularly honored, too.

World's smallest easels: Designing stamps

The U.S. Postal Service takes total responsibility for all postage stamp designs, but the government agency does not review or accept unsolicited artwork. A great deal of the reason for this approach is the vast number of inquiries and suggestions received annually. What it does accept, and even solicit, are ideas for stamp subjects.

The public suggests almost all subjects chosen to appear on U.S. stamps and postal stationery. Each year, Americans submit proposals, on literally thousands of different topics, to the postal service. Every stamp suggestion is considered, regardless of who makes it or how it is presented.

On behalf of the Postmaster General, the Citizens' Stamp Advisory Committee (CSAC) is tasked with evaluating the merits of all stamp proposals. The Committee's primary goal is to select subjects that are interesting and educational. The Committee recommends only 25 or

so stamp subjects each year. To get to that number, and to be certain each suggestion that the public makes is given equal consideration, the following 12 major areas have been adopted to guide subject selection:

It is a general policy that U.S. postage stamps and stationery feature primarily American or American-related subjects.

U.S. postage cannot portray, and thus honor, a living person.

Commemorative stamps or postal stationery items honoring individuals are usually issued on, or in conjunction with, significant anniversaries of their birth. But no postal item is issued sooner than ten years after the individual's death. The only exception to the ten-year rule is the issuance of stamps honoring deceased U.S. presidents. They may be honored with a memorial stamp on the first birth anniversary following death.

Events of historical significance are considered for commemoration only on anniversaries in multiples of 50 years.

Only events and themes of widespread national appeal and significance are considered for commemoration. A philatelic or special postal cancellation, which may be arranged through the local postmaster, may recognize events or themes of local or regional significance.

Stamps or stationery items are not issued to honor fraternal, political, sectarian, or service/charitable organizations. Stamps or stationery cannot be issued to promote or advertise commercial enterprises or products. Commercial products or enterprises may, however, be used to illustrate more general concepts related to American culture.

Stamps or stationery items cannot honor cities, towns, municipalities, counties, primary or secondary schools, hospitals, libraries, or similar institutions. Due to the limitations placed on annual postal programs and the vast number of such locales, organizations, and institutions in existence, it would be difficult to single out any one for commemoration.

Requests for observance of statehood anniversaries are considered for commemorative postage stamps only at intervals of 50 years from the date of the state's first entry into the Union. Requests for observance of other state-related or regional anniversaries are considered only as subjects for postal stationery, and again only at intervals of 50 years from the date of the event.

Stamps or stationery items are not issued to honor religious institutions or individuals whose principal achievements are associated with religious undertakings or beliefs.

Stamps or postal stationery items with added values, referred to as "semipostals," are issued every two years in accordance with Public Law 106253. Semipostals are not considered as part of the commemorative program and separate criteria apply.

Requests for commemoration of universities and other institutions of higher education are considered only for stamped cards and only in connection with the 200th anniversaries of their founding.

No stamp is considered for issuance if one treating the same subject has been issued in the past 50 years. The only exceptions to this rule are traditional themes, such as national symbols and holidays.

Ideas for stamp subjects that meet the criteria may be addressed to the Citizens' Stamp Advisory Committee, c/o Stamp Development, U.S. Postal Service, 475 L'Enfant Plaza, SW, Room 5670, Washington, DC 20260-2437. Subjects should be submitted at least three years in advance of the proposed date of issue to allow sufficient time for consideration and for design and production if the subject is approved. Although the U.S. Postal Service relies heavily on the Citizens' Stamp Advisory Committee, it has the exclusive and final authority to determine both subject matter and designs for U.S. postal stamps and postal stationery.

The task of converting an idea for a stamp subject to an actual design is not easy. If existing art is considered for reproduction, how it will appear in postage-stamp size is critical. For many stamp designs, original art is commissioned that must be both attractive and a proper depiction of the concept of the stamp subject. No matter how much work goes into each design, liked and disliked by many . . . such is art!

Scenes of major events in the American Revolution are reduced to postage-stamp size, as are key events of the Civil War. The American Revolution was remembered on stamps leading up to and during the Bicentennial celebration in 1976. Other military actions, likewise, are the subject of postage-stamp designs, including a multisheetlet set issued over a five-year period to remember World War II.

You can find out about Pennsylvania Toleware, hand-carved carousel animals, and Navajo blankets as an introduction to the study of American folk art. These are just a few of the doors opened to the mind through stamp collecting. Stamps can take you on an entertaining and educational journey through history, art, politics, science, and society because stamps commemorate the events, people, and achievements that have shaped our world and our lives. Each little piece of paper has an image that may serve to illustrate a feature that you saw on last night's television news presentation or read in your local newspaper, or it can provide a little more meaning to a child's school lesson on virtually any subject.

Along the way, the government contracted private printing firms to produce U.S. stamps. Then, after the U.S. Bureau of Engraving and Printing began producing postage stamps, stamp production involved a combination of private firms and the government agency. Production moved from stamps with no perforations that had to be cut or torn apart, to those with perforations, to those now that are die cut and self-stick. Single-color, hand-engraved works of art are still produced in postage-stamp form, but they are not a minority to lavishly designed and mega colored small posters.

Collecting the stamps of the country that you reside in truly immerses you in them. The stamps, collected and placed in an album, take on a magnitude larger than their physical size, becoming a historical and cultural record.

Posting the U.S. Stamps

When you hear words "postage stamp," you probably think of that little piece of paper you put onto the corner of the envelope containing grandmother's birthday card or the rent check. You heretofore had little reason to know or care that each country normally has an array of postage stamps, many of which the average person never uses or even sees. Here's a rundown of the various types of U.S. postage stamps you may encounter:

  ✔ **Regular Postage:** These are the stamps that you normally use when paying your utility bill or sending a greeting card to your favorite wealthy aunt. This group breaks into two subcategories. With contemporary production capability being what it is, the ability to distinguish between the two types purely on sight is not as easy a task as it was a few decades ago.

- *Commemoratives* are normally on sale for a lesser period of time than definitives. Commemoratives honor a person, place, thing, or event and are generally larger in physical size than definitives.

- *Definitives* are generally part of a set issued over a period of time. Definitives remain on sale for years and they're of a smaller format than commemoratives. These U.S. stamps are seen far more often than commemoratives, too.

✔ **Airmail:** A faster service than regular mail, airmail is no longer a domestic service. For many years, however, the U.S. offered domestic airmail at a postage premium over ground service (see Figure 11-4). Today, the U.S. still produces airmail stamps for international mail. Issued quite infrequently, airmail stamps have the word *airmail* as part of the stamp's inscription.

✔ **Parcel post:** Although the U.S. issued only a single set of parcel-post stamps, the set has become quite popular (see Figure 11-5). The rate structure for packages is so complex, with so many different services offered (FedEx, UPS, RPS, and so on), that you need to complete a small questionnaire to determine what is best for each package. Having specific stamps for this type of service is nearly impossible — a situation that was realized many years ago.

Figure 11-4:
The first U.S. airmail stamp.

Figure 11-5:
U.S. parcel-
post stamp.

✔ **Postage due:** A postage-due stamp is not an actual service, but a *bill* from the postal service (see Figure 11-6). Postage due stamps are applied by postal employees to tell the recipient that the letter or package bearing the postage-due stamp requires an additional payment to cover the total postage for that letter or package. The postage-due stamp has fallen into disuse because it was replaced by a simple hand-stamp that allows space to write in the amount of postage needed.

Figure 11-6:
U.S.
postage-
due stamp.

Many other types of U.S. stamps exist, and you may come to discover them as your collection grows. For example, the U.S. once issued a stamp to cover the cost of registering a letter, and another stamp to cover the cost of certified mail. Neither stamp had a successor.

Although you may generally collect single copies of each stamp to get started, here are four examples of stamp multiples that you need to know. Please check the Glossary of this book for many more important definitions. In the case of these stamp multiples, you should not separate them to retrieve a single stamp for your collection — at least not until such time as you do it from a position of understanding.

✔ **Booklet pane:** An unseparated block of stamps printed and cut especially for use in booklets (see Figure 11-7). The booklets are a convenient way to carry stamps, and they come complete with their own protective cover.

U.S. Stamps

EXPLORING THE SOLAR SYSTEM

© 2000 USPS

© 1978 USPS

© 2000 USPS

U.S. Stamps

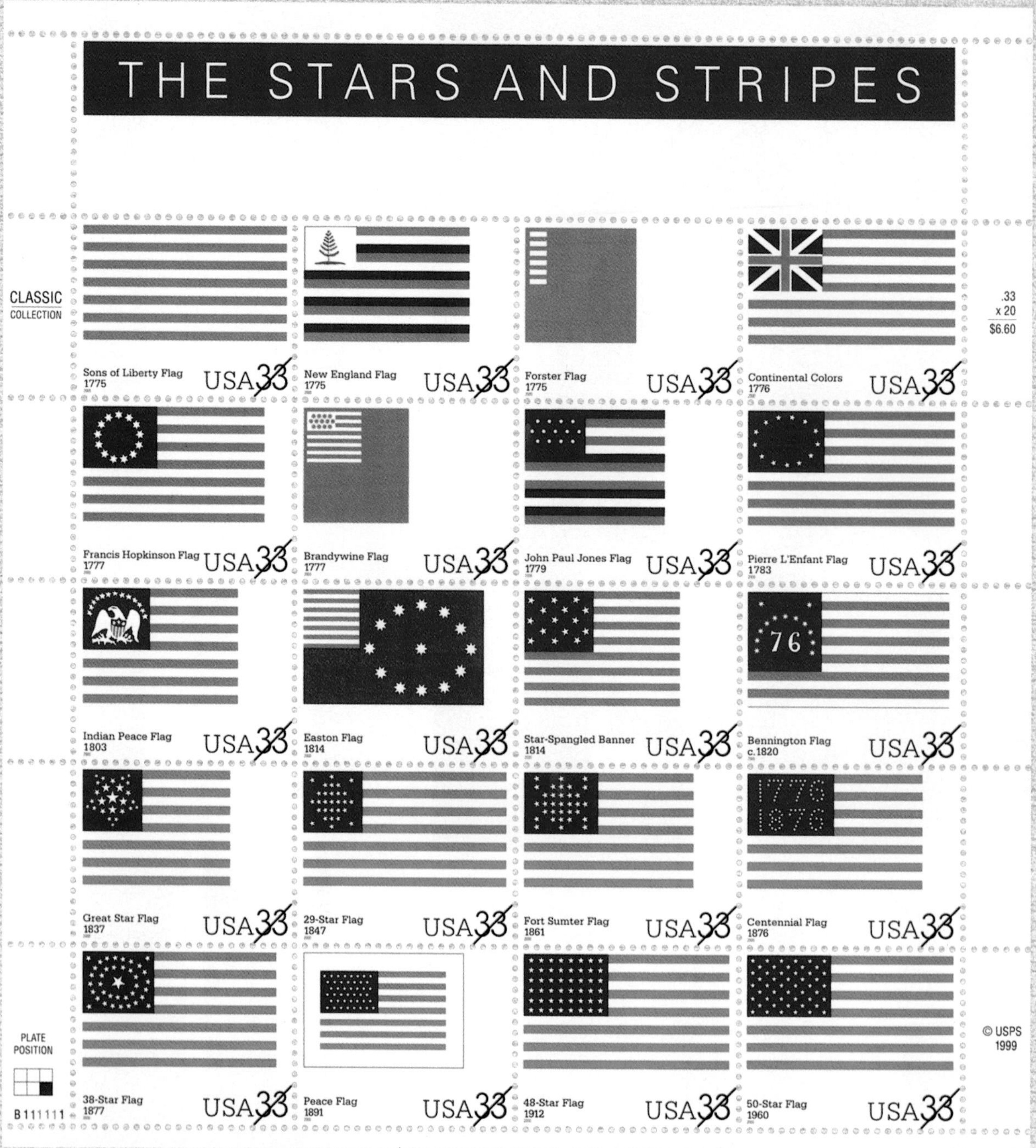

THE STARS AND STRIPES

CLASSIC
COLLECTION

.33
x 20
$6.60

Sons of Liberty Flag 1775	New England Flag 1775	Forster Flag 1775	Continental Colors 1776
Francis Hopkinson Flag 1777	Brandywine Flag 1777	John Paul Jones Flag 1779	Pierre L'Enfant Flag 1783
Indian Peace Flag 1803	Easton Flag 1814	Star-Spangled Banner 1814	Bennington Flag c.1820
Great Star Flag 1837	29-Star Flag 1847	Fort Sumter Flag 1861	Centennial Flag 1876
38-Star Flag 1877	Peace Flag 1891	48-Star Flag 1912	50-Star Flag 1960

USA 33

© USPS
1999

PLATE
POSITION

B 111111

© 2000 USPS

U.S. Stamps

TECHNOLOGY • ENTERTAINMENT • SCIENCE •

HISTORICAL EVENTS • POLITICAL FIGURES • LIFESTYLE • ART • SPORTS •

1980s
CELEBRATE THE CENTURY®

Space Shuttle Program — 33 USA

Cable TV — 33 USA

Vietnam Veterans Memorial — 33 USA

San Francisco 49ers — 33 USA

Hostages Come Home — 33 USA

Figure Skating — 33 USA

Compact Discs — 33 USA

Fall of the Berlin Wall — 33 USA

Video Games — 33 USA

Personal Computers — 33 USA

Hip-hop Culture — 33 USA

Space Shuttle Launched, Berlin Wall Falls

The space shuttle *Columbia*, the first reusable spacecraft, was originally launched April 12, 1981. Sandra Day O'Connor became the first female justice on the U.S. Supreme Court, and Sally Ride became the first American woman in space. The Iran-Contra hearings made headlines.

Several events signaled the easing of international tensions. In December 1987 President Ronald Reagan and Soviet leader Mikhail Gorbachev signed a nuclear arms reduction treaty. The fall of the Berlin Wall in November 1989 presaged the end of the Cold War. The Vietnam Veterans Memorial was dedicated November 13, 1982. A new national holiday, Martin Luther King Day, was first celebrated in January 1986.

The growth of cable television, video games, and compact discs had a major impact on home entertainment. *Dallas* and *The Cosby Show* topped TV ratings. Hip-hop culture and music videos gained popularity.

New Words: yuppie, infomercial, biodiversity

BOLIVIA
ISSUES OF 1953-54

Foreign Stamps

Theme or Topical Stamps

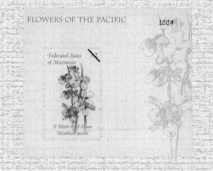

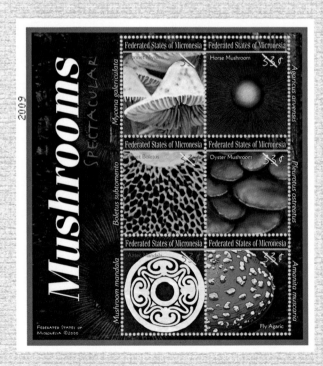

Theme or Topical Stamps

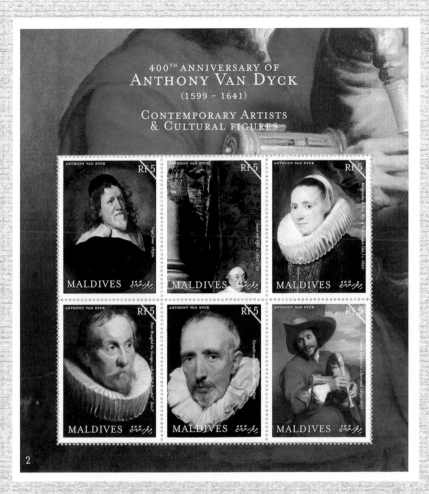

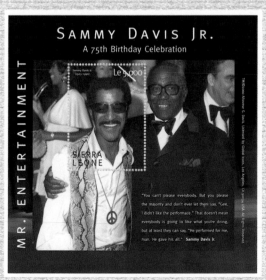

Theme or Topical Stamps

Figure 11-7:
Booklet
pane.

✔ **Coil pair or plate number coil strip:** Coil stamps are produced in roll form for use in vending machines — where you insert money for the stamps — or dispensing machines, which may be for office use. A coil usually contains 100 or 500 (or more) stamps of a single denomination and design. Perforations on parallel sides of a stamp, running horizontally or vertically, distinguish U.S. coil stamps. For more information on perforations, see Chapter 3. U.S. coil stamps produced since 1981 show a plate number appearing at the bottom of the stamp at certain intervals. The current, common practice is to collect these plate number coil stamps in strips of five, with the plate number on the middle stamp.

✔ **Plate block:** This block of stamps has the sheet margin attached showing the plate number used in printing that sheet (see Figure 11-8). The block is no less than four stamps (two by two) and large enough to be two stamps deep next to each plate number in the margin. For a period of time, U.S. stamp panes bore multiple plate numbers, and the size of the plate block became quite large.

✔ **Se-tenant (say-ten-*awnt*) grouping:** This grouping features two or more unseparated stamps having different colors, denominations, or designs. See Figure 11-9. Se-tenant is French for "joined together." Se-tenant pairs, blocks, strips, and sheetlets have become a popular way to produce a larger number of different designs at one time, as well as to commemorate more people, places, or events with a single stamp issue.

Figure 11-8:
Plate block.

Enough talk. Now it's time to go out and do it. Don't be in any rush to fill spaces in your album (if that's how you plan to house your newfound collectibles). There are plenty of stamps to go around, particularly the more recent ones. (Look at Figure 11-10 to see a typical starter album.) Have plenty of fun with your start, and expect to make mistakes — everybody does.

THE SUBMARINE STAMPS
U.S. Navy Submarines
A Century of Service to America

USS *Holland*, the U.S. Navy's first submarine, was purchased in 1900.

S-class submarines were designed during WWI.

***Gato* class** submarines played a key role in the destruction of Japanese maritime power in the Pacific during WWII.

***Los Angeles* class** attack submarines, armed with "smart" torpedoes and cruise missiles, are nuclear powered.

***Ohio* class** submarines—also nuclear powered—carry more than half of America's strategic weapons, making them a vital part of America's nuclear deterrence.

Figure 11-9:
Current
se-tenant
sheetlet.

Figure 11-10:
U.S. starter
album.

Cozying Up to Your Postal Clerk

Perhaps the title of my favorite song from *The Wiz,* "Ease on Down the Road," reflects the best approach to crossing something that has the appearance of a daunting threshold — from wanting to begin a stamp collection to actually doing so.

No matter how you begin or in which direction you go, round up all your incoming envelopes and parcels and ask all your relatives and friends to save their envelopes and parcel covers for you, too. Even if you plan to collect mint stamps only, all the used varieties you obtain can help you see what is available and provide you with material you can use for trade. And, if you are fortunate, you may find something particularly neat in the mail that you can show to your friends. After the first time that happens — whether it's a particularly nice, pictorial postmark or a badly printed stamp (your first freak!) — and you show it off, you may find that interest among friends and relatives picks up considerably.

Somewhere between many to most new U.S. Stamp issues are available at your local post office. I hesitate to say *all* are available, because it's a rare situation. Nevertheless, you cannot find a more convenient place to do your stamp shopping. Leave it to the U.S. Postal Service to have a store in every town!

When you begin to purchase stamps for a collection, be sure to tell the postal clerk. In fact, tell each postal clerk as you utilize his or her services. No doubt you will find that one clerk tends to take better care of the stamp collectors, while another may show no interest at all. Servicing the needs and wants of stamp collectors is generally far down on a clerk's priority list of services to offer, but the basic good nature of some clerks may help you. Today, each clerk has his own consignment of postage stamps, and one clerk's stash may include more commemoratives or something else neat, while another may opt for the more basic designs. The U.S. Postal Service considers postage stamps "accountable paper," and each clerk must account for all the stamps consigned to him. **Note:** If you seek a particular stamp at a post office counter and your clerk does not have it, but another clerk nearby does, the two clerks may literally swap stamps of the same denomination.

By all means, *don't* press the clerk for special service. You, as a stamp collector in a normal queue of postal patrons, rate nothing extra. Perhaps commenting, however, on how nicely the USPS-issued sweatshirt complements the clerk's eye color may rate some extra help. It certainly has worked for me.

Chances are not good that your favorite postal clerk has commemorative stamps that go back more than a few months. Your favorite clerk may not have a wide selection of definitive stamps beyond that specific to the current, first-class mail rate. So, your favorite clerk may have stamps that cover the current one-ounce rate for first-class mail, stamps to cover the rate for additional ounces, perhaps stamps to cover the postal card rate, and perhaps some one-cent stamps. The USPS handy-dandy, self-stick, postage meter strip and scale can easily handle any other rates that the clerk needs to cover. This all-purpose, computerized device, which is known commonly among postal clerks as *POS,* an acronym for "Point of Sale," translates the weight of the item that you have to mail, along with the rate class (Priority Mail, book rate, and so on, and destination, if pertinent). The screen shows the postage amount needed, and *POS* prints a self-stick meter (label) that the clerk affixes to your parcel.

Few clerks now carry a stock of express-mail stamps, Priority Mail stamps, and airmail stamps. For more information about various stamp types, see Chapter 2.

Because other collectors no doubt also frequent the same post office, an interested postal clerk may be an ad hoc information source on local stamp clubs or other activities. Further, check the bulletin boards for any stamp-collecting related notices. While looking, see if I am yet among those folks whose photos are posted. My side view is better than my front view. Notices of upcoming stamp issues may also be posted, and you may even find a schedule for upcoming issues through the end of the year.

Make your stamp purchases, return home, and find a safe place for your bounty. Take a look at Chapter 14 for guidance on how to keep your stamps safe and happy. For the purposes of your rapid development, and before you complete that chapter, be sure that you have chosen a preprinted album or that you have a current stamp catalogue with a listing and illustration of each stamp. Until you decide to go your own way — which is not expected — filling up a stamp album is a good goal. Although, the nice part is that you are under no obligation to fill all the spaces on every page.

Until you decide how you want to store your stamps for the long-term, at least for now, keep them dry, flat, dry, at room temperature, and dry.

After doing all this schmoozing at the local PO, you will have enough mint stamp sources to decide if you want to continue collecting them. And, presuming your response is a resounding "yes," press on. The U.S. Postal Service offers traditional-mail and Internet-based ordering from its Kansas City, Missouri depository. The mailing address is USPS, Stamp Fulfillment Services, P.O. Box 219424, Kansas City, MO 64121-9424, and the Web site address is http://shop.usps.com. Ask to be put on the mailing list for the free quarterly publication, *USA Philatelic,* which depicts all U.S. stamps currently available from the USPS mail-order division.

Dealing without Vegas

It's time for you to meet your first postage-stamp dealer, a person whose business is providing you with the postage stamps that you need to build your collection. The vast majority of stamp dealers who specialize in U.S. stamps operate on a very small scale — usually a part-time, sole proprietor. The dealer purchases newer material directly from the U.S. Postal Service in somewhat the same ways suggested to you earlier in this chapter: at the post office or from the Kansas City depository. In addition, the stamp dealer also purchases collections and accumulations from stamp collectors, and bulk lots and other material from other dealers.

Until you have some experience in stamp collecting, work with dealers who are members of the nation's largest dealers' organization or the nation's largest collectors' organization. Both maintain a list of dealer members that you can tap:

✔ **American Stamp Dealers Association,** 3 School St., Suite 205, Glen Cove, NY 11542-2548; Internet: www.asdaonline.com.

✔ **American Philatelic Society,** P.O. Box 8000, State College, PA 16803; Internet: www.stamps.org.

Dealing with dealers

Working with a stamp dealer is not the same as purchasing electrical tape at the local hardware store. A good dealer takes an interest in what you are collecting, keeps an eye out for items that you still need, and generally goes a long way toward keeping the spark in the hobby for you. All dealers, however, are not saint like. You may find some you wouldn't like to be your neighbor. At the same time, they play a tremendous role in maintaining the hobby's stability.

Before you find the one or more "good dealers" who will help you through your stamp-collecting odyssey, you will want to shop a bit. If there is but one stamp dealer in your town, or at least close enough to visit, you need to cultivate a relationship. If you have more than one stamp dealer from which to choose, so much the better. In general, though, you will find that stamp dealers are like any other small businessperson: some are neighborly, some are a pain in the sensitive parts of your body, and others are all business with no personality at all. Compare them to the owners of various small shops within a few miles of where you live . . . it's the same run of people.

I have known dealers and collectors who have formed a relationship so strong that their families vacation together. The key, to me, is that the dealer is your commercial contact to stamp collecting, and the most important issue to resolve is a relationship that allows you to obtain the material you seek.

While you are trying to find a dealer who you can trust, the dealer is also seeking out trustworthy collectors — like a courtship leading to stamp-collecting wedlock. A dealer's membership in his national stamp dealers' organization or national stamp collectors' federation is important, but it is not a single determining factor. The reasons for not being a member are varied and do not always mean the dealer has a serious character flaw, such as drugging and then tattooing his clients. If a dealer you would otherwise use is not a member, ask why.

Today's dealers pretty much all accept credit cards, and many take them in preference to a personal check. Other dealers prefer checks, but only accept them after they get to know you. Dealers are also subject to being bad businesspeople themselves. One of my favorite dealers, and arguably the most knowledgeable in the area of worldwide postal markings and their market value, went from stamp dealing one month to truck driving the next. I have not heard of him since. Pity.

Dealers are both merchants and financial advisors — the latter in an unregulated environment but still affecting items that you may purchase now and hope to sell later at some sort of profit. Just as you are cautious when purchasing anything of value about which you know less than the seller (the dealer), you need to find out about any dealer before you purchase anything that costs a large sum of money from him. Reputations are critical in stamp collecting; don't be afraid to ask other collectors about dealers you frequent.

You can also find dealer advertisements in the various stamp periodicals, the two largest of which are listed here.

- ✔ **Linn's Stamp News,** P.O. Box 29, Sidney, OH 45365; Internet: www.linns.com.

- ✔ **Stamp Collector,** 700 E. State St., Iola, WI 54990; Internet: www.krause.com/stamps/sc.

The stamp periodicals also list upcoming stamp shows, a major part of which are the dealer booths. Stamp shows are a great place to meet dealers face to face. You can read more about exhibits in Chapter 10.

Add the local post office, the U.S. Postal Service ordering facilities, and stamp dealers to your sources, along with your own incoming mail and what you can obtain from friends and relatives, and you have your supply channels firmly in place.

Chapter 12

Globe-trotting

· ·

In This Chapter

▶ Speaking stamp language

▶ Swapping and dealing stamps

▶ Locating your sources

▶ Challenging you in different ways: Foreign relations

· ·

*M*ore than 260 countries currently issue postage stamps. As the world continues to change, with nations combining, breaking apart, and changing governments, the number of stamp-issuing countries is constantly subject to change. Add to that total some 400 additional countries that at one time or another issued their own stamps. Those countries may exist today under a new name, broken into parts, with each part attached to a different current country, or as a combination of earlier stamp-issuing countries. The range of what is open to you is close to endless.

Stamps are printed, as you would expect, in the language of the issuing country. Some countries may include an additional language. Although fluency or even being conversant in the language of the country whose stamps you are collecting is not imperative, knowing the language is certainly a plus. At the very least, you need to understand key words in the language and have some guide that allows you to pick out and identify characters if the country's language does not involve an alphabet that is similar to English.

Collectors of U.S. stamps who live in the U.S. can visit their local post office for many of the new stamp issues, and perhaps for a few of the older ones. However, if you collect the stamps of Costa Rica and live in Oklahoma City, Oklahoma, don't expect to visit a Costa Rican post office in your favorite shopping mall — you won't find one. Collecting stamps of a country other than your own does present some interesting challenges. So, you need to develop a solid source to supply you with stamps.

Speaking Lingua Philatelica

Within the world of stamp collecting, language comes into play in ways that are amplified when collecting the stamps of a country other than yours and other than one that's home to a major stamp-catalogue publisher. The major publishers — for obvious reasons — are based in countries with the largest concentration of stamp collectors. (Although this can, on mulling it over, turn into a wicked case of which came first, the chicken versus the egg.) Thus, if you are interested in collecting the stamps of Germany, you can find that much of the information, literature, references, and so on, are in German. Duh.

Collecting Romanian stamps, on the other hand, presents you with somewhat of a different situation. Knowing the Romanian language can help you tremendously, but it won't provide all the assistance you may expect.

When in Rome, speak as the Romans do

You cannot underestimate the importance of knowing the language of the country whose stamps you want to collect. At the same time, not knowing the language does not make you a second-class citizen when it comes to being a collector of foreign stamps. I make that brash statement from personal and ongoing experience.

Without getting into my own collecting interests, I want to share that I neither speak nor read the language of the country whose stamps I collect. To compensate for that deficiency, I have put together

- ✔ **Reference materials** (printed) that help me understand overprints on that nation's stamps. If nothing else, a dictionary that relates words of one language to another, as well as a guide to a non-Latin alphabet to note the letters for an easier time checking words in a foreign dictionary.

- ✔ **A transparent ruler** that allows me to measure overprints and transparencies of the alphabet used in this country, so I can make a closer match when a difference in a letter provides me with a new variety for my collection.

- ✔ **Specialized catalogues** of that country's stamps, which provide far more detail than do the more general catalogues of the larger publishers.

- ✔ **A stamp identifier** that allows me to check the stamp's origin based on what was printed on it originally, what the overprint reads, or sometimes an illustration. The stamps of some countries — for a specific time frame — bore a specific ornament or graphic illustration. Japan used a lotus blossom as a decorative ornament for quite a few years, and Great Britain always has an image of the monarch and no country name.

- ✔ **Online guides** that tend to be more current.

Remember the U.S.S.R.?

If I were to collect the stamps of the country of my ancestors on my grandfather's side, Lithuania, I would be seeking postal emissions of Pre-World War I Lithuania and stamps issued by the same country after the breaking apart of the U.S.S.R. But what of that period from the time Lithuania ceased to exist as a sovereign nation until the U.S.S.R. breakup? Read on for one person's approach.

These are my choices, but they are certainly not a requirement for everyone. When trying to help someone identify a stamp that is outside my immediate area of knowledge, I rely on some standard references that are easy to obtain and use. A dealer who still has one or more stamp identifiers (no print versions have been published in seven years or so) may sell one to you. Check the Internet (www.askphil.org/b28.htm) for an extensive listing of wording that you can find on the world's stamps, along with the country of origin and the meaning. Other listings are also available on the Internet, as individual collectors and stamp-collecting specialty organizations post listing information on Web sites for their own members (and others) to share.

Foreign philatelic phrases

The other language area with which you may flounder for a moment is stamp-collecting terminology. When collecting stamps of a country whose language is English, you're assured that the bulk of the literature and references about those stamps is in English — or a large enough percentage is in English — so you will not have a problem.

Stamp catalogues naturally use the language of the country in which they are printed for those words that describe the characteristics of a stamp. Normally, you have no problem discerning what is meant. Although, from time to time, you may need to have one or more words translated for you. I've seen printed listings of stamp-collecting terms in more than one language. Apparently, philatelic terminology lists are not in enough demand to require their ready availability.

Another form of help is already in place! Not only do larger stamp-collecting reference books have a glossary to help you, but you can also find references that are nothing but glossaries. Online glossaries are easy to find; using an Internet search engine to find "stamp+glossary" returns quite a listing. To speed your search, you may go directly to the Web site www.askphil.org/b25.htm for AskPhil.org's extensive presentation.

Online glossaries have the advantage of frequent updating; words are added as they become important to the hobby. With newer forms of production, terms such as die cut, hologram, and self-adhesive — and any derivatives — may be added quickly, and you won't have to wait for a new printing of a traditional book.

Knowing where to go for help eases many concerns about understanding something new.

Amassing a Melting Pot of Stamp Sources

Even if you receive mail regularly from the country whose stamps you plan to collect, and you also have relatives and friends who frequently correspond with people in that country, you cannot pull together as many different stamps as you can from the country in which you live. Thus, you need to set up an acquisition program — sort of a fancy way to say that you need to have additional sources of material.

With a proper road map, you should have little difficulty getting what you want.

Postal administrations love stamp collectors

The U.S. Postal Service regularly conducts market studies about what percentage of postage stamps sold are never used and, therefore, are presumed to be in the hands of stamp collectors. Such studies have looked at the total number of stamps, broken the total into commemorative and definitive stamps, and also checked on some specific issues with an eye toward how to plan future stamp issues.

Even with all that checking, as long as postage stamps sold by the USPS remain in this country, the chance that the stamps will be used for postage still exists. Essentially, the money paid for them is not a total profit.

Not so with countries that primarily sell their stamps abroad to collectors. Chances are exceedingly slim that stamps of a South Pacific island sold to collectors in the U.S. or Western Europe will be used as postage. Visiting the country of Kiribati so that I can send Kiribati stamps home on postcards would be great, but I just don't see that happening in the immediate future. Stamp collectors accept the fact that some of the stamps issued in the world today end up in a philatelic collection rather than a mailbox.

Lists of postal administration mailing and electronic addresses are readily available, although they may be more easily obtainable on the Internet. Most postal administrations of the world are equipped to sell their stamps directly to collectors. Although this may be a slower, and sometimes more frustrating, way to purchase the new issues of a country, it can be enjoyable to pick up the daily mail to see a letter to you from your favorite island. Check out www.askphil.org/b38a.htm for an extensive listing. You can purchase available stamps directly from the postal administration, or you can sub-scribe to receive new issues as they become available. Each country has its own policies and approach to such sales. You need to be sure that you under-stand the rules of the game before proceeding.

Stamp dealers also love stamp collectors

Just as the term *grocery store* includes a wide range of retail outlets from the largest chain-owned, megastores to the most intimate specialty or cuisine-based food boutique, so it is with the term *stamp dealer*. Some stamp dealers may possibly offer you more than one of the services listed just ahead in this chapter. Likewise, some stamp dealers may limit their work to but a single service, and perhaps even a single service for the stamps of a single country.

Your search, then, will be for one or more stamp dealers who can help you with what you seek and in the manner you desire to build your collection. Here are several types of stamp-dealer services for foreign-stamp collectors:

- ✔ **New Issue Service:** You tell a dealer which country (or countries) you want, or which topic, and the dealer sends the material to you at regular intervals — an excellent way to stay current with the stamps of a country. You always run the risk of the dealer missing something, but you probably can do better with this service type than with trying to purchase all the items individually yourself.

- ✔ **Want Lists:** You provide a dealer with a list of specific items you want and the dealer sends them to you with a bill.

- ✔ **Approvals:** A dealer sends you a stamp selection that he expects to be of interest to you. You keep the ones you want and return payment for them along with those you chose not to purchase. Upon the return of the material, the dealer prepares and sends another selection.

- ✔ **Collections or other bulk lots:** A great collection starter, these large stamp groupings of a country can probably cover a large percentage of the really inexpensive material. This serves as an excellent way to get a country collection started without having to order many stamps individ-ually and pay for them as individual items. Bulk lots normally provide you with the least cost-per-stamp rate you can find. Then, after you're really into your country collection, bulk lots are a great way to search through many, many stamps in search of elusive varieties that someone else has missed.

Like-minded collectors, gather 'round

A great stamp-collecting feature is the flexibility you're allowed. Unless you are working from a tightly scripted "collection program," (such as purchasing stamps only to fill the spaces in your album), you can, from the wide array of different stamps produced since 1840, personalize your collection to make it unique. That stated again: The same attributes of the hobby that promote flexibility sometimes make it difficult to find others with the same general interests.

Easing that problem is an amazing group of organizations, each made up of people who have a similar collecting interest. These specialty groups, with names ranging from the Aerophilately of Mexico Study Unit (specializing in Mexico airmail issues), to the Concorde Study Circle (interested in stamps and postal markings depicting the Concorde airplane), to the St. Pierre & Miquelon Philatelic Society (collecting stamps and postal history relating to the small French-owned islands off the East Coast of Canada).

A group may include only a handful of members, or it may include thousands of members, sometimes drawn from all over the world. It has been said — only somewhat facetiously — that a specialty group needs only a minimum of three members: president, secretary, and newsletter editor.

The largest single listing of such groups — found on the Internet at www. askphil.org/b02.htm — shows nearly 550 such groups.

After you have settled in on a country whose stamps you want to collect, find a specialty group with the same interest. The country or region that does not have at least one group's interest is rare. If there is nothing, and you begin to subscribe to any of the stamp-collecting periodicals, keep alert to the possibility of such a group starting, or even make an effort to start one yourself.

Not only does membership in a specialty group bring you into contact with others with a similar collecting interest, but you can see references to and advertising from dealers who specialize in the stamps of that area (via whatever periodical the group produces). Look on your specialty group membership as warm and fuzzy.

Specialty groups often have annual meetings in conjunction with a stamp show. Some groups with larger memberships even have regional meetings. Very few specialty groups have local chapters that meet on a regular basis. You have the opportunity to have considerable personal interaction, or you may be as introverted as you choose. The key word is *choose*. See Chapter 8 for more on friendly assistance.

The sultan of swap

From those childhood days of trading bubble gum cards, clothes, or toys, you are now prepared to enter the world of adult stamp trading (hold the trumpets, please). Unlike the childhood days of "I will give you two red marbles for your large blue one," you may find more formality when it comes to stamps.

Organized trading clubs exist. Such groups may range in size from a few to many participants, and each has its own rules of engagement. Without attempting to sort out how one or many work, my best recommendation is to be sure that you understand and can work within the rules of a given trading group. Appendix A can get you off to a good start.

Some trading clubs, for example, may ask you to keep track of the stamps you send for trade and those you keep. Other trading clubs may require that you make trades on a stamp-for-stamp basis; you give ten stamps and get ten stamps in return. Or, you may find clubs that work on a catalogue-value basis, where you give a quantity of stamps that total ten dollars and receive a like value of stamps in return. As long as no one in the group seeks to take advantage of the others, either approach may work well.

Joining a specialty group puts you in contact with others who share your general collecting interest. These collectors may well be your best contacts for trading, because they have sorted their material more closely along the lines of how stamps from your country of interest are generally sorted. If you are not lucky enough to find a trading partner who shares your specific interest, take what you can find. Receiving many stamps that fit your collecting interest is second only to receiving the many stamps that you still need to fill spaces.

Local stamp clubs also present swapping possibilities. Many clubs schedule swap sessions as part of regular club programming, or members may just come to the meetings early to trade among themselves. As you can see, the toys may become more sophisticated, but the childhood habits remain.

No matter where or how you participate in stamp swapping, the key is to play it straight. Normally, trading is conducted with inexpensive material; each participant is seeking to rapidly increase his collection with a minimum cash outlay. Rather than attempt to be a "winner," when there is no competition, be sure that the material you are offering is sound and not all the lowest possible grade. Getting a reputation as a bad swapper does not help your overall standing within your immediate stamp-collecting circle.

Challenging You

Before you begin to consider how you can store the stamps that you collect from your favorite country, consider how and what you are actually seeking. (For more information about storing your collection, see Chapter 14.) That is, some countries have issued few enough stamps, that preprinted albums are reasonable in both size and price. Some countries' stamps, however, are so prolific that albums run into multiple volumes with accompanying higher costs.

Keeping you on your geographic toes, countries with tentative boundaries, seemingly drawn in pencil on a map, complicate matters. If your family came from a country where territorial control was based on which day of the week it was, you may want more than the postage stamps of the region. In addition, you may want to stay alert for envelopes (stamp collectors know them as *covers*) postmarked from towns in the disputed territory. You may find postmarks from the same town covering stamps from different countries. This sort of situation sends you to your history book and gazetteer.

The following guidelines should help you get a grip on foreign stamp collecting:

1. **Select your country of choice.** Several things can point you to collecting a country's stamps:

   • Emigration from or immigration to a country

   • Your first vacation outside of your home country

   • Your most memorable foreign trip if you are a veteran traveler (Chances are excellent that you can find stamps depicting the places that you visited or scenes that you viewed personally while traveling abroad.)

   • Country where you would like to visit

   • You were stationed there with the military

   • You do business with people or firms in that country (see Figure 12-1)

Figure 12-1:
Country with
a stable
monarchy.

2. Set boundaries (such as time or place) for your country's collection.

Are you really interested in all the country's stamps, or merely those covering a time period that has some special significance? If your grandparents emigrated from that country, do you want to stop your collection with stamps approximating the year of their emigration? Or, is there some other event that would set a beginning or ending point to your collection?

If I were to begin a Lithuanian stamp collection, I would stop with issues of about the time my maternal grandfather left the country for the New World. That small collection would represent to me what the country was like at the time of his departure. I am proud of the heritage, and would see that collection as one small way to hang onto that heritage. (Skip ahead to Figure 12-2.) You may view your own situation differently, wanting to keep a tangible memory of a country's significant political change. See Figure 12-3 as an example.

To keep things personal for a moment longer, my daughter spent a year in a Scandinavian country while still in high school. Her experience was so good, that I can see her (or me) beginning a stamp collection of that country solely to have postage-stamp-size prompts to memories of a wonderful experience.

3. Seek out sources.

See "Amassing a Melting Pot of Stamp Sources" earlier in this chapter for more ways to get your grubbies on foreign stamps.

The real point here is that collecting the stamps of a certain country does not obligate you to seek out all stamps from the first country issues through to the present. Rather, you choose what you want for your own reasons.

If nothing else, firmly understand that your collection is *your* collection, that you are not alone, and that you have help and many, many stamp sources. Move as rapidly as you want, remembering all the while that prizes for reaching a specific point in your collection before anyone else does are nonexistent.

Figure 12-2:
Stamps
showing
local/region
al heritage.

Figure 12-3:
Bringing
in a new
constitution.

Balking at territories

Stamp collectors often obtain stamps that have come about because of some tragic, natural disaster, such as typhoons, earthquakes, or volcanic eruption, or because of man-made crises, such as war or transportation disasters (see Figure 12-3). Normally, collectors hold on to overprinted stamps (noting a military government or a premium for disaster relief) and covers with censor markings or notation that the item was pulled from a train or airplane wreck to show them off as something different.

Much more rare are the items that result from a pleasant major change. With the breakup of the U.S.S.R. came "new" stamp-issuing entities, many of which had issued their own postage stamps prior to the Russian Revolution, such as the Balkans. With their independence following the U.S.S.R. breakup came a return to their own postal system and their own postal stamps. But, for a short period, until the new stamps were available at every post office, stamps of the U.S.S.R. were used successfully. No matter how easily I can attribute this usage to a loyalist unwilling to accept the change, the realist within me screams that the U.S.S.R. stamp was the remaining stamp in the user's house when the letter was finished and ready for mailing: No thought was given to its origin or possible symbolism.

Chapter 13

Planning and Theming

• •

• •

*I*f you are collecting a particular country's stamps, you seek out stamps that are identified as being issued by that country. If you are collecting a topic (or, as known in Europe, a *thematic*), you seek out stamps that have, as part of their design, a recognizable depiction of the person, place, thing, or event that you are collecting. If you are comfortable with that definition, read on to see just how complicated collecting for a theme can be.

Finding the material you want is always the challenge. You need to know what is available, as well as where to find it. Fortunately for you, the tremendous increase in topical stamp collecting in the past few years has spawned many topical stamp dealerships. To find topical dealers, look at Chapter 7.

After the material that you want starts flowing in, you must decide what to do with it. With a country collection, the accepted approach is to keep your stamps in chronological order (or, at least, close to that). With a topical collection, no *accepted* approach exists. So, I'll demonstrate one way to put together a topical collection. I will not be at all surprised if you take the same stamps and form the collection so that it looks different. Seeing one approach take form, as it once did for me, may well ease any butterflies you may have, unless, of course, they are butterflies depicted on stamps.

Collecting What Interests You

Topical collecting is truly the free-form part of stamp collecting. You, the collector, can first set the topic you want to pursue, lay down your own parameters, and then seek out the items that you believe match those parameters.

Unless you are interested in building a topical collection for participation in competitive exhibits, you have absolutely no rules to follow other than those that you set for yourself. Competitive exhibits and other exhibits are discussed in Chapter 10.

Knowing and going after what you like

No one is able to choose a topical collecting area for you as well as you are. Only you know what you like well enough to want to spend countless hours searching for stamps, choosing how to arrange them, and then putting an album together to display them. You may be a full-time forest ranger, but your personal interests lean toward rugby. So, begin a stamp collection that features the sport of rugby.

You have a colleague, however, who is fascinated with trees native to a country and is knowledgeable on the subject. So, your colleague builds a topical stamp collection based on trees that are native to the country issuing the stamp. For example, if the Norwegian pine is shown on a stamp, but the tree is not native to the country issuing that stamp, your colleague will not be interested in the stamp. You may not want your collection to be that refined, but this example does illustrate the level of choice open to you.

Although you may not choose from among the most popular topical collecting areas, you have an opportunity to build a meaningful collection that becomes personal. Do not attempt to build a topical collection because you believe it will become a good investment. I am not aware of any stamp that greatly increased in value purely because of what is printed on it. Some stamps may double or triple in value because they are in demand by both those collecting it for a country collection and those collecting it for the topic(s). When the initial value is well under one dollar, however, a dramatic increase does not convert to financial return.

Some popular collecting areas remain on top from year to year, and others are somewhat trendy. Long-term favorites include (but certainly are not limited to)

- Aircraft
- Art
- Birds
- Christmas
- Flowers
- Insects (including butterflies)
- Prehistoric animals
- Religion
- Science
- Scouting
- Ships
- Space
- Sports
- Trains

Some of the more trendy topical areas have been

- ✔ Halley's Comet
- ✔ Princess Di
- ✔ Royal babies
- ✔ Royal weddings
- ✔ Rock stars

You certainly are not limited to these lists, or even my personal listing of about 1,050 possible topical areas — which is always undergoing revision. The fictitious colleague mentioned earlier in this chapter who collects stamps depicting trees native to the country issuing the stamp does not have a topic that will show up on any formal list because it is probably one of a kind. You may choose to start a stamp collection based on dinosaurs, however, which has many adherents, and still end up with a collection unlike any of the others.

Creating collection boundaries

If you are collecting flags on stamps, you can easily pick out the red-white-and-blue U.S. flag. The U.S. has issued dozens of stamps depicting Old Glory. Thus, any time you see a U.S. stamp with the familiar symbol, you add the stamp to your collection. Most U.S. stamps depicting the U.S. flag show the flag as a major part of the stamp design. (Skip ahead to Figure 13-1 to see a topical stamp.) Just as the U.S. has many stamp issues depicting its flag — the U.S. Postal Service tries to have at least one stamp with a flag always on sale — just about every other country does the same.

So, you may look for a single flag on as many stamps as possible; you may seek an example of every national flag ever shown on a stamp; or you may generally collect as many stamps showing flags as you can find. This is not buck-passing; it is personalization.

But what about those stamp designs of a ship with a flag flying where the flag is in the shadows or is too small to have all the stars and bars delineated? You know from the situation that the flag *must* be a U.S. flag, but you cannot identify the flag under a high-powered magnifying glass (see Figure 13-2). Is this a stamp for your flags-on-stamps collection? Are you expecting me to tell you whether it is or not? No. That is a decision for you alone. Here are some issues to consider when making decisions for your own collection, if for no other reason than to promote some level of consistency:

- ✔ Seek stamps where your topic dominates the design.
- ✔ Broaden your scope to include stamps where anything meeting your topic is easily identifiable.

✔ Include logic in your collection, thus collecting stamps that contain a topical item, unidentifiable by sight but identifiable on the basis of some external factor. For example, if a ship on a stamp is identified as British, the flag flying from the ship *must* be a British flag. If you know what brand of bicycle a particular national Olympic team rides, and that team is identified on a stamp honoring that Olympic sport, then the bicycles the team members are riding *must* be that brand.

Figure 13-1: I'm betting on horse number 3.

Figure 13-2: Ship with small flag.

Some topical collectors save only those stamps where their topic dominates the stamp design. Others collect those where the topic is prominent (which, of course, includes dominant). And, others, knowing from their research that the tiny item fits their topic, collect those stamps that feature a diminutive version of the topic.

Matching parameters with finds

You can find stamps in a variety of forms. The same design that you find on a single stamp may also be on a souvenir sheet, and/or part of a miniature sheet. You may also find a stamp, normally earlier ones, with different perforations.

Just to make things more complicated, I'll give you another decision to make: A stamp that you want was issued as part of a set, and dealers will only sell the complete set. What do you do?

Breaking up is hard to do

You have settled on the topic of spiders, to go along with your lifelong interest in spiders, and finding stamps depicting spiders has been going well for you. Then you happen to find a set of five stamps that you must purchase as a set because none of the dealers that you contacted would break the set for you. Unfortunately, only two of the stamps depict spiders and the other three show other forms of creepy-crawlies (as you can see, I don't share your love for spiders).

What do you do with the three stamps that are not part of the set?

✔ Discard them into your pile of material for trading purposes?

✔ Mount them in your album with the spider stamps because they were issued as part of the set that includes the spider stamps?

✔ Add a second *supplementary* page to your album page and mount the nonspider stamps there, referencing their relationship as part of the set?

The correct answer in this case is "Yes." Again, you have the choice, and all I am doing is offering suggestions.

Along similar lines, you certainly will find sheetlets with stamps of different designs where at least one stamp depicts a spider and the other stamps do not. What do you do? In this case, because the sheetlet is a complete unit, topical collectors will generally keep the sheetlet intact and mount it in the spider-stamp album.

Go (con)figure

When the world was a simpler place, stamp collecting consisted of collecting stamps, each issued in sheets that contained multiple copies of the same design. The only varieties that resulted were from a different perforation measurement, different paper, or a change in the stamp's color or shade.

Stamp collecting is a little more complex now. Here is a rundown of various configurations that you may expect to encounter in your topical stamp shopping:

✔ **Single stamp:** This is the traditional item. One stamp with something in its design that causes you to want to include it in your topical collection.

✔ **Se-tenant:** Two or more stamps with different designs printed together on the same sheet.

✔ **Block:** An even number of stamps — 4, 6, 8, and so on — still attached. These may be se-tenant or all the same design (see Figure 13-3).

Figure 13-3:
Block of
four horses.

✔ **Margin block:** A block of stamps from the edge of the sheet, with the selvage — the unprinted paper on the edge, or margin, of a sheet of stamps.

✔ **Plate number block**: A block of stamps from the edge of a U.S. pane of stamps that includes the plate number designation.

✔ **Sheetlet:** A small (smaller than the normal-size sheet of stamps of a given country) sheet containing more than one stamp, with selvage adding little, if anything, to the stamp subject (see Figure 13-4).

✔ **Souvenir sheet:** A small sheet of one or more stamps where the nonstamp margin continues or enhances the commemoration (see Figure 13-5).

There are other stamp configurations that you will encounter, many of which are described in the Glossary at the end of this book.

With your collection's formatting basics in hand, note that a single stamp design may be available to you in more than one format. That is, a stamp that is part of a four-stamp set may also join the three other stamps as part of a souvenir sheet. Stamp catalogues normally list each configuration of the stamp as a different item. It is very possible — and definitely not advisable — that if you remove the stamp from the souvenir sheet and compare it up close and personal with the stamp that is part of the four-stamp set, you will not find any differences. Often, however, there may be differences.

There is absolutely no reason to argue if the two stamps are different. Different or not, you still have the option of including one, the other, or both in your collection. Most topicalists will save both.

Figure 13-4:
Sheetlet.

Figure 13-5:
Souvenir
sheet with
horse in
selvage.

Hunting for Treasure

You jump right into the new topical collection by purchasing every stamp you
find that fits. If you are collecting horses on stamps, you are ready to purchase

everything that includes a horse. You may even be fortunate and find an accumulation of horse stamps. Even without that good luck, however, you can find yourself with quite a few stamps for your new collection.

If you are like most other new topical collectors, or at least stamp collectors with a new topical collection, you can go through all the stamps you currently possess a couple of times just to see what you have. Then, you may begin to wonder what else there may be.

Rather, focus on how you can cut the odds a bit so that you have a fair shot at getting all the stamps that you want for your collection.

First the bad news: For the most part, all postage stamp catalogues — the formal documents that list each variety of stamp — are country based and not topical based. Only in the past few years have the first topical catalogues become available. There are perhaps a dozen or so topical-stamp catalogues, covering some of the larger topics.

Now, the good news: It is quite easy to tap into an existing network of information that can provide you not only with a whole lot of camaraderie, but also with some solid information. Nearly 500 topical-stamp checklists, an additional 45 or so handbooks each providing information on a single topic, and an ever-increasing number of Web sites devoted to single topics can keep you up-to-date and supply you with savvy.

What you may perceive losing in formality, you certainly make up for in the heart and soul of the hobby of stamp collecting: friendship and human interaction.

Many avenues are open to you. With these avenues, you can find information on what material is available.

American Topical Association

The American Topical Association (P.O. Box 50820, Albuquerque, NM 87181-0820; Internet: `http://home.prcn.org/~pauld/ata`), or ATA, is the most compact single source of information for the topical stamp collector. Services include more than 450 (and growing) individual checklists available in print form or in computer spreadsheet format. These checklists cover some rather esoteric areas and range in size from a few dozen stamps to more than 8,000. The ATA also has about 50 larger publications covering more extensive topical areas, a bimonthly journal devoted to topical stamp collecting, and sponsorship of its own annual exhibition. The ATA, which participates in many stamp shows around the country, also has chapters, each of which is devoted to a specific topical area.

Major stamp periodicals

Four major stamp periodicals in this country provide information on new issues (as do quite a few smaller ones).

- *Linn's Stamp News*
- *Global Stamp News*
- *Scott Stamp Monthly*
- *Stamp Collector*

Global Stamp News is particularly good for new collectors. Contact information for each is found in Appendix A. You can get a free sample copy of each publication just by asking for it.

If you are fortunate enough to find a specialty group that covers your topic, that group's own periodical may have the information you need. The more general periodicals will be more timely, but have far more information than you may want to wade through.

Philatelic libraries

Another source of solid information is the philatelic libraries, specialized libraries with books and periodicals dealing only with stamp collecting. The most visible philatelic library in the U.S. is the American Philatelic Research Library (P.O. Box 8000, State College, PA 16803; Internet: www.stamps.org). There are others in the U.S. and in many other countries. A list may be found on the Internet at www.askphil.org/b36.htm.

A philatelic library may be stand-alone, such as the American Philatelic Library, or part of a larger library. The Wineburgh Library is part of the library at the University of Texas-Dallas. In either case, you can use them in person. Some may suggest, or even require, prior notification. After you're there, you have access to the same sort of cart-catalogue system available in your local public library, and the works are shelved. Some of the philatelic libraries in the U.S., the American Philatelic Research Library for example, loan material directly through the mail and also through interlibrary loan. You cannot realize how research-based stamp collecting is until you have prowled the shelves of a philatelic library.

Topical stamp-collecting dealers

Stamp dealers specializing in topical stamps are also a great resource for information. Because topical-stamp information is not as formalized as its country-based collecting cousin, stamp dealers become more of an information source due to their immersion in the area.

Dealers not only have stamps on hand from which you may purchase, but they may also offer a new-issue service to which you may subscribe. How such a service is configured is left to each dealer. But new-issue services generally allow you to leave instructions for a dealer to send you upcoming new stamp issues that meet your topical area, along with an invoice. Some dealers may require an advance deposit. Pros and cons for a new-issue subscription exist:

- ✔ **Disadvantage:** You are dependent on the dealer to make the decision for you as to what fits your topic.
- ✔ **Advantage:** You are assured that at least most of the new issues covering your topic — and perhaps even all — will be covered by the new-issue service. Over the years I have used them quite successfully.

Putting It All Together

Before you get piles and piles of stamps and your task appears too daunting, consider just how you want to put this topical collection together.

You need some guidelines for what to include and exclude from your collection — sort of like putting together the guest list for a family social event. There is always an uncle and aunt who are not related by blood but who are considered part of the family. At the same time, there is that hard-to-stomach cousin whose invitation will be lost in the mail. Use the same approach with your collection — except this time there will be no hard feelings.

The 'clusions: In and ex

When talking about a topical stamp collection in generalities, nod knowingly and proceed with the discussion. When you actually get down to dealing with those little pieces of paper, small pangs of reality may reach out and slap you a bit. The first pang: What do I want to include in this collection? Before moving into a more generalized checklist of steps to take, here is what went on in my house for our stable of horses on stamps.

When it comes to the horses-on-stamps collection, I know the best. That discussion has already been completed and a set of rough guidelines drawn. The *starter* collection I purchased includes some material that was quickly ruled out. The current collection does *not* include zebras or anything from the donkey family. The collection I purchased included both. I chose to remove them.

Is this a significant decision? Perhaps not to you. It really wasn't of much importance to me. But, to the person who actually was going to take that material and build on it, the decision was quite important. Next came a discussion revolving around statues of horses, or more precisely, statues that included horses (see the statue of a horse on a stamp in Figure 13-6). After a spirit of give and take, the decision was to keep them in the collection (see Figure 13-7). Lose the donkeys and zebras; keep the statues. A topical stamp collection's direction is forged. Similar decisions, no matter how consciously they are made, revolve around most any topical collection.

Figure 13-6:
Statue
including a
horse.

Figure 13-7:
Is there a
horse? Of
course not.

After you have acquired some material for your topical collection, and before you get deep into your situation, pause for a moment and consider just what you want to include and exclude.

Here, then, is a brief checklist for you as you begin your topical collection.

✔ Choose your topic.

✔ Go through all the stamps you currently possess and find all that fit the chosen topic.

✔ Begin to log your stamps that fit the topic. Starting this process before you have hundreds (or thousands) allows you to set your log to your particular needs. Note, at least as a starting point, country of origin, date of issue, catalogue number, and a brief description of the stamp.

✔ Unless you have quite a few stamps from your own holdings, purchase a *starter* collection. This may be in the form of a packet of "200 different whatevers" (or more), or it may be album pages from material that a dealer purchased from a collector who had the same topical interest.

✔ From the material now at hand, see if you do not want to keep any individual items — or types — because they do not fit what you want your topical collection to be. (Earlier in this section, I discuss how donkeys and zebras were cast out of the horse collection, although other collectors of similar material may choose to keep that material.)

Arresting arrangements

Psst. Have you thought about how you plan to arrange your topical stamps in your album? "I didn't have to," you say? You know exactly what you want?

Good for you. Or, at least, good for you right now. At the same time, you may want to spend at least a few minutes considering if there are any alternate ways of arranging your collection. Here are some thoughts:

✔ Arrange by country, then by issue date within the country. This is very close to an actual country collection and is logical.

✔ Trace the history of your topic and make your arrangement a colorful history *book*. A stamp's country of issue or date of issue are not important here.

✔ Make your arrangement a *how-to* or an identifier. Perhaps an archaeology topic depicts various "digs." A collection of flowers (or, more precisely, of orchids) may serve as an identifier of types.

✔ Make your collection into a history, with many asides offering detailed examples of the topic in action. If you were collecting airplanes on stamps, a history of flight and examples of all identifiable aircraft would be the main part of the collection. Then, you may want to do a few pages showing the many uses of the Boeing 727 or the fabled Piper Cub. The former has both military and civilian uses; the latter has wide-ranging uses from pleasure riding, to crop-dusting, to military courier.

Horsing around

When I was first introduced to the concept of topical collecting, because my own stamp-collecting background is country based, my first belief was that I would procure as many stamps within that topical that I could find and then lay them out in an album (of my own making) by country in chronological order. Then I would be able to show my success in finding all those stamps. Wait! That turned out to be the wrong approach for me. There is nothing in that scenario that pertains to the topic itself, merely that I chose a topic and then got many stamps but no story.

When presenting the same stamps to someone with no previous stamp-collecting background, the hundreds of horse stamps were an opportunity to tell a story of some sort. Why not, I was asked in an instructional tone of voice, separate the stamps by what the horse was doing on the stamp and then begin some sort of further arrangement? So, I had piles of military horses, racing horses, pleasure horses, farm horses, horse "portraits" that merely showed the breed, and horses doing other work (see Figures 13-8 and 13-9).

Within each of those subcategories, there was further sorting in such a way that the original pile of a few hundred stamps began to have a life of its own. The subpile of breeds became smaller piles by breed, such as, American saddlebred, appaloosa, quarter horse, Arabian, and so on.

The other subpiles were sorted likewise, and the plan for an album literally developed itself. Nowhere along the way was there concern for which country issued a given stamp or in what year it was issued.

Please understand, I only encourage you to consider just what you want to say and do with your topical collection, not how to go about doing it. A different topical area can easily be arranged differently. A collection of Panda bears on stamps may be arranged along the lines of the life of a Panda, beginning with stamps showing cubs and moving through various aspects of a Panda's life. Great buildings of Western Europe may be arranged by year of completion, by country, by function, by style of architecture, or perhaps in some other way.

Adding to your album

A topical collection begs to be seen. Visual by nature, a topical collection really should be housed in such a way that it is easily available for view. Look at Chapter 14 for various types of albums and even some nonalbum methods of storing your collection.

You are fortunate if you can find a preprinted album that has images of stamps on its pages to match your topical collecting interest. There are very few such albums. Your options will pretty much be an album you build yourself — very much a majority situation within topical collecting — or stock pages that allow you to move stamps about easily.

Stock pages (thick pages with clear strips evenly spaced and pasted to the backing to provide pockets for your stamps to stay safe) are particularly good to keep on hand at least for temporary storage of material until you decide on a final page layout. You are able to adjust stamps on a stock page in seconds without having to worry about the stamps beginning to curl or perforations getting banged up — or most any other danger to those fragile paper items.

As you begin to assemble your pages, remember that stamp sets make up items with and without your topic. If you are going to keep the nontopical stamps with your collection, now is the time to settle on how you will do this. Be sure to review Chapter 14.

Be particularly careful with larger souvenir sheets and sheetlets. You will need to test how you have them mounted before formalizing your approach. Because souvenir sheets and sheetlets are so floppy, you have a great risk of a crease or a corner becoming dinged from the normal opening and closing of an album. So, after you have each sheetlet on an album page or stock page, and part of the album itself, carefully open and close the pages.

Part V
Protecting Your Collection

The 5th Wave — By Rich Tennant

It was supposed to be a simple deck remodeling. Then we had our stamp collection appraised...

In this part . . .

This part discusses two major areas to take major steps toward protecting your collection. The manner in which you store your stamps is critical to their long-term health. You can gain an understanding, with suggestions, of the various approaches you may take to keep your collection safe and orderly. Beyond the utility of what sort of system you employ is the issue of how well your storage approach displays your collection. You may be interested in the aesthetics of presentation, or you may only be concerned with the orderliness.

You can find that not much time passes in your stamp-collecting life before the value of your collection begins to mount. Further, you can have the opportunity to purchase individual items for your collection — the type that fall into the *must-have* category. Before purchasing anything that causes you to gulp once and wonder if you *really* want to take that step, you need to be sure the item you are purchasing is sound and not a fake. The second chapter in the part helps you become aware, armed, and ready to look at future purchases with the properly jaundiced eye. Knowledge is power.

Chapter 14

Housing Your Stamps

*I*f you have ever built a home, had a home built for you, or watched construction of any building, you know that site preparation and building a proper foundation are essential to the overall structure. Before the labor on the aesthetic elements of the building begins, considerable thought and work are devoted to a proper start. So it is with choosing how you house your stamps.

Laying the Foundation

Before you plan how to keep your collection — or, *house* your collection — you need to do some preplanning, which is similar to a home builder preparing a site and putting in the foundation.

Be certain that your storage location is dry and not subject to extreme temperatures. Therefore, keep your stamps in an attic that has temperature and humidity control.

✔ Have some idea of just what you're planning to store (even though you may be new at all this).

If you collect only single postage stamps, your stamp housing should be specific to your single-stamp collection. If you collect multiples of postage stamps, such as a block of four stamps, large strips, or even complete sheets, you need to house those multiples to accommodate larger, more floppy items. And, if you collect covers — first-day covers, event covers, or inauguration covers — you need to provide a home that accommodates the bulk of items that are multiple thicknesses of paper each. As I lay out the various options you have, you can see how well each may be applied to various types of collections.

✔ If you have friends already collecting stamps, observe how they house their collections and inquire why that particular approach was taken.

I do not want to overplay procuring an album or supplies to make your own album. But after you begin to shop and notice that it is possible to spend more for an album than for the stamps that go into it, you may want to know why certain types of albums are better or worse for your needs.

The more planning you do, the easier choosing the proper items for your needs can be. And, if you are planning a combination of foundation-laying methods, that's also fine. Your additional planning would be to predict in advance if you want matching album binders — or anything that matches — or if you can be content with the best individual items you can obtain, where *best* may relate to quality, price, availability, or something else.

Here are some basic, before-you-start issues to consider, if only long enough to determine they just don't apply to you:

✔ Just what is available in the marketplace? You may plot out exactly what you want, only to find it is not available.

✔ How expensive are various types of album and album-making supplies? If you are not purchasing locally, be certain to consider shipping costs.

✔ If you want matching album binders across the board, what is available?

✔ How easily can you update your album pages with new issues or varieties of the older material?

Finally, before beginning the housing process, here is a list of items to keep away from your stamps and covers. Many of these are common office supplies that you may have handy, particularly if you choose to make your own album or other type of storage system.

✔ **Ballpoint pens:** You must press hard to write. Therefore, you may leave an impression on anything under the pen's point. If you like detective stories, then you know how much of a trail a ballpoint pen can leave. Don't write on any stamps or covers with anything. Write on envelopes in which you keep stamps or on slips of paper that you keep with the stamps.

✔ **Clear plastic tape:** Neither the permanent nor the removable type is good. The permanent tape type leaves an easily visible and touchable residue that renders your stamp or cover valueless. Incidentally, the removable type of tape may leave the same residue. Tape and stamps don't mix at all.

✔ **Masking tape:** Although seemingly removable, the longer the tape is attached, the more permanent this tape becomes. Trying to remove dried-up masking tape is not a pretty sight. This is a recording: Tape and stamps don't mix at all.

✔ **Paper clips:** These all-too-common items, along with any other metal fasteners, leave creases in your paper items. If left attached for a long time, paper clips also may leave an oxidation residue, *rust* to us lowbrow readers. If you need to keep items together, keep them in something (a larger envelope) rather than holding them together. Any marks left may downgrade the value of a stamp.

✔ **Peelable labels:** Although the label may be removed, the residue may not be visible to the naked eye. Some types of labels degrade over time and their residue may migrate beyond the item to which it was originally affixed. In other words, fear the migrating label. The adhesive is similar to removable tape. In case you missed the two previous warnings: Tape and stamps don't mix at all.

✔ **Photo albums:** The magnetic pages are adhesive-coated papers that use PVC and acidic adhesives that enhance the rapid degradation of stamp paper. The acid's capability to migrate to stamps or covers attached to the page has been proven. Although you may not care how the back of your family photo appears, your postage-stamp backs are important. Use only materials suitable for stamps and not something else merely because it appears to be a convenience.

✔ **Rubber elastic bands:** If these are used to keep a group of envelopes together, you run the risk of leaving creases, other markings, or even tears. Further, rubber bands tend to degrade themselves in the air in a relatively short time, doing nothing good to the paper they are touching at the time. To keep stamps or covers together, use a larger envelope.

✔ **Rubber cement:** This may also induce a chemical reaction that will destroy the value of your material.

Building the Structure

For your first album — the word *first* is a major clue here — you probably want to consider an album with preprinted pages (see Figure 14-1). That is, you want an album with spaces already in place for you to cover with actual stamps. The stamp collector who begins with an album that he carries through his whole collecting career is rare. Normally after a period of collecting, you will find that the album has become too small for your collection or your collecting interests have moved in a different direction from what was covered by your first album. Remember that you won't be alone.

Entering this escapade, you have many decisions to make, the first of which is whether you want a preprinted album or prefer to make your own. If the latter, the remainder of this section can help you plan for that do-it-yourself effort. You still need to understand some of the stamp-album basics, no matter which direction you proceed in. If you want to begin with a preprinted album, here's some key options to consider.

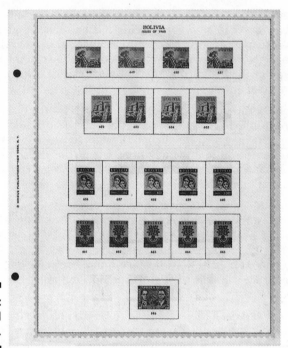

© MINKUS PUBLICATIONS—NEW YORK, N.Y.

Figure 14-1:
Preprinted
album page.

Printed on one side or printed on both sides

Certainly you can get more stamps into an album if you can mount them on both sides of a page. And the cost for the album will be less, also. The other side of the coin is that unless you have a glassine sheet (nearly transparent, see discussion of glassine envelopes later in this chapter) in between every page, you run the risk of damaging stamps that get caught on each other. Also, if you choose to use stamp mounts rather than hinges, a double-sided page is subject to far more stress than a page with mounts on only one side. *Stamp mounts,* explained and shown later in this chapter, are individualized containers for a stamp.

Page- and binder-hole size

This is a difficult issue to phrase and a messy one to answer. It (accurately) suggests there are no real standards relative to album-page dimensions and the hole configuration used. Some U.S. publishers of preprinted albums offer their product on a standard 8½-x-11-inch format with the traditional three holes. Most use nonstandard paper dimensions and/or hole configurations. Even the nice and rather pricey foreign hingeless albums — more about them soon — seemingly with holes all the way down one side of a page, each have a different number of holes. Thus, the pages of one publisher of these albums do not fit the binder of another publisher. The answer to your resounding "Why?" comes from the sales/marketing area: After you have any sort of investment in album pages and binders from one publisher, you are less inclined to change *systems* and absorb the accompanying expense.

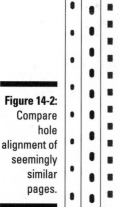

Figure 14-2:
Compare hole alignment of seemingly similar pages.

When beginning, do so with an understanding of whether you are purchasing an album to test the waters of your collecting interest or if you are purchasing an album you fully intend (intent at the time of purchase, for you may well change your mind months or years down the line) to expand on to accommodate a growing stamp collection. If your intent is to expand, then, at the time that you are shopping, be sure to investigate the availability and cost of blank pages and empty binders to accommodate items that you cannot plan for now.

Single-country, regional, or worldwide albums

The title of this section refers to stamp albums designed to house the stamps of only one country, a group of countries from the same geographic region (Benelux or British North America), or the stamps of the whole world. Note that I did not include *topical* album in this section. Simply, there just are not enough of them yet to consider them as a full category. If you are fortunate enough to find a topical album that matches your collection, then by all means, get that album and enjoy it.

Single-country albums are not the smallest grouping that you can find. For example, finding albums for only the semipostal stamps of Switzerland, booklet stamps, commemoratives only, definitives only, and so on, is possible. For purposes of starting out, however, I am not recommending consideration of that album type. Although available, albums covering regions, the world, or even more than one country are not nearly as plentiful as they were when no more than 12,000 total stamps were issued in a single year.

Low-priced worldwide albums are still available; though there is no question they are designed for the beginner only. Someone really serious about collecting all the world's stamps requires the Scott International Album series. That series, unique in the world, requires about 60 *parts* that number into the hundreds of pages each. The total suggested retail price for the set is in the neighborhood of $6,500 — enough discounting exists that no one will actually pay that amount. The total, however, does show the project's immensity.

Your options for a preprinted album run the gamut from a few dollars to a few thousand.

Hingeless or regular

Here is yet another question that requires some explanation before a real discussion may continue. When you bring your first album home, you are faced with the issue of how to attach (stamp collectors prefer *affix*) the stamps to the album pages. Certainly cellophane tape, staples, and quick-setting glue are not under consideration for this task.

When working with a preprinted album, you have two principal options: stamp hinges (see Figure 14-3) and stamp mounts (see Figure 14-4). The former is the historic method. In recent years two issues have weighed heavily against hinge usage:

Figure 14-3:
Stamp
hinge.

✔ Hinge quality is not what it was. What had been *peelable* hinges now often are difficult to remove from stamps or album pages without leaving a remnant or damaging the stamp.

✔ The marketplace puts a premium on *never-hinged* mint stamps. Thus, a mint stamp with any sign of hinge usage downgrades in value. For your current commemorative stamps, which will probably never increase in value anyway, such a downgrading is not financially significant. For that rare stamp with inverted image that you purchased the day after receiving your lottery winnings, one little stamp hinge may cost you thousands of dollars.

Short of potential damage, which may be easily controlled through careful use, hinges are not nearly as much of a problem for used stamps.

Figure 14-4:
Stamp
mount.

Made of a plastic substance that doesn't hurt stamps, *stamp mounts* offer protection (see Figure 14-4). It is even possible to re-use a mount, if care is taken at every step. There is a downside however:

✔ **Cost:** The cost per mount can be more than the cost per stamp. Precut mounts are more expensive per mount than strips from which you cut the exact width you need. Even then, however, the cost can (pardon me for this) mount up rapidly.

✔ **Sizing:** You must understand how to measure mounts to fit your stamps. Most mount manufacturers provide a guide that helps you, and by all means, use one when you have the opportunity. A too-tight mount does bad things to the perforations; a mount that is too loose may lose its stamp as pages are turned. In the spirit of Goldilocks in *The Three Bears,* you want a stamp mount that fits "just right."

✔ **Weight:** If you have an album printed on both sides, you run the risk of overloading the page's weight capacity that can lead to tearing the page when turning it. If you have such a scenario with your album, be very careful how you turn the pages.

✔ **Bulk:** A stamp mount itself is essentially the equivalent of two stamp thicknesses. Add the stamp itself and the result literally is something close to an appendage on the page. Multiply that extra thickness by the number of pages in your album, and you will realize that an album binder that houses pages with stamp mounts can handle fewer pages than one with stamps attached by hinges.

Even with all the issues, you want to consider using stamp mounts for mint stamps priced at above the minimum catalogue value.

Figure 14-5:
Hingeless
album page.

Now we arrive at the actual issue at hand: hingeless albums or regular.

✔ **Hingeless albums:** It's just what the term *hingeless* suggests — an album page with stamp mounts is already in place (see Figure 14-5 in this chapter).

Here are the pros:

- There is tremendous convenience in this approach.

- You save time.

- The mounts are the proper size for the stamps to go in them.

- The page itself is designed to accommodate stamp mounts. That is, some preprinted pages display the stamps so close together that it is difficult to fit mounts for individual stamps in a horizontal row because mounts add about five millimeters to the width and height. Although this is not common, it certainly is known.

And the cons:

- You'll spend more money. You have to calculate the cost of purchasing stamp mounts and add in the cost of the regular preprinted album itself to see if the actual cost is more or less. There is no question, however, that hingeless albums are more costly than regular. Only if you are purchasing stamp mounts at a premium is the hingeless album page equal to or less.

- Selection is even more limited than with preprinted albums, and it is more difficult to add items that are not illustrated.

Paper quality

Stamps are made from exceptionally good paper. If the paper is stored properly, the stamp paper can probably last for something like 400 years. The fact that many healthy, old stamps are still around testifies to the long-lasting quality of stamp paper. Paper researchers can evaluate the projected longevity of all forms of paper, and have done so for most of the papers used in preprinted albums.

Although the results are not consistent, only a few paper types used for albums have come in at the 100-year level or so. Suffice to say that when you get to really inexpensive stamp albums, you may find the less-quality paper. That is the bad news. The good news is that such albums are normally the first such type you would outgrow in just a few years, probably before any actual damage to your stamps takes place.

After you are committed to building a stamp collection and realize that — for reasons other than the quality of the paper — your stamp album is just not suited to you, when you plan for an upgrade be sure to take paper quality into strong consideration.

Today, you are foolish if you do not require a new album to be printed on acid-free paper. Further, if you are making your own album pages, purchase only acid-free paper. Acid in paper is the great destroyer, both of the page itself and any other paper it touches.

Perhaps the best advice here is to become concerned with the paper used in your stamp album when you begin to purchase stamps at a price level that doesn't accommodate signs of problems in 20 years or so. An advantage of using stamp mounts is that the stamp does not touch the album page.

Expandable

Unless you have chosen a collecting area where no new stamps are forthcoming — a dead country or U.S. commemoratives through 1950 — you face a situation with your prospective new album about what to do with stamps not yet issued. That is, you purchase an album knowing it probably does not have spaces for stamps issued within the past few months and cannot be expected to have spaces for stamps to be issued over the next few months. Then what do you do?

At least for the short term, you may find room on pages to tuck those stamps for safekeeping. Some albums provide blank spaces for such stamps. For your consideration, other albums have

- ✔ Enough unused area on pages to allow new stamps or even varieties of older stamps, to be placed.

- ✔ Matching blank pages for you to use, as you would like.

- ✔ Both regular supplements and matching blank pages. Supplements are issued on a regular basis, normally every year, to accommodate stamps issued since the last supplement. Supplements match the album and provide illustrations of stamps. Blank pages match the album pages when it comes to paper size, stock, and border design. Beyond that, the page is blank, and you are free to use it however you choose.

In time, you want something better that allows you to present a more attractive page. When looking for your album, look into how that album handles such an overload. Albums covering areas where new stamps are anticipated normally produce annual supplements — pages that are an extension of the album you originally purchased — which is by far the neatest resolution to the issue.

With all this information, you're a better-prepared consumer when it comes to choosing a preprinted album.

Making Your Own Album

Making your own album can be a rather time-consuming venture. Stamp collecting is a hobby though, and hobbies are expected to take plenty of time. So, you need three principal items — in addition to time — to begin to build your own stamp album:

- ✔ The stamps you want to mount in that album

- ✔ An accurate measuring device for the stamps

- ✔ A means of producing the actual album page

The process is rather straightforward. You determine beforehand what you want as a continuing title, if anything, for the album pages. Examples may be *United States* or *Upland Gorillas*. Consider how you want to handle headers for each stamp issue, and if you want any additional text to describe the stamps further. Some collectors like an abundance of information on the background of a stamp. Other collectors only want such philatelic information as its perforation measurement, watermark, printing method, and so on. And still other collectors only want a catalogue number printed under the stamp that is mounted on the album page.

This is a good time for experimenting with various approaches. To do this, take the same group of stamps — perhaps enough for at least three pages — and set up a few different arrangements on a page. Even go so far as to produce final pages and merely lay the stamps on each to see which is more appealing to you. After all, this is for you. While you are testing, experiment with page titles, page borders, and whether you want a box around each stamp.

Do-it-yourselfers

If you are proficient with drawing tools, you are now on your way. But so many more decisions need to be made!

- ✔ Have enough of the same color ink to produce *many* pages. If you are using pen and ink, you will be handling any borders, boxes around stamps, and all writing on the pages. Better to have too much ink on hand rather than too little, unless you are using a name brand that you know is available any time you need it.

- ✔ Decide if you will be using text and how you will be producing it.

  Some collectors handprint all the words, others use a typewriter, and some use a simple computer word-processing program to generate the text in position, and then do the hand drawing. As you can see, there are no real rules to follow. Which type of pen, drawing aids, or even ink color you use is your decision. The options are nearly endless, and you literally can personalize each page.

- ✔ Use a paper stock that does not produce *feathering* (where the ink is not absorbed uniformly and appears fuzzy).

- ✔ Specify acid-free stock.

  If you have the opportunity to use paper goods for some 400 years, by all means take it. Then, take care of yourself, exercise, and watch your diet in an effort to outlive your stamp-album pages.

About the only thing to steer clear of in this process is generating pages with a photocopy machine or computer laser printer. Some-to-many collectors continue to be of the belief that the toner used in these processes should not be touching postage stamps for any length of time. Although I am not aware of any formal testing of the potential hazards, I am cautious enough with my little loved ones to be wary of the unknown. For my own work, I use an inkjet printer, and I am certain each page is dry before allowing any of my stamps near it.

Software for those who smash their thumbs

Computer-aided album-page design has lept from nonexistent to nearly totally automated in just the past few years. Presuming you already have the computer and printer, your software options are quite broad. Although the Macintosh family of personal computers has the reputation for being dominant when it comes to graphic arts, the most specialized software I have seen for building stamp-album pages is written for the Windows-based systems.

You are not, however, required to use a stamp-album-page generator. Quite a few other approaches exist, ranging from free-drawing programs to high-end programs suitable for producing book-length manuscripts including all the graphics. Candidly, spending $800 for software that you will only use to produce album pages lacks logic. If, however, you have such a program already, you are well on your way.

High-end programs

The high-end programs, such as PageMaker and Quark Express, allow you to make your album as you would lay out a book. Both are available for both Windows and Macintosh platforms.

Although drawing boxes for each stamp on a page is simple enough, you will find these feature-rich page layout programs allow you to draw and keep boxes for the most common sizes in your collection apart from the active area of your work and copy them to the active area as you need them. This will save you considerable time and guarantee consistent sizing. You also have more control over the "live" area of a page and are able to set parameters for all the pages to assure consistency. The difference between this type of program and a low-end freebee may well be similar to comparing a 1941 Army Jeep and a contemporary SUV: both get you to where you want to go, but with the SUV you enjoyed the ride more.

Free is good

Many excellent, free software programs perform the tasks you require. Each program may have quirks, and perhaps one less bell or whistle than the high-end software. If you come upon a lower-end package with which you are comfortable, you have just saved yourself a fair amount of money that you can spend on more stamps for your collection. The real key to page layout or draw software is finding the one that you like. Most do the job — not all can do it in a way that is comfortable to you.

Enter the specialized software made just for you. A few programs specifically designed to produce stamp album pages appeared in the recent past. Because a single entrepreneur or, at best, a small firm produces these specialized programs, the programs tend to come and go rather rapidly. If you are in the market for such a program, check out the Internet: `www.execpc.com/ ~joeluft/resource.html`, click Software, and prepare to be amazed. The listings, shown in Figure 14-6, show Web sites promoting various stamp-collecting software offerings, including album-page-building packages.

Figure 14-6:
Joe knows
software.

The Home Page is on a whole different topic, but his reputation has come from the resource area. My favorite type of automated album-building software allows you to construct a database, including stamp measurements, and then lays out the pages for you. Meanwhile, you have provided instructions on page titles, headings for stamp sets, and even text for the individual stamps if you so choose. What you may lose in flexibility — and I have not put the software totally through its paces yet — you certainly pick up in speed. As you add a new stamp to your collection, and also to your database, you can push a mouse button and generate revised pages.

Your options are wide ranging, from totally manual, where the artist within you controls the action, to just about totally automated. Then all that's left is some brief words (some repeated) relative to supplies for computer-generated album pages.

✔ If at all possible, use an inkjet printer.

 ✔ Choose archival-quality paper. Think 400 years.

 ✔ Choose paper that easily goes through your printer. Some printers require paper to take a nasty U-turn, which is simple for lightweight stock used for everyday printing. Thicker paper may cause a problem. Read the printer instruction manual (you know, that small document that came with the printer and at which you scoffed) for recommended paper specifications. When in doubt, test. After you have returned home with three or four reams of beautiful paper that you found on sale for $50 a ream is not the time to test your printer.

The upside of producing your own album is that you can produce it just as you want it. Also, if you do not include your time spent in the calculation, you should be able to build your own album for less cost than purchasing one. If you're attempting to complete a collection of a country or a time period of one country's issues, then the do-it-yourself approach requires you to have another source of information (such as a current or recent catalogue or a good checklist) about what stamps are available and how close you are to completion. Album manufacturers must be up-to-date on such information.

Expressing Creativity with Stamp Album Alternatives

Ruling out your dresser drawer or sitting loose in a closet shoe box as ameans of storing stamps, two alternatives to traditional stamp-album storage are worth considering. Even if you rule out both of them for the bulk of your collection, still consider these possibilities for that extra material that always becomes part of your stamp holdings.

Glassine envelopes

Glassine envelopes, or *glassines,* are your friend (see Figure 14-7). I keep the bulk of my collection in glassine envelopes, sorted by catalogue number and stored in matching boxes designed for industrial-parts picking. Although definitely not pretty, I know my material is safe and easy to access. When I do my killer album, I will have all the stamps ordered in a way that will make mounting rather simple.

Figure 14-7:
Glassine
envelope
selection.

Just as you choose your album paper wisely, you need to be certain that the little envelopes you select actually are glassine and not made of something else. I also have seen clear cellophane-like envelopes, the safety of which has not been tested for stamps. Unless you are assured that something other than glassine is safe, stick with the tried-and-true.

Stock pages

Stock pages have evolved over the years. They are pretty much little stamp shelves (see Figure 14-8). Where they were once made-from-manila stock, similar to that used for file folders, now nearly all are produced from some form of plastic.

The newer plastic models, most with clear horizontal strips so you can view the complete stamp, make a wonderful storage facility. Some collectors choose stock pages to house their collection rather than paper-based album pages. Be certain, if you are going to use stock pages for long-term storage, that you have assurances about the safety of the plastic. These pages afford you the flexibility of being able to move the stamps about as you are adding to your collection. Thus, stock pages are excellent for the early stages of building a collection.

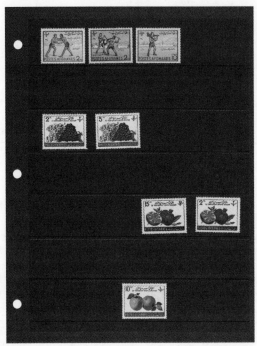

Figure 14-8:
Stock
pages.

Also, stock pages come in a variety of configurations such that you are literally able to customize your presentation to your every desired detail. Generally, stock pages are available to fit a three-ring binder. Some manufacturers offer stock pages with hole configurations to match their proprietary binders. You can find enough of a variety to fit a standard binder to keep you wondering just how you can use each configuration.

Your options on how to house your collection are nearly as varied as what sort of collection to begin in the first place. That is a positive situation, whether you are ready to accept that right now or down the collecting road. Begin carefully and, again, have fun!

Chapter 15

Faking It

• •

In This Chapter

▶ Recognizing a fraud: Altered coloring

▶ Detecting an overprint and uneven perforations

▶ Forgeries come in all sizes and colors

▶ Faking versus enhancing

▶ Getting an expert's opinion

• •

*Y*ou will very possibly collect stamps for a long time, enjoy collecting immensely, and never come upon a faked stamp. But if you are faced with one, what about the stamp may raise your suspicions? I can assure you that a fake will not come with a little, sticky-back tag that reads, "Beware of me."

Along similar paths of stamp collecting's dark side — stamp collecting is made up of people, and fortunately only a very few are not to be trusted — are those stamps that were repaired skillfully or otherwise *enhanced* without any sort of note to that effect.

Nothing is better than building your own level of knowledge so that you can separate the good from the bad. Information enables you to build your own knowledge base. Even then, however, you may still need to seek help. What help is there for you? This is the sobering chapter that touches on these subjects with the hope that you can set out to keep from being victimized. I am not an alarmist, and I certainly do not want you to shift immediately into a totally defensive mode. Just as you go to a grocery store without even thinking of something being unfresh to the point of causing harm, you will go through stamp collecting with that same positive attitude. At the same time, when you see an opened jar on the grocery-store shelf or a section in the frozen foods that is warm to the touch, your antennae are raised. Consider this chapter an introduction to antennae raising.

Forgering Ahead

Two principal types of forgeries occur:

- **Postal:** Items produced to defraud the government
- **Philatelic:** Items produced to defraud stamp collectors

The postal service does not have much of a sense of humor when it comes to postal forgeries. I have never had a solid answer as to whether retaining a postal forgery for a stamp collection is permissible. Normally, if the postal service believes that fake stamps are still running loose in the kingdom, a couple of postal inspectors are dispatched to retrieve them.

Should you have a forgery in your home, and the postal service catches wind of it, here's what goes down:

1. The postal inspectors, the law enforcement arm of the postal service, appear at a stamp collector's door.

2. The inspectors identify themselves and ask to see the postal forgeries, or the inspectors ask if the collector possesses them. (I know of two instances in which this actually happened, and in each case the collector would dutifully produce the forgeries for the inspectors.)

3. After the forgeries are in the inspectors' hands, the inspectors thank the collector and leave — with the forgeries.

   In retrospect, I am not aware of any demands for the collector to turn them over. At the same time, I would react the same as my acquaintances: compliance with the request.

Philatelic forgeries, on the other hand, do not normally attract the attention of people carrying badges and weapons, unless an attempt to sell the forgeries is made without noting they are fake. In fact, collecting fakes and forgeries is popular.

To start, you may want to find out the key parts of a stamp where the forger plies his trade. This chapter cannot cover all the ways to spot a forgery but serves primarily as the basis for your lengthy discovery process.

Perferted

As you build your collection, you already have or soon will come upon two stamps with the same design and different perforation configurations. The difference may be two different perforation measurements, such as perf 11 for one stamp and perf 10 for another. The difference may also be that one stamp is perforated and the other is imperforate. Or, one is a coil stamp (perforated on two parallel sides) and the other one is perforated on four sides or imperforate. See Chapter 3 to read more about perforations and Chapter 11 about coil stamps.

Further, within the two, one stamp has significantly more value than another does. When a pair of stamps meets such conditions, the stage is set for the possibility of a forgery. This is based on changing the perforation of the lesser-value stamp to that of the greater-value stamp (see Figure 15-1). In the overwhelming number of such situations, no forgery exists. When you are paying a large (for you) sum of money for an item, however, you deserve to know it actually is what it is said to be.

Your key responsibility — a responsibility easily met by looking carefully at catalogue listings after noting the design similarity — is to know that two or more different perforation gauges are known for the same stamp design. Then, you need to check the perforations on the stamps *very* carefully to be sure that they were placed there at the time the stamp was produced and not later by a deceitful creature working under a bright light in the middle of the night. If you cannot tell if the stamp has been reperforated — and still fear it may have been — then you need to seek assistance.

If you do not know which stamps in your collection are subject to forging, you may not realize you have any fakes until you are ready to sell. Not only will you be offered a lesser amount for your collection than you had hoped, but the collection itself will be under far more scrutiny once a fake is spotted. On top of all that, years probably have gone by and you have no chance of going back to the person from whom you obtained the fake stamp for a full refund. I certainly am glad that only a few stamps are faked, and many collectors will never be faced with having to worry about it at all.

Figure 15-1:
Reperfed
single
from the
Washington/
Franklin
Series.

Making money the hard way

I always question the sanity of people who choose to produce postal forgeries. Think about it: producing stamps that match in design, color, paper type, gum type, and perforation, and the forged stamp still may only have a value of a few dollars. I remember a forger of then-current six-cent stamps. At 100 stamps per sheet, you are into the 17th sheet before the total value reaches $100, the same as five $20 bills.

Some stamp features may easily indicate a forgery, but other characteristics may make forgery identification difficult.

- **A narrower stamp:** To get from a perforated stamp to an imperforate stamp of the same design, the forger carefully slices away the line of perforations. If a stamp that is obviously narrower than the *good* stamp results, the forger has failed. When the stamp being sliced is a little wider than average in the first place, the forger has a better chance of a plausible finished product. You, as a newcomer, are not expected to recognize the second attempt, but an expert is. More on experts later.

- **Uneven perforations:** If the perforated stamp is more valuable than the imperforate version, the forger will then trim the imperforate stamp to the proper size and proceed to add perforations. *Reperforating,* as the method is known, is a meticulous process requiring a steady eye and hand. Many attempts are so crude that even someone with no stamp-collecting experience recognizes the result as a forgery. Other attempts require another visit to our expert. Reperforated stamps tend to have perforations that are uneven. The more even the perforations, the better the forger. Work to improve your skills so that you are not only able to identify the easy items, but also some of the more difficult ones.

Overprints, including surcharges, are another forger's playground. Often the overprinted stamp has a higher value than the same stamp without the overprint. A forger, then, will stock up on the original stamps and begin to apply a fake overprint.

Detecting fake overprints can be difficult (see Figures 15-2 and 15-3), particularly if the original stamp is recent and the forger is using contemporary printing methods. Early attempts may be cruder, although there are still quite a few excellent fakes running around the countryside masquerading as legitimate. Although you can often detect a fake overprint by comparing it to a "good" one printed in a journal article or in a stamp catalogue, you have no guarantee that the catalogue reproduction is accurate. Merely transferring the image of an overprint from a real example to a catalogue illustration can bring about enough of a change to cause misunderstanding. That is, if you compare a legitimate copy of an overprinted stamp to a printed guide and find a difference, do not jump to the conclusion that you have a fake because there is no match. Get a second opinion from another collector or dealer first.

Fortunately, there is not enough fakery to cause alarm. Still, it may happen.

The best comparison is from your own reference collection. For suspect overprints — and certainly not all, or even many, are suspect — obtain a stamp with a known good copy of the overprint or surcharge. This reference may be on a low-value stamp that has the same overprint, or a damaged stamp that has little market value but still permits a good view of the overprint. Then run a direct comparison on your own stamp desk. Your "reference" copy need only serve one purpose: a guide to a correct overprint.

Figure 15-2:
Legitimate
stamp with
fake
Hungarian
(Fiume)
overprint.
Identifying
the fake
overprint is
difficult
without
some
form of
reference.

Look for any of the following:

- **Ink of a different color or shade:** Although it is possible that not all the same overprints are applied with the same ink density, you should be able to denote different shades.

- **Different type or font:** Look at each letter carefully for an exact match. Also, if the overprint includes some sort of illustration, compare the two *very* carefully.

- **Irregular letter spacing:** The letter spacing within words and spacing between words must match perfectly. If the overprint is made from handset type, then spacing within a word often may be difficult to match.

- **Irregular line spacing:** If the overprint has more than one line of type, measure the line spacing.

The list certainly is not all-inclusive, but it starts you on your way toward self-expertizing your own material.

Sometimes a forger with more brashness than intelligence will apply a fake overprint to a used stamp. One way to identify this attempt at fakery is to look at the overprint under a magnifier to see if the overprint has been applied *over* the cancellation. Certainly, if the cancellation is under the overprint, the cancel was not applied before the stamp was used. Chapter 3 can direct you to the tools that you need here.

Covering the gray

A forger with some expertise in chemistry may immerse the stamp in a specific liquid or gas known to affect a particular ink to alter the stamp's color. Although this is an esoteric form of forgery, it does conjure up a sinister vision of the rogue-forger romping about his laboratory (pronounced, la-BOR-a-tory) with various beakers of chemicals in the background, each containing a single stamp.

Color *changelings* do exist, however, and you need to know when color alterations are a possibility.

- If two stamps have identical designs (produced from the same plates, but different colors and one color has a much higher-market value than the other).

- The lesser-value stamp can be recolored to the greater-value stamp by chemical means. This is not a common occurrence, but it does happen.

Color-missing does not mean "color-not-apparent-to-the-naked-eye." That is, if you look at an item believed to be missing a color, you must ascertain whether absolutely no sign of that color is on the stamp at all. If a multicolor stamp is thought to be missing a color, you must not be able to see any small dots of that color under a 10X glass. It is possible the ink color in question was running low in the production process and a full portion of ink was not applied to one or more stamps. But, if *any* ink was applied, what you have is merely an ugly stamp — not an error, but an ugly stamp with little value.

Reprinting the classics

Reprints of original stamps are yet another form of fakery, but only if the items are not sold as reprints. The country originally issuing the more valuable stamps produces some reprints. Such reprints are often listed in stamp catalogues, and usually with footnotes that explain how to tell the original (and more valuable) items from the lesser-value reprints.

Other reprints are privately produced and, unless produced expressly to defraud, merely is a way for the average collector to have some sort of copy of the extremely valuable stamps. I remember, as a child, getting such a reprint of the famed one-penny British Guiana, then the world's most valuable stamp. I paid ten cents for the reprint, certainly not an item produced to defraud.

Currently I possess a couple of sets (copies, unfortunately) of the first three stamps issued by Buenos Aires. See the following Figure 15-4 to see what Buenos Aires reprints look like. The *real* stamps of this type were issued in 1858, during a period when what is the now the capital of Argentina maintained an independent government. Catalogue value of the actual first three stamps is about $2,000.

To ink is human

Human intervention often encourages color-missing errors. Some inks change color, or even seem to disappear when exposed to sunlight. For a period of time, one type of red ink used on U.S. commemorative stamps would vanish if left in the bright sun for a reasonably short period of time. Until that phenomenon was understood, a rash of "color-missing" stamps was offered in the marketplace at a nice premium over the regular stamp. As an experiment, take two common current (and inexpensive) stamps; place one near a window that gets direct sunlight for a large part of the day and the other in a drawer.

After four or five days compare the two. A difference between the two shows you what the sun can do to inks.

The first of these color-missing items was discovered by accident and no evil intent was apparent. Before the facts become known, some with less-than-ethical intentions came onto the secret and made a tidy profit before word was blasted throughout the realm. So, be careful with any color-missing item that you are offered to be sure the color was left out at the time of printing and not removed later.

Figure 15-4:
Set of
Buenos
Aires
reprints.

Caveating your emptor

How you discover an item is another clue to its past. If you are offered a stamp . . .

✔ In top condition, for just a small percentage of its high-catalogue value, then be suspicious. Legitimate, sound postage stamps areonly sold at amazing discounts in unusual situations.

✔ That has suspicious markings by someone you don't know, then don't take candy from strangers! Inquire about the seller before closing the deal.

✔ In an online sale, whether retail or via auctions, then pay with a credit card to protect yourself. Online sales are a potential problem area.

✔ As a part of a large lot, then do some checking. Most of the forgeries I have found were part of large lots that I purchased. That is, among all the common items emerges an item with a catalogue value of $1,000. Your first emotion is elation. Then, I hope, comes the doubt. And, then comes the checking.

The forger himself may not be guilty of "salting" the lot with what appears to be high-value stamps. Rather, someone along the way probably noted they were not real, placed them with stamps to be discarded without first marking them as fakes, and after a few decades any memory was lost. The person selling the large lot may not have seen the items at all when preparing the material for sale; or, he did notice them, was suspicious, but chose not to say anything nor use those items as some sort of come-on hyping overall value. So, you end up purchasing the large lot, including the fakes, but not under the guise of legitimate stamps. When you begin to check the material you come upon individual stamps with values (if real) each more than what you paid for the lot.

I remember paying about $500 for a lot of material and pulling out a dozen or so stamps with a total catalogue value of about $25,000. Fortunately I did not put a down payment on an Italian roadster before I did some checking: Every stamp that I thought was valuable was actually a fake. I still have them, but they are in an envelope marked "FAKE."

Many years ago, as I was building my own collection, I purchased mystery boxes of stamps regularly from a dealer that I liked. The lots were sold as- is, and normally had a retail price in the $75 to $90 range. From those boxes I would extract stamps totaling four to six times the catalogue value, perhaps more. I particularly remember one box, priced at the same amount, in which I found items with a total-catalogue value of about $25,000! Wheeee!Of course, after I took out all the fakes and forgeries, I was back to the usual value. In the meantime, the learning experience was tremendous. I checked a pair of German inflation stamps first with a catalogue value of about $1,500, then. I showed the German stamps to a dealer specializing in Germany with the hope he would make a good offer for the items (not something I would want for my own collection). He smiled knowingly, handed them back to me, and explained that the German stamps were fakes. I was crushed.

Needless to report, I was much more cautious with all the other high-value items I found. By the time I checked all of them with friends, my understanding of fakes jumped manyfold. It turned out to be a great experience, although not necessarily one that I recommend for all new stamp collectors.

Faking versus Improving

In some industries and hobbies, enhancing an older item is just part of doing business; in stamp collecting it is considered unethical. To rephrase, refinishing antique furniture is an art form; refinishing an antique stamp and offering it for sale as genuine can lead to jail time. Continuing the morality-play opening to this section, after a stamp has been repaired or otherwise enhanced in quality, notation of what has been done to the stamp should travel with that stamp forevermore. The notation may be in the form of a formal opinion (certificate) from a recognized expert, a less-formal note from the person selling, or even a hand-scrawled warning next to the stamp in your album or on the envelope in which the stamp is kept. Selling a repaired stamp as if it is in original condition is fraud.

Many forms of enhancement are possible, of which these are only a sampling:

- Perforating a single straight edge stamp (no perforations), which was originally produced on the edge of a sheet that was trimmed.

- Removing a postal marking chemically, such that no marks are visible to the naked eye.

- Repairing tears, cleaner than any plastic surgery.

- Replacing a stamp's missing corner by going to another damaged stamp of the same design for the appropriate body part. Missing chunks of a stamp are also replaced.

Two tools can help you immensely in your effort to identify these repairs: a long-wave ultraviolet (UV) lamp and your watermark fluid and tray. Watermark fluid is described in Chapter 3. This use of a UV lamp is not a tool in the same sense, although UV lamps are used in stamp collecting for identification purposes. UV light is part of the light spectrum, and is valuable for seeing things not visible under regular light.

Shortwave UV light (UV lightbulbs are all properly marked) is useful in detecting fluorescence and luminescence on stamps. Longwave UV light is useful for spotting repairs to paper, attempts to remove a cancellation, or reconstructive surgery to a stamp.

First use a little common sense. Probably no stamp with a catalogue value of under $10 or even $50 is a candidate for chicanery. Then, look at potential purchases carefully. Be a nit-picker! If you are not certain whether a stamp has been repaired, ask the seller to immerse the stamp in watermark fluid. The repaired area should jump out at you like a neon light outside your motel window.

Watermark fluid is showing you where the density of the stamp's paper is different — where the watermark has been impressed into the paper during manufacture. Any work repairing a tear or adding a corner naturally affects the thickness of the paper.

A longwave UV lamp can bring a postal marking (ink) to life that was thought to have been removed. Seeing the cancellation come up before you can give you an eerie feeling. Immediately, thoughts of a television series, *Tales of the Stamp Sleuth,* come to mind. Be certain to use a longwave UV for this task, while remembering that a shortwave UV lamp is used primarily to determine if the stamp is *tagged* or is printed on phosphorescent paper that activates high-speed automatic-canceling equipment. The equipment "looks" for the tagged stamp and, if found, cancels the envelope. If a tagged stamp is not found, the envelope is kicked out of the automated system for manual inspection and canceling.

Never look directly at a UV lamp — longwave or shortwave. I advise not using them for extended periods. UV light can be dangerous, so be certain to read all warnings that come with any light that you purchase.

Wearing the White Hat and In This Corner . . .

At some point in a person's life, someone else who will listen to that person's problems is needed. Stamp collecting builds that provision into its world in the form of an *expert*. Years of study and then collegial acceptance as one who knows much about one or more aspects of stamp collecting earns this formal title.

A person may be considered an expert on the stamps of a whole country, or a date range of a country's stamps, or even a single complex set of stamps. How broad the area of expertise is not the issue. Peer recognition determines whether or not a person is an expert.

Experts are called on to offer an *opinion* on the stamp's authenticity, or to identify a stamp that may cause others to be unsure, specifically regarding whether that stamp is genuine. An expert's clarification may be based on identifying the paper used for printing, the watermark, the printing method, or which die was used, or color — all the individual facets that collectively make up the identification of a stamp. See Chapter 16 for what you can do before you may need an expert's help.

In reality, these experts are just like you and me with the exception that they have taken the time to really study. Coupled with that study is a pretty good aptitude for how to identify a stamp. Experts also have a strong reference collection covering the material they know well, along with a solid library to back up their work. You, too, can become an expert. The identification tips presented in this chapter, as well as throughout this book, are geared toward helping you lay the groundwork for your accession. In addition to Chapter 16, look at Chapter 3.

Even if you don't aspire for lofty heights, the more you know about your own material the less you need to go elsewhere for assistance.

In the meantime, should you have an identification question, or come across a stamp requiring an expert opinion, services are available that you may use. The two largest expert services in the United States are operated by the

- American Philatelic Society (P.O. Box 8000, State College, PA 16803-8000; Internet: www.stamps.org/Services/ser_SubmitItem.htm) The American Philatelic Society reviews any material.

- Philatelic Foundation (21 East 40th St., New York, NY 10016). The Philatelic Foundation reviews all U.S. material and foreign stamps issued before 1940.With these two groups, or any other experts you may come upon in your stamp-collecting career, always obtain instructions on how to submit an item before you send it along. Each service has its own procedures and fee structure.

An extensive list of experts from around the world who review questionable material is on the Internet at AskPhil.Org (www.askphil.org/b35.htm). Note that a fee is involved when working with these experts, and normally what you receive back from the expert (or, in the case of an organization, *expert service*) is a certificate with the expert's opinion noted (see Figure 15-5). Only a few experts guarantee their opinions, the normal approach is to offer an opinion.

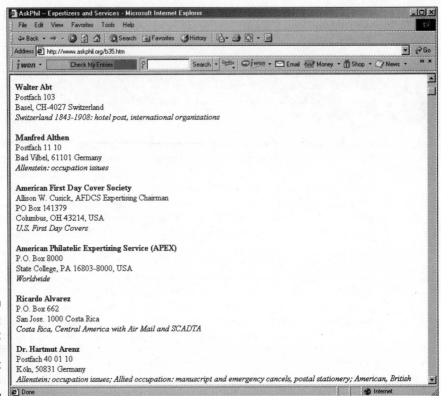

Walter Abt
Postfach 103
Basel, CH-4027 Switzerland
Switzerland 1843-1908: hotel post, international organizations

Manfred Althen
Postfach 11 10
Bad Vilbel, 61101 Germany
Allenstein: occupation issues

American First Day Cover Society
Allison W. Cusick, AFDCS Expertising Chairman
PO Box 141379
Columbus, OH 43214, USA
U.S. First Day Covers

American Philatelic Expertizing Service (APEX)
P.O. Box 8000
State College, PA 16803-8000, USA
Worldwide

Ricardo Alvarez
P.O. Box 662
San Jose. 1000 Costa Rica
Costa Rica, Central America with Air Mail and SCADTA

Dr. Hartmut Arenz
Postfach 40 01 10
Köln, 50831 Germany
Allenstein: occupation issues; Allied occupation: manuscript and emergency cancels, postal stationery; American, British

Figure 15-5:
Screenshot
of *AskPhil*
expert
listing.

In all cases, before you actually send material for *expertizing,* communicate with the expert or service to be certain how to submit the material and what the fee will be. Often the fee is based on the anticipated catalogue value of the item if found to be good. Each expert/service sets its own fee. Expertizing certificates are normally sought for specific types of material at the time of sale, with arrangements as to who pays — buyer or seller — in each situation. Expertizing certificates are only important relative to stamps that tend to be faked, mistakenly identified, or suspected of being altered.

Part VI
The Parts of Ten

The 5th Wave   By Rich Tennant

The Jack Nicholson Terrier

"I don't think we should make him lick
the stamps anymore!"

In this part . . .

This part lays out some useful information in bite-size chunks — information designed to assist you when you are in the midst of a decision-making situation. First is a list of ten keys to identify a stamp. You do not need to use all of them each time you are in an identification mode. Which keys you will need is based on the stamp. Next is a list of methods to dispose of part or all your collection. If you decide to specialize, you may want to get rid of your more general collection; or, you may have purchased a large collection just to obtain the part you need, with the desire of selling the remainder. Or (horrors!) you may want to dispose of your collection in favor of finally paddling your canoe from Traverse City, Michigan, to Pier 52 in New York City's Manhattan, and you need a spare oar. Whatever your reason, you will have the need at some point to decrease your stamp holdings. If you are at all like me, often an actual real-life situation hits closer to home than the presentation of a lot of theory. The final chapter of this part is a series of actual questions from stamp-collecting beginners — whether they are total newcomers to the hobby or merely to the subject area.

Chapter 16

Ten Keys to Stamp Identification

*L*ook at any stamp on an envelope from your incoming daily mail. Chances are that you know what it is, or you say to yourself, "This must be a new one. I haven't seen it yet." Your mind processes some of the points raised in this chapter to reach those conclusions. The tips presented here formalize the process for you, flesh it out a bit, and provide a concise guide to get you from "What is this?" to "I know just where to put it in my album."

Not all the tips noted here apply to every stamp you seek to identify, but enough of the information will indeed assist you through those trying times. Likewise, you need not attempt to identify a stamp using the tips presented here in any particular order. Your larger task is to be sure that you consider — no matter how briefly — all the stamp's characteristics that may apply to identifying that particular stamp. This is an exercise in free-form troubleshooting.

Is the Design Unique?

Considering all the stamps issued by all the countries of the world, most stamp designs are unique. Seventy-five countries may issue a stamp near the same date for the same commemoration, but chances are extremely high that each of those 75 stamp issues have a variation in the design.

You won't need any special tools to assist you in identifying a stamp on the basis of its design only, which should speed up your effort. If you are trying to find where the item fits into your preprinted album, all you need to do is match up the stamp design with the smaller illustration of the stamp in the album. Chapter 14 discusses albums. If the stamp design includes a date, searching for the illustration in the album is even easier. Many countries include a date of issue as part of the overall stamp design, normally in small type at the bottom or side of the actual design. U.S. stamps, although the United States came late to this practice, also now include the date.

Always begin with the design to zero in quickly.

What Is Its Nickname?

By their nature, nicknames are identification shortcuts. Collectors and dealers reference postage-stamp nicknames to speed up their identification. Referring to the *5-dollar Prexie* is easier than the *Calvin Coolidge, 5-dollar value, in the Presidential Series of 1938*. Stamp collectors have all heard of the *Upside-down Airmail* or the *Inverted Jenny* and immediately recognize the stamp (this one qualifies for two nicknames) as the 24-cent of the 1918 first airmail series of the United States.

Not only can using nicknames make you feel *in the know,* but also it's a rapid way of referencing a particular stamp.

To begin to find out about these shortcuts, you may want to attend local stamp club meetings (see Chapter 8), read stamp periodicals (see Appendix A), and start to understand some of the major regular-issue series issued by the country of your particular interest. Although commemorative stamps (see Chapter 1) are normally the more attractive stamps of any country, the more studious stamp collectors usually focus on the regular issues, or *definitives*. Each U.S. definitive series has a name, as do lengthier sets of other countries. The postal administration may have assigned the name at the time of issue, or collectors may have affixed it to the set after issue. Here are some of the most prominent examples:

- ✔ **U.S. Americana Issue (of 1975-81)** is a lengthy series from one-cent to five-dollar denominations with a consistent design element that allows them to be recognized easily.

- ✔ **U.S. issues of 1938 showing deceased presidents** (and Ben Franklin, Martha Washington, and the White House) to that point known as the *Prexies*.

- ✔ **Great Britain *Machins*** are an extended set of regular-issue stamps with a profile of Queen Elizabeth II rendered as a plaster cast by Arnold Machin. His design won a 1965 competition.

- ✔ **Canada's *Admirals*** is a lengthy set of regular-issue stamps with the same view of King George V in the uniform of a Navy admiral.

Nearly every country has sets of stamps that have taken on their own nick-names. As you choose to move into a collecting specialty, that form of short-hand becomes second nature to you.

Is It an Overprint?

Overprints — an additional printing on a stamp that was not part of the origi-nal design — is considered a new stamp. After the overprint is applied, the stamp takes on a new identity. In fact, a stamp that's been overprinted is listed under that new identity in the postage stamp catalogues. Some coun-tries make more use of overprints than others do. An overprint may be applied as a commemoration, to show a change of government, or to make a stamp that was originally destined to provide a particular type of mailing ser-vice, provide another instead.

For collectors of U.S. stamps, overprints are a minor item applied as a com-memoration or as a security device. On stamped envelopes, however, over-prints have been used extensively over the years for purposes of revaluing when the postage rate is changed. While new rates are normally more, I have seen examples of postage rates decreasing.

The 1928 Molly Pitcher overprint turned a common two-cent definitive stamp depicting George Washington into an honor for the heroine of the Revolutionary War Battle of Monmouth. (Mary Ludwig married John Casper Hays, but she came to be known as Molly Pitcher because of the pitchers of water that she brought to the thirsty soldiers during the cruel Battle of Monmouth.) Thus, that stamp is normally identified as the Molly Pitcher Stamp, a commemorative stamp dressed as a definitive.

At about the same time, post office burglaries in Kansas and Nebraska prompted the Post Office Department to authorize overprinting 11 issues from the then-current definitive series with *Kans.* or *Nebr.* to reduce the opportunity that the stolen stamps be used in the states where they were taken. For a period of time, only stamps overprinted *Kans.* were available for sale in that state, and only *Nebr.* overprints were available for sale in Nebraska. If stamps were stolen and taken across state lines, they could not be melded easily into the unoverprinted stamp supply of another state. Collectors know these stamps as the *Kansas-Nebraska Overprints.* A single item might be called the *One-cent Kansas Overprint.*

Many countries, particularly if their currency has been devalued or a new regime has changed the currency, surcharge a stamp. A surcharge is an over-print for the express purpose of changing the face value of the stamp, such as the amount of postage it represents. Because currency changes may come about more quickly than a supply of stamps with new currency designations, postal administrations have relied upon sometimes the closest printing press to apply a surcharge. From the standpoint of a stamp collector, a surcharged stamp is a totally different stamp from the unsurcharged variety.

What Are Its Colors?

Color is the most difficult attribute of a stamp to pin down. Sometimes color names do not conjure up the color itself. For example, *lake* is a dark red and has no resemblance to any color associated with a body of water. You must also contend with colors that are close to each other, such as red, carmine, and rose; or vermilion and orange; or bistre, bistre brown, and olive bistre.

Several things can complicate your ability to properly determine a stamp's color:

- A stamp can change color in the process of aging.
- Sometimes an overly dominant cancellation can change some or all of a stamp's color.
- Each catalogue system has its own color-naming convention.

That is the bad news.

This is the good news: An easy project helps you through the color maze — the reference collection. Seldom is a color only used on one stamp. And, often there is an inexpensive stamp known in only one color that is one of the many colors that you are trying to identify for another stamp. Therefore, you obtain a clean copy of the inexpensive stamp for your reference collection and compare questionable stamps to it. An unstated benefit of a reference collection for colors is that the stamps used for reference usually are of the same vintage as the stamps that you are attempting to identify. Thus, the effects of aging are minimized.

A small caveat: Printed color guides are more often a problem than a solution because they tend to fade. For colors that are close, color guides lose their effectiveness. Stick with the reference collection as much as you can. If you begin to collect U.S. stamps, you'll discover the three-cent George Washington of 1861. It is known in a number of colors/shades, the most famous of which is *pigeon-blood pink*. Before you race to your local pigeon hangout to do a blood letting, I am here to tell you that there is absolutely no relationship between the name of the stamp's color and the blood of a pigeon. Oh yes. I found that piece of information second hand; I will not perform the test myself.

What Are Its Measurements?
Size Matters

A fraction of a millimeter can make a difference. Knowing the correct measurement of a stamp's design is a key to identification in two major arenas. Some countries have produced two stamp series with the same design, with one series being substantially larger than the other series. Although it is almost impossible to mistakenly identify a stamp in one of the sets if you have examples of both sets in front of you — a part of your reference collection — you may not instantly recognize to which set the item belongs if you are looking at the same one without a reference stamp for comparison.

Your trusty millimeter-measuring gauge can come to your rescue. However, where one stamp is, say, 33 percent or 50 percent larger than the other stamp is, your gauge really is more of a crutch than a critical piece of your identification arsenal. Still, the millimeter-measuring gauge normally allows you to measure more precisely than a common ruler designed for general office use. Early twentieth-century U.S. definitives, at the time when production methods were moving from the flat-plate press to the rotary-plate press, present an entirely different issue.

Design measurements are an essential element in stamp identification, with the measurements at fractions of a millimeter. Not only do you need a measuring gauge that is accurate and easy to read, but you also need to know how to use it. If you have a metal gauge, be certain that you place the gauge carefully over the stamp under consideration and look directly down over the measuring lines.

Do not look at the measurement at an angle, for you may be victimized by parallax with the result being a faulty reading. Remember, when measuring an item three different points need to line up perfectly: your eye, the point on the ruler that you are referencing, and the point on the item where you are measuring. The greater the distance between the latter two, the more chance the three points will not line up properly and you may obtain a misreading without realizing it.

Klutz that I am, my choice for a measuring gauge is one that is clear plastic with the printing on the bottom. Thus, I am looking through the plastic to see the small lines of the measuring gauge as well as the stamp itself. In this manner, the lines of the measuring gauge are literally touching the stamp, and I have little chance for a misread because I am not looking straight down. I have eliminated the parallax problem by bringing the distance between the second and third points (the point on the ruler and the point on the item) down to virtually nothing.

Particularly when measuring the design of a stamp accurately to the 0.25 or 0.50 millimeter, you need to consider the thickness of the lines on the measuring gauge. Do you read from the outside of the lines, the inside of the lines, from the same relative spot on the lines you are using, or does it matter at all? Given that you probably will be *reading* with the aid of a magnifying glass (at least I do), the thickness of the lines becomes more apparent. I generally try to use the same relative spot on the lines being used. Normally I line up what is being measured with the left-most edge of a line on the measuring gauge. Before you lock into that approach, however, test your own talent to do this close measurement and your device with any stamp for which exact design measurements are known.

See Chapter 3 for more information about other tools.

How Are Its Perforation States? The (W)hole Story

Happy is the collector whose only interaction with a perforation gauge is to identify stamps with perf 10½ or perf 12 measurement. It is extremely possible that after a little while, the collector may abandon the perforation gauge and be able to do as good (and faster) a job merely on sight. Just as puppies are trained to know when to go outside or which furniture to shun, stamp collecting trains collectors on other forms of repetitive activity. Chapter 3 discusses both stamp-collecting tools and perforations.

Determining whether a stamp in the U.S. definitive issues of 1922-32 are perf 11 or perf 11 x 10½ (first number is horizontal measurement of perforations across top and bottom of the stamp, the second number is vertical measurement of perforations across left and right sides of the stamp) is not as easy to spot on sight. Even then, however, the task itself is easy. The same is true for many issues of the world, including some of the earliest British stamps of 1854-58.

Beginning with the U.S. Great Americans issue of 1980-99, the plot thickens — sometimes it thickens into a brick. Perforation measurements for many U.S. definitives from that point forward may be to the tenths of a perf rather than the traditional quarter of a perf. Long-standing designs for perforation gauges are not effective for the finer measurements, and you need to move to one of the new types with fine lines emanating from a guideline. They are more difficult to use, but the newer gauges certainly provide the result you want. When you are ready for such an advanced gauge, have a more experienced collector or a stamp dealer help you choose one.

Is It Illuminating?

Without high-speed equipment to cancel and sort mail, the USPS probably could not handle the huge volume of mail it sorts. High-speed postal equipment must be able to *read* whether postage has been applied and position the envelope properly. The front of the envelope, which contains the address and the stamp, must face the canceling device to permit the address to be read automatically. *Reading* is based on the luminescent glow detected by the equipment. Luminescence — fluorescence or phosphorescence — is part of the stamp itself; the luminescence comes through the type of paper used or an inklike substance applied to stamps to generate ultraviolet (UV)-light-activated afterglow for the equipment to detect.

If the USPS uses ultraviolet (UV) light for its process, you can use it to see the same luminescence.

During the early days of testing and the initial implementation of *tagged* stamps — stamps produced with a nearly invisible ink — the tagged versions were what you were seeking. Later, you are seeking the *tagging omitted* versions. Without the UV light, it is impossible to know which is, or is not, tagged. The first tagged stamp is the eight-cent Jetliner-over-Capitol airmail stamp issued in 1962. The value of that stamp tagged and not tagged is about the same, but it's a historic item.

The early stamps, which are known as *tagged* and *untagged,* are noted in specialized U.S. catalogues, as are those later stamps known with tagging missing. Along the way, the USPS also began to use fluorescent or *Hi-Bright* paper. As you study luminescence, you will come to know how to distinguish the various types. This is a fascinating and specialized area of U.S. stamp collecting.

Great Britain also has tagged items: definitive stamps with phosphorescent bars. For these stamps, you look for how many bars are on a stamp, their position, and of course for errors, such as missing or shortened bars. Armed with a shortwave UV light, you can have plenty of fun on a small budget.

Do not look directly into the UV light. Further, you should avoid prolonged exposure to the light. You may want to use sunglasses that feature a UV block.

How Was It Printed?

Four principal printing methods are used to produce postage stamps. Other printing methods, which have been and are being used, are in the minority.

- ✔ **Engraved:** The metal is cut away by hand to produce a die or plate for use in the printing process. Also known as *Recess* or *Intaglio,* engraved printing lays the ink above the surface of the paper. This is the easiest printing method to recognize because of the ink ridges protruding above the paper. Often you can feel the ridges. When attempting to determine the printing method used on a stamp between engraved and something else, look for the raised ink.

- ✔ **Photogravure:** A process where Intaglio prints are made from flat plates having an irregular grain. Also known as *Gravure,* it's most often used for multicolor stamps. Photogravure uses images broken into small dots.

- ✔ **Lithography:** Also known as *Offset Lithography* or *Offset,* lithography is the most common and least expensive process for printing stamps. Lithography also uses images broken into small dots. Lithography is printing from plates impressed on a rubber-covered cylinder, also known as a blanket, from which they are transferred by the offset process to the paper.

- ✔ **Typography:** The art of typography involves choosing the type faces that will display to the best advantage the art to the finished plate. Also known as *Letterpress* in commercial printing, typography does not use small dots; its color is continuous.

Many good references can help you better identify the printing methods and use specific stamp examples.

Is Its Paper Wove or Laid?

Your initial need to identify stamps on the basis of paper type used will be based on your ability to differentiate wove paper from laid paper. Other types of paper tend to be based on which country issued the stamps under study. Chapter 3 tells you how each type of paper is made and how you can identify it.

Using a totally nonstamp example, here is my favorite explanation of the difference between wove and laid: Hold a piece of paper up to a bright-enough light source so you can see any sort of pattern in the paper itself. If the pattern you see is similar to the type of pattern seen on a common window screen (horizontal lines close together and of the same weight), you have wove paper. If you notice essentially the same overall pattern with the addition of larger and heavier parallel lines only running in one direction (not across each other) you have laid paper.

If you have one or more stamps printed on laid paper, by all means include one (even a damaged one) in your reference collection. If not, visit your local stationery store or office supply shop for paper advertised on its wrapper or box as *laid*. While you may have to purchase a box of stationery or a ream of paper to get your single-sheet example, you will at least have a live item to use for reference. See Chapter 3 for more of a discussion on paper.

As with any aspect of stamp production, the study of paper may become quite detailed. Excellent references exist for you to use for such study.

What Are Its Catalogue Numbers?

Each postage stamp ever issued and considered a separate variety has a unique catalogue number within a given catalogue system. That is, the U.S. *Scott Standard Postage Stamp Catalogue* assigns unique numbers, as well Great Britain's *Stanley Gibbons Stamp Catalogue,* or France's *Yvert & Tellier,* and Germany's *MICHEL* Catalogue. (See Appendix A for more information about these catalogues.) Those four firms continue to publish catalogues of the postage stamps of the world. Scott produces its set annually and the others on a less-frequent basis. Further, smaller publishers around the world produce catalogues of a single country or a region and each of these publishers has its own numbering system. Thus, a single stamp can have multiple (and usually different) catalogue numbers, one for each catalogue system. Although this may appear confusing, normally a collector is only using a single catalogue system overall and does not normally move among different systems.

A single stamp from Great Britain has catalogue numbers in at least four systems and perhaps more. How, then, do you know which to use?

If in the United States, and unless you know another system is being used, refer to the *Scott Standard Postage Stamp Catalogue*. If in Great Britain you normally refer to *Stanley Gibbons Stamp Catalogue,* and so on. One way to distinguish between systems is to note the system your dealer(s) use. The system being used in a country normally is a function of nationalism and practicality. Even then, you need to follow a basic protocol — nothing locked in stone, but I suggest it to guarantee that all concerned can equally understand the shorthand reference you make. If you're referencing the famed

Invert Jenny, use the reference "U.S. Scott C3a," which tells the other person(s) with whom you are communicating which country, which catalogue system, and which catalogue number, all in a concise manner. Take advantage of the shorthand provided. For something as famed as this stamp, no doubt you normally can refer to it — as if on a first name basis — as just "C3a." But, then, there are other C3a's in the stamp world, and if you were in the company of a group heavily into the stamps of India, that reference would mean something else.

Where the other identification tips presented in this section presumed that you have the stamp in hand and were trying to identify it, usage of a catalogue number is an ideal way to identify an item without actually possessing it. You can request a stamp from a dealer or in trade from another collector without the other person seeing the stamp you reference.

I have been at events where collectors have engaged in rapid-fire communication, tossing catalogue numbers back and forth to all except me, knowing exactly what was being discussed. I was not certain if the collectors were really deep into their hobby, or if they just did not have much else to do with their time. But, they *were* having fun.

Chapter 17

Ten Ways to Dispose of a Stamp or Collection

● ●

In This Chapter

▶ Bartering as an active sport

▶ Coming up with a reasonable price

▶ Advertising online: Get a security deposit

▶ Making fast friends: Donating to a newcomer

● ●

Disposing of *any* stamps is not in the nature of a stamp collector. Emotionally, a stamp collector does not really trade or sell an item, but the collector is really placing it in a good home. Nevertheless, the situation does occur sometimes under the following circumstances:

✔ You decide to specialize and dispose of all stamps not meeting the criteria for that specialty. Perhaps you sell the material, buy what you need/want, or you may even swap a bit for what you want.

✔ To obtain a large lot of material for this new specialty, you had to purchase an even larger lot with an overabundance of material that you did not want. You sell what you can to recoup some of the expense of what you just purchased.

✔ Alas, you conclude that stamp collecting is not for you . . . and you also have been accepted to Human Cannonball School. You want to sell your collection to finance your venture to a more sedate lifestyle.

Of the many ways possible to shed material from a collection, each has its own idiosyncrasies.

Trading with Another Collector

Trading with a fellow collector is perhaps the simplest and most straightforward of the trading possibilities. This is a throwback to childhood, when collectors would trade marbles, doll clothes, any other toys — or lunches.

Unless such stamp trades include material of some value, trading directly among collectors may be based on catalogue value. On the other hand, collectors may forsake value altogether and merely trade stamp for stamp. Not unusual, particularly among collectors with a worldwide interest, would be a conversation that goes something like, "My 100 Norway for your 100 France." On agreement, one collector counts out 100 Norwegian stamps and the other 100 French stamps, and they swap.

A great deal of stamp-for-stamp trading occurs among collectors at local stamp meetings. Collectors, having spent the period between two meetings picking up new material, come to the meeting with those items they are prepared to give up in exchange for getting a head start on the next month's new material. If you are trading by mail with another collector, be certain to *decorate* your outgoing envelope with commemorative stamps that your trading partner can soak and save — just one of the little extras that stamp collectors expect of each other.

Trading with a Stamp Dealer

A stamp dealer is in the business to buy and sell stamps, so why would he want to trade with a collector? If the collector is a good customer, then good customer relations dictate acceding to the customer's wishes as long as they are not unreasonable. In addition, and perhaps more often, the stamp that the collector offers to trade is more saleable to the dealer than the item that the collector wants in trade.

Normally, trades between dealers and collectors are stamp-for-stamp or for a small group, rather than a large group of stamps. Although a value increment on the basis of trade certainly exists, it may remain unstated with each party understanding the value involved and merely trying to negotiate the trade in such a way that it is comfortable to both parties. I found that trading material with dealers is quite easy. I entered with the feeling that trading with the dealer would work or it wouldn't, and if not, the situation would not end with any hard feelings on either side. After all, either of us could always make a cash offer for the material the other is offering in the trade.

Joining a Trading Club

Trading clubs, or *swap clubs,* can take a beginning collector from zero to an abundance of stamps in a hurry. Although a few swap clubs, from time to time, mention their existence on the Internet, and you can see them mentioned also in the stamp-collecting periodicals, I found that a simple Internet search got me off to a great start. Merely by entering "stamp+trading" into any of the better search engines, the Web brought up enough online possibilities to allow a thorough investigation. You can find more resources and Web sites in Appendix A at the end of this book.

Stamp trading clubs may come and go quickly because the individuals who run most of these clubs become bored or shut down for other reasons. I suggest you hold off searching for a trading club until you are ready to join one, so you get the most current information. Also ask any collector friends for trading clubs that they know and their impressions of them.

Because most trading clubs are small, one-person operations, each has its own personality. Begin slowly and see if you fit in. If so, increase your participation. If not, excuse yourself from the group and move on to another. Do not take an active role until you have read thoroughly, understand, and agree with the regulations. Some clubs have rules as loose as a neighborhood social gathering, where everyone brings food to share; others appear to be using cast-off regulations from a prison camp; and, then, you will see the clubs that operate somewhere in between — that vast middle ground.

Selling to Another Collector

As common as selling your material to another collector may be, for some reason I have the most trouble with this method of stamp disposal. Either you as the seller or the other collector as the prospective purchaser must set a price for the material that you are offering. For reasons I absolutely cannot explain, after mumbling what I want for the item(s) being offered, I always feel as if I am asking too much. Therefore, I tend not to use this approach myself.

The fact that I tend to avoid this disposal method shouldn't be a reason for you not to sell to another collector or purchase from one. If a collector has an available item that you want, and you have nothing to trade, then trade cash.

The purchase price may need to be set in the same manner as a dealer sets a price: Take the market value into consideration and then factor the market value up or down by the grade and condition of this specific item. If neither of you know the market value, as determined, for example, by current retail-sales prices, then you need to revert to the current-catalogue value. Try to come up with a reasonable price. See Chapter 5 for more on grade and condition, Chapter 6 for a discussion of value, and Chapter 7 for a larger discussion of stamp dealers.

Often the item being discussed is not listed in a catalogue specifically, nor has either of you seen a dealer offer the item. In such cases, one of you needs to relate it to something else for which you know a retail price or merely come up with something that is agreeable to the both of you.

Selling to a Dealer

Preferring not to include stamp collecting in my personal conflict-resolution situations, I probably am far too sensitive when attempting to sell material to a stamp dealer. Because I do not attempt to stay current on market prices, even those relative to my own collecting interest, I always fear that the price I quote will be embarrassingly high or so low that not giggling while writing the check will be all the dealer can do. So, I want the dealer to make an offer to me . . . the dealer is on top of the market, or so I presume given that the dealer is making all or part of his income from buying and selling stamps.

I have had situations where I would not take anything lower than a certain price, and I have so stated that. If the dealer wants to pay my price, fine; if not, I pack up tent and stamp and go my merry way with no hard feelings.

As you can see, I do not barter well. I know that, accept that, and factor that into my stamp dealings. If someone offers me something at a price higher than I am willing to pay, for whatever reason, I try to refuse the offer graciously. If I believe one is appropriate (and have the nerve at the time) to make a counteroffer, I will. Normally, however, I leave the item for another day. This fits into my own overall approach to stamp collecting — at least my own collection — as a hobby where I want to enjoy myself.

If you are one to whom bartering is a participation sport, have fun! This is the area for you, and certainly you will find more than enough dealers to engage. Be as tough or as gentle as you want, remembering that your own reputation is being cast with each transaction. If you notice that dealers do not want to barter with you, perhaps you need to back away from any high-pressure tactics, similar to those of the locals hawking souvenirs to tourists leaving cruise ships for a day ashore.

Cheating or attempting to cheat the other person is the absolute worst thing that you can do. Once it becomes known, you will be treated worse than Typhoid Mary.

Seeking Your Best Offer

I read classified advertising of all types for recreation. I particularly enjoy those ads that describe an item for sale, set a price, and add "OBO," (or best offer). You have that same opportunity with the items that you want to sell.

Classified ads that you pay for in the commercial stamp-collecting periodicals are among your options. You are certainly not going to pay $15 to advertise an item that you are selling for $1, although none of the periodicals will complain. Local clubs and specialty clubs publish many periodicals that accept ads. Sometimes ads in these small publications are gratis; at other times, a minimal fee may be charged. Larger publications can give your ad a broad circulation, but your audience may be sufficiently targeted to still make your sale (or trade) in a small periodical.

If you have been prowling about the various Internet-based message systems, you have noted classified-ad-type messages that are often free. You have more of a risk here. If you place an ad in a stamp-collecting periodical or a club-published newsletter, you can normally get at least some help if the prospective purchaser stiffs you. That is not the case with the Internet postings. You may want to require payment in advance.

Attending Traditional Stamp Auctions

Traditional refers to those firms that run their own auctions to which you send material to be sold by them. Until rather recently, stamp auction houses were *very* traditional and worked from printed catalogues to their own customer lists, augmented by advertisements in the stamp-collecting media. Now, more and more auction houses are utilizing the Internet to increase their customer base, with some even allowing bidding via the Internet.

You may have the option of selling your material outright to the auction firm, and then watching the material go through the sale process. If you accept that approach, you really are not participating in the auction process, but rather selling directly to a dealer. For more on auctions, see Chapter 7.

Each auction house has its own set of rules called *Terms of Sale* or *Conditions of Sale,* which are usually in front of their catalogue. You need to read and understand the rules before asking them to sell material for you. These rules include what fee is due to the auctioneer from you. There will probably be a seller's fee as a percentage of the hammer price (jargon for the price at which a lot sells), and possibly a lotting fee. Further, each auction house has its own set of practices relative to the minimum lot value that the auction house will handle.

If you have material suitable for sale at public auction, all you have to do is make financial arrangements with the auction house and ship the material. For better material, public auction is an ideal disposal method. For a list of auction firms that are members of the American Stamp Dealers Association or the American Philatelic Society, contact either group at the address found in Appendix A. Or, you can find a listing of worldwide auction firms on the Internet at www.askphil.org/auct06.htm.

The fees for consigning material to auctions are negotiable, depending on how much material you are consigning or the quality of the material. This can range from a low of 10 percent to a high of 25 percent. There are also collectors who pay no fees, whose material is sought by the auction firm as *classic* or hard to find, or simply if the auctioneer knows that his clientele includes customers for that category of philatelic offerings.

Joining Online Auctions

With eBay as the archetype for now, stamp collectors have a wide range of online auctions to use as an outlet for material to sell. Online auctions range from the all-inclusive eBay and those similar auction sites, to those that specialize and perhaps exclusively offer postage stamps. Most have a fee structure, but some of the newer and smaller online auctions charge nothing (at least at the beginning).

Before you commit to one

✔ Investigate all that appeal to you in any way. Check online auctions for what range and type of stamp-collecting material is being offered, as well as what sort of bid prices the material is drawing. The lure of a no-fee auction may be quite alluring, but if you get no bidders, you have gained nothing.

✔ Understand the meaning of the various fees that you may be charged. Various sites have a *lot fee* — a flat amount for posting the lot, or an amount that varies based on the beginning bid price that you post. You also may be subject to a fee that is a percentage of the winning bid price. Other fees may cover posting an illustration with a lot, storing that illustration on the auction site's server, having a reserve price, using larger or bolder type than usual, or for special placement of your lot on the site. I have no opinions relative to the fees other than to make sure that you know what you are buying or selling.

A reserve price on these sites is one below which the lot will not be sold, but which is not necessarily displayed. If you have a lot for which you note a minimum (opening) bid of $7.50 and a reserve price of $15, all the bidding action is visible on the site. But the winning bid needs to be $15 or more before the highest bid is actually designated as a *winning bid*. I do not like reserve prices in these circumstances. I choose to set my minimum bid at the least I will accept and then let the games begin. However, the choice is yours. See additional information on auctions in Chapter 7 and key addresses in Appendix A.

Because the cost is so low to the seller, experiment with online auctions before you jump in with all feet. Try the concept first with one online operation, and then experiment with others to see which feels better to you.

Donating to Charity

Many charitable institutions accept postage stamps as donations. These organizations often use the stamps as therapy or recreation for the people whom the organization serves. Others gather up the material for sale to a postage-stamp wholesaler. Whatever the material's final destiny, if the organization has proper tax-exempt status, then you may claim your donation as a deduction in your annual tussle with the IRS and your state equivalent (if you have one). For more information about tax exemptions, see *Taxes For Dummies* by Eric Tyson and David J. Silverman (Hungry Minds, Inc.).

The organization that receives your material can't give you a financial evaluation of your material. A stamp dealer or other knowledgeable individual or firm must do this. Simply ask the organization that receives your material to recommend someone for this purpose. The recommended assessor usually evaluates your material at no charge as a service to the group getting your donation.

Incidentally, the tax-exempt organization usually keeps the material for two years before selling it. This is a protection in case you receive a high evaluation, and the material sells for much less than your deduction from taxes. The organization can claim that market conditions have changed in the two-year period, which the IRS currently accepts.. However, most dealers, when evaluating the material being donated, are forthright, and only quote what they know is the current retail price.

Finding charitable organizations that accept stamps as donations is pretty easy. Here's where to look:

- **Stamp-collecting periodicals:** You should correspond with any of these before sending off material, both to be certain

  - You want to send the type of material they accept.

  - The group has the proper tax status. This can be verified if you ask if they have an IRS 501(c) 3 status.

  Some groups only accept bulk material; others accept better stamps for resale.

- **Your local Yellow Pages:** For instance, some extended-care facilities accept postage stamps as donations.

If you plan to donate to a tax-exempt institution, be certain that you receive a confirmation letter that lists what you sent. The recipient should acknowledge what you sent. The recipient does not value the material; that is your responsibility. Ask the organization to return your letter listing the contents of your donation with a *received* stamp, a signature, and date on it.

You must assign the value of the material for tax-deduction purposes. Market value is fine; sometimes catalogue value is fine. If you are not sure what to do, check with a tax professional.

Helping a Philatelic Newcomer

Unless the material being disposed of has some value to it that would make the income derived pay for more than a trip or two to the local waffle emporium, this is my favorite of all stamp-disposal methods. Share stamps of no value to you to help someone get a flying start into the hobby.

You may be hoarding all the stamps from the incoming mail that comes to your apartment house or your housing subdivision. Now, you have a garbage bag or two yet to be sorted. Along comes a newcomer wanting to know how to start. The light goes on over your head, and immediately you have a new stamp-collecting friend. Given that incoming mail normally has stamps of little monetary value, sharing the material cannot be a loss to you. If you share your time with the newcomer to go through the material, then you can also share the results and the thrill of any discoveries.

Disposing of your unneeded material in this manner — to close where I opened — you know you have placed the material in a good home. And, what a wonderful way to help a child enjoy the hobby you like so much!

Chapter 18

Ten Commonly Asked Questions About Postage Stamps

*N*ot all questions concerning postage stamps come from stamp collectors, or even from those who are considering taking up the hobby. Often a postage stamp that was found lodged in a dresser or desk drawer, purchased at a yard sale, provides the basis for a question; or a favorite relative bequeaths a stamp collection to a niece or nephew with no collecting experience. This chapter comprises the most popular questions asked over the past year to the question-and-answer section of AskPhil.Org, an online reference service about postage stamps and stamp collecting. All questions to that service are answered, but some replies are given directly and others are posted to the AskPhil Web site. See Appendix A for more stamp-collecting Web sites.

What Is It Worth?

The most common question by far and the most difficult one to answer concerns worth. Presuming the questioner describes the item properly — or you can look at the stamp up close — *worth* is still a relative term. Chapter 6 goes into detail about the various levels of value. Chapter 3 helps with identification.

When the question of worth comes up, my first question is: How much is the stamp worth *to whom?* For example, generally, U.S. stamps issued over the past 50 years have appreciated little in value. Small holes have been shot into that logic, however, on enough occasions to debunk it. Within the past week, I tried to purchase the same block of four (two stamps across and two deep, still attached) U.S. stamps — issued within the past 20 years. I remember purchasing the block at the post office for less than one dollar. Pricing from two different dealers was $5.50 and $13.00. Not a bad increase but this is not normal, as one of the dealers was quick to tell me.

The best response to the question about worth is to point to the latest catalogue value. If you use the *Scott Standard Postage Stamp Catalogue,* then that value essentially represents what you would expect to pay if you purchased that item, by itself, from a retail dealer. Purchase that stamp along with others at the same time, and you may pay less for each stamp because dealers often offer quantity discounts. To sell a stamp at whatever price is being offered, a stamp dealer must purchase it for less. The bottom line is that catalogue value states a stamp's price in relative terms, or the price is stated in real terms when you sell or buy it. Normally, buyers who know the catalogue price are content; then, relating that catalogue value for other material to current market price, they can presume what it's worth. Because collectible postage stamps do not enjoy a formal market — where buy and sell prices are set — what you pay depends on subjective criteria.

What's the Story Behind This Stamp?

This question is really two questions.

✔ The first answer responds to the literal question regarding the stamp's background. For example, what is the background of the stamp's commemoration?

Normally, the country issuing the stamp provides a brief explanation, which is picked up by stamp catalogue editors for identification purposes. Armed with that data, you can research the subject more deeply. Many stamps, particularly those issued by your country of residence, are easy to research. For instance, from your home in New Jersey, finding detailed information on the ninth president of the United States can be a bit easier than finding information on the ninth president of most any other country of the world.

✔ The second question is purely from the practical perspective as well as the physical characteristics of the stamp. What information is available on its production? Is the stamp available only as a sheet stamp? Is it also available in a booklet or as a self-adhesive?

If the stamp's face value is not the current first-class mail rate, why was its face value used? That is, if the current first-class mail rate for one ounce is 34 cents, then why was a 55-cent stamp used on that letter? The solution to this mystery may be simple. The first-class mail rate for two ounces (which is probably what the contents of the envelope must have weighed) is 55 cents.

Among other answers to the last question regarding the difference between the first-class mail rate and the stamp's face value are

- The stamp's face value may be the difference between the old first-class mail rate and a new rate. For example, the stamp could be a make-up stamp — the nondenominated stamp issued by the U.S. Postal Service at the time of a rate change to cover only the amount of the rate increase.

- Perhaps the stamp covers a specific rate without a corresponding inscription on the stamp (such as two or more ounces of first-class mail, Priority Mail, or express mail).

Even the most mundane postage stamp may have plenty of stories. Mysteries such as how to figure what rate was used on a given envelope or package wrapper can be fun. Some collectors revel in that challenge. Those are just the sort of questions that are great for a local stamp club meeting. If you cannot get help there, then you may need to find a specialty organization (see Chapter 8) or write to AskPhil. Some mysteries are embarrassingly simple to solve, others are just plain unsolvable and lead to debates long into the night after a club meeting ends. And you thought stamp collectors would have no basis for an argument!

Where Can I Purchase . . . ?

This question was much easier to field when all major cities and many smaller ones had stamp dealers with their own retail stores. Today, retail storefronts that sell stamps are far less prevalent. If a retail store that sells stamps is near to you, then become a frequent shopper to do your part to keep the breed alive. For everything but the most recent postage stamps available at your local post office, you need to know how to find stamp dealers who handle the type of material that you want. This book's Appendix A lists a number of stamp-purchase resources.

✔ Stamp-collecting periodicals are a good source of persons and places to purchase stamps from. These periodicals supply plenty of dealer advertising as well as listings of upcoming stamp shows and stamp bourses, where dealers have sales space. This book's Appendix A can help you with important addresses.

✔ The World Wide Web is another excellent source of stamp-selling sites. Appendix A at the back of this book also lists key Web addresses; you can also do a general search on stamp dealers, which can produce a list of Web sites numbering into the thousands. The particular search engine that you use can affect the number of responses, but any of the larger search engines should provide the desired results.

How Do I Get a First-Day Cover?

A first-day cover is an envelope (*cover*) with a newly issued stamp, postmarked on the stamp's first day of sale at a city designated by the postal service.

U.S. first-day covers (FDC) may be broken into two categories:

1. The U.S. Postal Service sells plain, unadorned envelopes with the new stamp and a First Day of Issue cancel.

2. A collector may send his own envelope, with or without a cachet (corresponding graphic and/or wording, usually on the left side of the envelope), with the new stamps already affixed, within 30 days of the date of issue. The U.S. Postal Service will service the envelope with the First Day of Issue cancellation.

   The envelopes submitted by a collector may be self-addressed, often with a removable label, or the collector may enclose a larger, postpaid self-addressed envelope for the return of his first day covers.

3. Collectors may also purchase completely-prepared first day covers from commercial firms who take care of affixing the stamp, printing the cachet, and getting the FDCs serviced by the USPS.

Certainly dealers who specialize in first-day covers have what you want. Many even have current covers the day they're available. Some dealers offer subscription programs that guarantee an FDC of each stamp as it is issued. For the do-it-yourselfer (and you definitely are not alone), every U.S. Postal Service press/information release on a new stamp, postal card, or stamped envelope includes information on obtaining your own FDC. Those releases may be available at

✔ **Your local post office:** Ask the postal clerk for information on the upcoming and latest stamp releases.

✔ **Online at** `http://shop.usps.com`: This Web site (see Figure 18-1) lists the most current stamp issues. Click any of them to get information on how to obtain a first-day-of-issue cancellation . . . as long as you are not beyond the deadline.

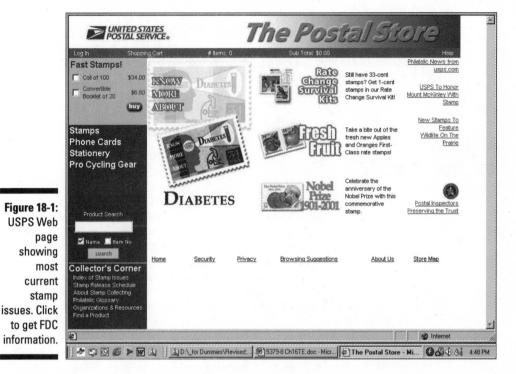

Figure 18-1: USPS Web page showing most current stamp issues. Click to get FDC information.

How Do I Separate My Mint Stamps That Are Stuck Together and Preserve Their Value?

After stamps get stuck together, the gum side of (at least) one of them has been disturbed and may no longer be considered *original gum.* If the stamps are stuck gum to gum, then the gum sides of both stamps are affected. If the stamps are stuck gum to face, gum has been deposited on the front of one of the stamps, negatively affecting its value. For more on storing your stamps to keep these situations from occurring, see Chapter 14.

After your stamps have stuck, little can be done to preserve the value of the stamps. The best you can expect is to soak the stamps free. (See Chapter 7 for more on soaking stamps.) If the stamps in question are modern and not of great value, they're available at least for postage and all is not lost. If the stamps are older and have some value, you can take a hit. Better to be the bearer of bad news, at least in this case, before the fact.

I responded to this question when a book of U.S. postage sheets that came directly from the post office were stuck to the point of making a three-dimensional block of stamps — many, many sheets were stuck together. This whole discussion is an object lesson on why you must be aware of the climatic conditions in which your mint stamps reside.

I Inherited a Stamp Collection. What Now?

There are collections, and there are collections. First, you need to know the scope of what you have. If, for example, you have a complete run of used U.S. commemorative stamps from 1950 to the present, you have quite an interesting collection that lacks much monetary value. A commemorative stamp collection is worth keeping intact and expanding, whether by you or someone to whom you give it. Or, if the collection consisted of all nineteenth-century stamps neatly mounted in a beautiful album, you still want to know what you have. In this case, your next step probably would be to decide if you wanted to sell the material or adopt it and begin a new hobby. Choosing to sell harkens back to Chapter 6. Prior to making any decision with the newfound stamps, discover and know what you have. This knowledge comes in handy if you decide to sell the material in future years.

What Present Should I Buy for a Stamp Collector?

This is the question I hope to get from a loved one, but it hasn't happened yet. If you know what the person collects and what's missing from their collection, then something that fits into the collection is perfect. You may check with a stamp dealer who knows your friend's collection, and may even know of one or more items the collector is seeking at the time. If that's out of the question, then see what sort of supplies the collector uses and add to them. The gift may be a package of stock pages, a bottle of watermark fluid, a new pair of stamp tongs, a top-of-the-line perforation gauge, or a gift certificate from a stamp dealer. Admittedly, these presents do not compare with roses or a fine bottle of wine. To a stamp collector, however, these gifts are quite meaningful.

Some of My Stamps Are Stained; What Do I Do?

If liquid soaks into the paper and causes a stain, you have few options. Staining is considered a *fault*, which negatively affects the value of the stamp. (See Chapter 6 for more information about value.)

Some stains can be removed chemically, which can easily cross over to being an unethical act that is detectable (perhaps by a UV light), and therefore it's fraudulent. (See Chapter 15 for more information about fraud.) If the stain is a pencil mark, perhaps you can remove it by carefully using a soft rubber eraser. A stained stamp may not be totally without value. You may have reason to use it in your reference collection as a color reference, or to check paper, or for its perforation measurement.

How Do I Get My Kids Interested in Stamp Collecting?

Simply share the fun of collecting stamps with your children. (See Chapter 9 for a more detailed discussion.)

- Begin with a starter album and a bunch of stamps.
- Start with an album of your own country so that they can find plenty of new stamps in the incoming mail; or, with a topical area the child likes apart from stamps.
- Go into sorting stamps, putting the stamps on an album page, and so on.

From the beginning, share with the children what the designs on the stamps mean: who the people or places are and why they're being honored. Make the stamps come alive. Also, match stamps with other interests the child may have: a favorite sport, animal, or place they may have visited or want to visit. With about 450,000 different stamps issued since 1840, you and the child have much to choose from.

Where Do I Find Information about the 1980 U.S. Olympic Commemoratives Taken Out of Circulation When U.S. President Carter Announced the Boycott?

Yes, the U.S. 1980 Olympics commemoratives were taken off the market at the time President Carter announced that the United States would not be participating in the summer games that year. But, the commemorative stamps were put back on sale about a month later. So, the current catalogue value for those stamps is no different than for those issued in the same time frame — no premium. For a brief period the market value of those stamps jumped considerably. Once the stamps were again available from the U.S. Postal Service, the market value for the stamps plummeted to the same level as other current stamps of the period.

Part VII

Appendixes

The 5th Wave   By Rich Tennant

Small differences can be significant in stamp collecting, just as it was for Capt. Hook and his twin brother, Capt. Pen.

In this part . . .

You do not want to have the appendixes in this part surgically removed. One appendix is a listing of major resources that will get you off to a flying start. The second is a lengthy glossary of stamp-collecting terms. Note that the glossary contains words that you may use fairly often in everyday conversation, but which have different meanings when applied to stamp collecting.

Appendix A

Rooting Through Resources

• •

Stamp collection has a larger body of literature than any other hobby. Specialized stamp-collecting libraries, which are open as research facilities, may have handbooks and monographs numbering well into the thousands and may receive upwards of 500 different periodicals on a regular basis. Largest and easiest to use — principally because of its online card catalogue and article index — is the American Philatelic Research Library. Its Internet address is www.stamps.org, and click Library. Then add to that wealth of information the impact of electronic publishing and communication.

Due to the abundance of philatelic information that's available, this Appendix is necessarily a selective listing of periodicals, Web sites, and national-level stamp shows.

Supporting Stamp Collecting: Catalogues, Magazines, and Journals

From the more inclusive listing of periodicals and catalogues within stamp collecting that follows, you can get a good overview of the hobby in general, as well as information on the many other more specialized periodicals. And, if you're interested in a similar listing of periodicals outside of the United States and Canada, point your Internet browser to www.askphil.org/b33.htm, AskPhil's listing of Principal Stamp Publications of the World. Also, when looking up the Web sites, you'll probably run into an http:// prefix.

The American Philatelist
American Philatelic Society
P. O. Box 8000
State College, PA 16803
Internet: www.stamps.org/Services/ser_AP_contents.htm

Australasian Stamps
The Australian Stamp Monthly Pty. Ltd.
P.O. Box 254
Sutherland, NSW 1499, AUSTRALIA
E-mail: Editor@shirelife.com

Canadian Stamp News
103 Lakeshore Road - Suite 202
St. Catherines, ON LN2 2T6, CANADA
Internet: www.canadianstampnews.com

Collectors Club Philatelist, The
Collectors Club of New York
22 East 35 St.
New York, NY 10016-3806
Internet: www.collectorsclub.org/Philatelist.html

Deutsche Briefmarken Zeitung/DBZ
Postfach 1363
D-56373 Nassau, GERMANY

First Days
American First Day Cover Society
P.O. Box 65960
Tucson, AZ 85728-5960
Internet: www.afdcs.org/First_Days_Journal/
first_days_journal.html

Gibbons Stamp Monthly
Stanley Gibbons Stamp Catalogue
5 Parkside, Christchurch Road
Ringwood, Hampshire BH24 3SH, ENGLAND
Internet: www.stangib.com/publications.html

Global Stamp News
P.O. Box 97
110 N. Ohio Ave.
Sidney, OH 45365-0097
Internet: www.gregmanning.com/content/stamps/global.asp

Ind Dak
No 84, P&T Colony
RT Nagar
Bangalore 560032, INDIA

L'Écho de la Timbrologie
37 rue des Jacobins
F-80036 Amiens - Cedex 1, FRANCE

Linn's Stamp News
P.O. Box 29
911 Vandemark Road
Sidney, OH 45365-0065
Internet: www.linns.com

London Philatelist
Royal Philatelic Society - London
41 Devonshire Place
London W1N 1PE, ENGLAND
Internet: www.rpsl.org.uk/philatelist.html

Mekeel's and Stamps Magazine
P.O. Box 5050
White Plains, NY 10602-5050, USA
Internet: www.stampnews.com/page7.htm

MICHEL Rundschau
Schwaneberger Verlag GmbH
Muthmanstrasse 4
D-80939 Munich, GERMANY
Internet: www.michel.de/kontakt

Philatelic Exporter
P.O. Box 137
Hatfield, Hertfordshire AL10 9DB, ENGLAND
Internet: www.philatelicexporter.com/

Philatélie Québec
454 Avenue Pierre de Coubertin
C.P. 1000 Succursale M
Montréal, PQ H1V 3R2, CANADA

Philatelist and PJGB, The
Christie's Robson Lowe
8 King Street, St. James's
London SW1Y 6QT, ENGLAND

Philately in Japan
Japan Philatelic Society Foundation
P.O. Box 1, Shinjuku
Tokyo 163-91, JAPAN
Internet: http://yushu.or.jp/english/e_kaiin/pj81.htm

Scott Stamp Monthly
Scott Publishing Co.
P. O. Box 828
Sidney, Ohio 45365, USA
Internet: www.scottonline.com

South African Philatelist, The
P O Box 375
Johannesburg 2000
SOUTH AFRICA

Stamp Collector
700 East State Street
Iola, WI 54990-0001, USA
Internet: www.krause.com/stamps/sc

Stamp Lover
National Philatelic Society, British Philatelic Centre
107 Charterhouse Street
London EC1M 6PT, ENGLAND
Internet: www.ukphilately.org.uk/nps/lover/lover.htm

Stamp Magazine
Link House, Dingwall Avenue
Croydon CR9 2TA, ENGLAND
Tel: **[44] 181 686-2599**
Fax: [44] 181 781-6044

Stamp News
P.O. Box 1410
Dubbo, NSW 2830, AUSTRALIA
E-mail: elainee@hannan.com.au

Stamps World
GPO Box 9773
HONG KONG

Timbroscopie
33 Rue de Chazelles
F-75850 Paris Cedex 17, FRANCE

Topical Time
American Topical Association
P.O. Box 50820
Albuquerque, NM 87181-0820
Internet: http://home.prcn.org/~pauld/ata/journal.htm

United States Specialist, The
United States Stamp Society
P.O. Box 6634
Katy, TX 77491-6634
Internet: www.usstamps.org/journal.html

Surfing for Stamps: Web Pages

Web sites tend to come and go because they're relatively easy to develop, but then a site may fade from lack of interest or usage. Although to guarantee how long any of the Web sites listed here will remain is impossible, each site was picked for what it offers you as well as my estimate of its longevity. Some of those listed have been around for years, and others have evolved from one-person, works of love to more developed joint or association-sponsored projects.

General reference

The Web sites in the following list are excellent starting points for a romp through the digital side of the hobby:

- ✔ www.askphil.org — The Collector's Club of Chicago sponsors AskPhil, a noncommercial, totally free information site, which is often cited in this book. The site offers basic information and addresses, both on and apart from the Web. It also has a Want List Service for you to post items you want/need for your collection.

- ✔ www.execpc.com/~joeluft/resource.html — Joseph Luft produces the granddaddy of stamp collecting Web links. This list, which continues to grow and become more and more user-friendly, is a keeper.

- ✔ www.stamp2.com/ — A Singapore-based list of stamp collecting links that, too, has grown over the years. Francis Chan is the developer.

- ✔ www.pgacon.com/stampcol.asp — Not only is this Web site an excellent list of philatelic links, Peter Aitken has a superb tutorial on digital scanning as it pertains to reproducing your stamps to their best advantage.

- ✔ www.yvert-et-tellier.fr/yvert/page_accueil.htm — The Web site for the stamp reference catalogue of France, *Yvert & Tellier*.

Big kahunas

These collecting Web sites are sometimes maintained by large organizations:

- ✔ www.stamps.org — Web site of the American Philatelic Society and the American Philatelic Research Library.

- ✔ www.linns.com — Growing site produced by the publisher of the weekly *Linn's Stamp News*.

✔ www.krause.com/stamps — Home of Stamp Collector, a biweekly stamp periodical, and other Krause stamp ventures.

✔ www.stampville.com — Relative newcomer that features contemporary subjects depicted on stamps and a wide range of allied micro Web sites.

✔ www.stamps.net — Billing itself as an Internet Magazine for Stamp Collectors, this is an independent Internet-only news and information source.

✔ http://shop.usps.com — The U.S. Postal Service Web site for stamp information and purchasing online. The site includes information for stamp collectors.

✔ www.delphi.com — Delphi is a large operation with many forums. This URL is the opening page, which includes a search box. Search *stamp* and from the list returned to you at least visit The Virtual Stamp Club and Stamp Collecting Forum.

✔ go.compuserve.com/collectibles — Probably the longest running of the online stamp gathering points, this site was around before the Internet was so popular. You need to log in the first time and select a screen name and password.

Fun, fun, fun

These Web sites are just plain cool and offer peeks into more specialized areas of the hobby. The sites noted here have been subjectively selected purely on the basis of what I believe to be examples of why stamp collecting is such an interesting hobby. If you run a generalized Web search on *stamp collecting* or *postage stamps,* I assure you that you will come up with your own similar list, which may not include any of the Web sites that follow. Enjoy.

✔ www.ioa.com/~ggayland/junior — A long-time Web site that's solely intended to interest younger collectors and to help juniors become interested in stamp collecting.

✔ www.essayproof.net/epco/index.html — Billing itself as the Museum of United States Essays and Proofs, this site shows off projected stamp designs that never were (essays) and proofs of early stamp designs that actually were produced. You probably cannot find a more striking presentation of early stamps — with all their hand-engraved craftsmanship and beauty — anywhere.

✔ www.sossi.org/badges/badges.htm — The specialty group Scouts on Stamps Society International produces this site, which shows the badge requirements for Boy Scouts, Girl Scouts, and Girl Guides from a variety of countries.

> ✔ www.south-pole.com — If you want to see the integration of stamp collecting and the real world, this site with the simple title *Antarctic Philately* can do it for you. This site has potato-chip qualities: You can't just see one page.

Showing off: Expos and the Like

Stamps shows of all sizes are scheduled for nearly every weekend of the year. Stamp-collecting periodicals carry listings with the specific dates, locations, times, and sponsors of the shows. Many Web sites also have such listings. No one listing, however, is all-inclusive. Nevertheless, you can easily get a solid idea of what is available near you by honing in on one or more of the major lists as a starter. The following groups of shows are considered national level; the largest shows other than the once-a-decade International Exhibitions or the USPS-sponsored shows, which take place about every five years.

This list is presented in a calendar-year arrangement, beginning with those shows normally scheduled for January.

SANDICAL
San Diego Philatelic Council
P.O. Box 80004
San Diego, CA 92138-0004
late January

Sarasota National Stamp Exhibition
Sarasota Philatelic Club
P.O. Box 99
Sarasota, FL 34230-0099
early February

ARIPEX
Show rotates between Tucson and Phoenix, Arizona
early March

COLOPEX
Columbus Philatelic Society
1068 Medhurst Road
Columbus, OH 43220
early March
Internet: http://ourworld.compuserve.com/homepages/wbeau

St. Louis Stamp Expo
St. Louis-area stamp clubs
Regency Stamps Ltd.
10411 Clayton Rd. #106
St. Louis, MO 63131
early March
Internet: www.mophil.org/stampexp.htm

ROPEX
Rochester Philatelic Association Inc.
P.O. Box 10206
Brighton Station
Rochester, NY 14610-0206
mid March
Internet: http://rpa.homepage.com

Garfield-Perry March Party
Garfield-Perry Stamp Club (Cleveland, OH)
c/o Holiday Inn Lakeside
1111 Lakeside at East 12th St.
Cleveland, OH 44114
late March
Internet: http://members.aol.com/gpstamp/gpsc.html

Postage Stamp Mega Event (New York City)
American Stamp Dealers Association
P.O. Box 8000
State College, PA 16803
early April

TEXPEX
Southwest Philatelic Foundation
Wineburgh Philatelic Research Library
University of Texas at Dallas
P.O. Box 830643
Dallas, TX 75083-0643
early April
Internet: www.flash.net/~jstamp/stamp1.html

The Plymouth Show (Michigan)
West Suburban Stamp Club
P.O. Box 700049
Plymouth, MI 48170
late April
Internet: www.oeonline.com/~pnj/plymshow.html

WESTPEX (San Francisco)
Western Philatelic Exhibitions
late April
Internet: www.westpex.com

OKPEX
Oklahoma City Stamp Club
early May

Philatelic Show (Boxborough, MA)
Northeastern Federation of Stamp Clubs
early May
Internet: www.nefed.org/show01/show2001.htm

ROMPEX
Rocky Mountain Philatelic Exhibition, Inc. (Denver, CO)
mid May
Internet: www.collectors-mall.com/shows/stamp/rompex.html

NOJEX
North Jersey Federated Stamp Clubs, Inc.
P.O. Box 1945
Morristown, NJ 07962
late May

NAPEX
National Philatelic Exhibitions of Washington, D.C
early June
Internet: www.wdn.com/napex

PIPEX
(Show locations moves among cities of Pacific Northwest)
Northwest Federation of Stamp Clubs
6616 140th Pl., N.E.
Redmond, WA 98052-4649
early June

National Topical Stamp Show
American Topical Association
P. O. Box 50820
Albuquerque, NM 87181-0820
late June
Internet: home.prcn.org/~pauld/ata/show.htm

INDYPEX
Indiana Stamp Club
P.O. Box 40792
Indianapolis, IN 46240
mid July
Internet: hometown.aol.com/indypex/isc/index.html

Minnesota Stamp Expo
Twin Cities Philatelic Society
3350 Rosewood Lane
Plymouth, MN 55441
late July

AMERICOVER
American First Day Cover Society
P.O. Box 1335
Maplewood, NJ 07040-0456
early August, each year in a different city
Internet: www.afdcs.org

STAMPSHOW (different city each year)
American Philatelic Society
P.O. Box 8000
State College, PA 16803
August
Internet: www.stamps.org/directories/dir_StampShow_intro.htm

BALPEX
Baltimore Philatelic Society
684 Shore Drive
Severna Park, MD 21244
Labor Day weekend
Internet: www.balpex.org

MILCOPEX
Milwaukee Philatelic Society
P.O. Box 1980
Milwaukee, WI 53201-1980
mid September

AIRPEX
Dayton Stamp Club
P.O. Box 1574
Dayton, OH 45401-1574
late September

Omaha Stamp Show
Omaha Philatelic Society
9201 Parkview Blvd.
La Vista, NE 68128
late September

Peach State Stamp Show
Georgia Federation of Stamp Clubs
late September

Philadelphia National Stamp Exhibition
Associated Stamps Clubs of Southeastern Pennsylvania & Delaware, Inc.
P.O. Box 358
Broomall, PA 19008-0358
late September
Internet: home.att.net/~pnse/index.html

SESCAL
Federated Philatelic Stamp Clubs of Southern California
P.O. Box 3391
Fullerton, CA 92634
early October
Internet: www.sescal.org

CHICAGOPEX
Chicago Philatelic Society
Post Office Box A3953
Chicago, IL 60690
mid November
Internet: www.mcs.com/~andyo/webbt/splash.html

VAPEX
Virginia Philatelic Federation
P.O. Box 5367
Virginia Beach, VA 23455-0367
mid November
Internet: http://members.aol.com/vashow

Appendix B

Glossary

• •

*S*tamp term got you stumped and not listed here? Go to
www.askPhil.org Q&A and ask Mr. PHILately.

AAT: Australia Antarctic Territory.

ABNC, ABNCo.: American Bank Note Company.

acacia gum: A water-soluble gum obtained from several species of the acacia tree, especially *Acacia Senegal* and *A. Arabica*, and used in the manufacture of adhesives.

accessories: Products used by the stamp collector to aid stamp identification and handling.

accountable mail: Mail that requires the addressee's signature on receipt to provide proof of delivery.

acid-free paper: Paper manufactured under neutral conditions with a pH greater than 7.0 and containing no acidic additives.

Acknowledgement of receipt stamp (A.R.): Spanish-language stamp issued to pay the fee for postal notification that the mail piece was delivered to the addressee.

across-the-lines mails: U.S. Civil War term for mail carried by private express firms between the North and South.

Admirals: 1 In 1912 and 1925, Canadian stamps series showing King George V in full-dress uniform as an admiral of the Royal Navy; **2** 1926 New Zealand issue; **3** From 1924 to 1930, the first stamps of Southern Rhodesia.

advertising cover: Envelope that advertises a commercial product, hotel, service, place, agency, or organization.

A.E.F.: 1 French Equatorial Africa (Afrique Equatoriale Francaise); **2** American Expeditionary Forces established in World War I; AEF Mail, AEF Post Offices, and AEF Booklets.

aereo: (Sp.) Airmail overprint or inscription.

aérogramme: (Fr.) Official Universal Postal Union (UPU) name for air letter sheet; lightweight paper with gummed flaps, usually with an imprinted stamp indicia, transported by air to other countries.

agency: A commercial firm that promotes and sells the postal products of the country or countries it represents; a post office maintained in one country's territory by another country.

air label: Labels inscribed _Par Avion_ or equivalent that means _by air._ France had the first example in black on red paper on Aug. 17, 1918; the U.P.U. adopted a standard blue color in 1922 for affixing to material carried by air.

airmail stamp: Stamp intended to prepay airmail postage; the first recorded is the 25-cent rose, Italian express stamp, 200,000 of which were overprinted in 1917.

albino: Die impression on a stamp or stamped envelope where the ink has not been transferred to the paper.

allied military post: British and American zones used these stamps; 1946 saw three general issues of these stamps, same design; America (Bureau of Engraving and Printing); Britain (Harrison & Sons Ltd.) and Germany (G. Westermann).

Andorra: Independent state between France and Spain that does not charge for internal mail. Before 1928, Spanish and French stamps were used. In 1928, the Spanish postal service established the _Correos Andorra_ overprint. The French postal service established a postage-due French stamp overprint, _Andorre,_ in 1931, which both nations accepted as postage.

á payer: (Fr.) Belgium and Luxembourg, on postage-due stamps.

ATM: Automatic Teller Machine. In reference to stamp collecting, an ATM that also dispenses stamps.

backstamp: Postmark applied to back of incoming mail to show date and time of receipt at the receiving post office.

balloon mail: Mail carried by balloon. This method of transportation was used in the Siege of Paris during the War of 1870 and the letters carried are called Balloon Monte.

bank mixture: Stamp assortment, usually on paper, collected from the incoming mail of financial institutions.

banknote issues: From 1870 to 1887, the American, Continental, and National Bank Note Companies printed these stamps.

BEP: Bureau of Engraving and Printing, Washington, D.C., where all U.S. currency and almost all U.S. postage stamps have been produced since 1894.

bisect: A stamp cut in half that has been used to pay the postage at half the face value of the original stamp. A bisect is collected on the original cover with the postmark or cancellation covering the cut.

block: An unseparated group of stamps at least two high and two wide. If the block is larger than four stamps, it is referred to as a block of six, block of eight, and so forth.

BNA: British North America

booklet: A stamp booklet that contains one or more panes of stamps.

booklet pane: An uncut block of stamps especially printed and cut for use in booklets. The booklets are a convenient way to carry stamps.

bourse: A market place, such as a stamp show, where stamps are bought, sold, or exchanged.

bull's-eye cancellation: a postmark in which the city, state, and dates have been placed directly on the center of a stamp or block of stamps.

bureau issues: Stamps produced by the U.S. Bureau of Engraving and Printing.

bureau precancels: Stamps that are precanceled at the Bureau of Engraving and Printing at Washington, D.C.

cachet: A rubber stamp or printed impression on an envelope that describes the event for which the envelope was mailed. Cachets are used for first days of issue, first flights, naval events, stamp exhibitions, and so on.

cancel to order (CTO): Stamps cancelled by postal authorities without having been used for postage. They are less desirable than stamps that have seen postal duty.

cancellation: A mark placed on a stamp by a postal authority to deface the stamp and prevent its re-use.

catalogue value: The price established by recognized postage-stamp catalogues. This is usually used as a guide for retail or wholesale prices.

centering: Location of the stamp design on the piece of paper it is printed on. If it is exactly in the center, it is a "perfectly centered stamp."

chalky paper: Stamp paper that has a coating of chalk or clay on the surface. Used in various British colonies.

changeling: An ink color change due to exposure to bright light, chemical fumes, heat, or other causes. Greens, reds, violets, and yellows are especially prone to change.

Cinderella: A stamplike label produced by a nongovernmental body.

Citizens Stamp Advisory Committee (CSAC): A group of citizens appointed by the U.S. Postmaster General to review more than 40,000 suggestions for stamp subjects that the USPS receives each year.

coil-line pair: Pair of U.S. coil stamps showing a colored line caused by a gap where the curved printing plate is joined.

coils: Stamps that are produced in roll form for use in vending, stamp affixing, or dispensing machines. A coil usually contains 100, 500, or more stamps of a single denomination and design.

color error: An item printed in the wrong color, or color omitted.

commemorative: These stamps generally have a more interesting design and honor a person (other than the heads of government or state), place, thing, or event. Commemoratives are on sale for a more limited time and, therefore, are produced in lesser quantities than regular or *definitive* stamps.

compound perforations: When there are two different perforation measurements on different sides. For example, a stamp of the 1938 U.S. Presidential Series is perforated 10½ on top and bottom and 11 on both sides. Such stamps are said to be perf. 10½ x 11.

correos: Spanish for POSTS.

crash cover: A cover saved from a plane, train, or other vehicle with a postal marking explaining the damaged condition.

dead country: A country that no longer issues stamps.

dead letter: Term for a mail item that is undeliverable due to a poor address, or the addressee is deceased or untraceable.

die cut: A die penetrates the stamp paper surrounding the printed stamp, permitting the removal of individual self-adhesive stamps from the liner.

double impression: Two impressions of the stamp design.

DPO: Discontinued Post Office

EFO: Errors, freaks, and oddities.

embossed: Stamps, usually envelope stamps that are raised in low relief in relationship to the surface of the paper on which they are printed.

engraved stamps: Stamps printed from plates into which a design is cut or chemically etched. The plate is applied under heavy pressure to the paper being printed, leaving the ink raised above the surface of the paper.

envelope cut square: The stamp portion of a stamped envelope that has been cut from the envelope in a square or rectangular shape.

expertize: To have a stamp or cover examined by one who is qualified to pronounce a stamp or cover genuine or otherwise.

face value: The monetary value of a postage stamp as printed in its design.

facsimile: A reproduction intended for souvenir value and not meant to defraud.

fake: A genuine stamp altered as to color, design, or value, and so on, to increase its monetary value,

first-day cover: A newly issued stamp affixed to an envelope and postmarked on the first day of sale at a city designated by the postal service.

first day of issue: The day on which a stamp is first placed on sale.

first-flight cover: An envelope bearing a cancellation and usually having a special descriptive cachet affixed, which has been at the point of origin and carried on a first flight, opening a new airmail route.

flat plate: A stamp printed on a flat bed press. This process is slower than the rotary press method of printing from curved plates.

fluorescent: An optical brightener that emits a distinctive, intense glow when viewed with a long or shortwave ultraviolet light. Fluorescent tubes in fixtures can emit damaging quantities of UV light that can discolor stamps and covers.

forgery: Imitation of a stamp made to defraud the postal service and/or collectors.

Frank: An indication on the front of an envelope that it is to be carried free of postage. This is usually limited to official correspondence such as that of Members of Congress or the President, and it also applies to servicemen's mail while serving in war zones.

freak: An irregularity in a stamp, such as color shifts, streaks, smears, double print, and so on.

general collection: A collection of the entire world rather than a specialized collection of one or more countries or topics.

glassine: A semitransparent paper used to make envelopes for stamp and cover storage; also used for album interleaving.

gum: The coating of glue on the reverse of an unused or mint postage stamp.

handback service: A cancelled cover or other item returned directly to the postal customer instead of processing it through the mail.

handstamped: Postmarked or canceled by hand, usually by a rubber stamp, may also be a steel device.

Hill, Sir Rowland: The man who instituted the penny-postage system in England and is considered the Father of the Postage Stamp.

hinges: Small pieces of gummed glassine or parchment paper used by collectors for mounting stamps on album pages.

imperforate (imperf.): Stamps without separating holes. They are usually separated by scissors and are collected in pairs.

imperforate between: A pair of stamps with perforations on all four sides with the horizontal or vertical perforations completely omitted.

inscription: Any lettering or numbers on a postage stamp.

invert: Usually a multicolored stamp in which one of the colors or the design has been printed upside down. For example, the 24-cent airmail issue of 1918 in which the airplane, printed in blue, is upside down.

inverted center: Stamp in which the central design is upside down in relation to the frame of the stamp.

Inverted Jenny: 1918 24-cent U.S. airmail error.

invisible gum: Colorless and tasteless gum on the reverse of a stamp.

issue: Act of a new stamp, or series of stamps, being released by a postal authority.

joint issue: Two or more countries issuing and releasing a stamp or set of stamps with a similar design on the same day.

jumbo stamps: Stamps with wide margins. Also referred to as Boardwalk Margins.

killer: Any obliterating postmark that renders re-use of a stamp impossible.

label: Any stamplike adhesive that is not a postage or revenue stamp.

laid paper: A paper showing light and dark lines when held to the light or put in watermark fluid.

lithography: Also known as *Offset Lithography* or *Offset,* lithography is the most common and least expensive process for printing stamps. Lithography also uses images broken into small dots. Lithography is the printing from plates impressed on a rubber-covered cylinder, also known as a blanket, from which they are transferred by the offset process to the paper.

local post: Service performed by a nonofficial body and used to carry mail within a certain area.

luminescence: A coating applied to a stamp that emits a glow when viewed with an ultraviolet lamp.

major varieties: A variation in stamp make-up, such as a color change, new paper, watermark, or different perforation.

microprinting: Tiny lettering that appears as a message under magnification. Originated as a security device by postal administrations.

minor varieties: A slight variation in color, a break in the line of the design, or a speck on the stamp can be considered a *minor* variety.

Mint, never hinged: An unhinged and uncanceled stamp as issued by the government printing office with full gum.

mission mixture: An assortment of low-quality stamps on paper sold by the pound and usually collected by a charitable mission or institution.

mixture: A mixture of stamps, usually on original envelope clippings, containing duplicates. May contain varieties of shades, perforations, and minor varieties.

Mulready cover: Named for the designer of Britain's first postal envelope in 1839. The decorated postal stationery was so ridiculed that it had a short life.

mute: Term applied to postage stamps or cancellations that do not indicate country or place of origin.

never hinged: Stamp with original gum in post-office condition.

new issue: The latest issue of stamps to come from a country.

nondemoninated stamp: Stamp without a value issued during period of a rate change.

nonprofit mail: Reduced-rate, third-class bulk mail for specially qualified groups.

numeral cancellations: Cancels that use numbers to identify office of mailing.

obliteration: Term used to denote a cancellation marking.

obsolete: Stamps that are no longer sold by the postal service.

occupation stamps: Stamps issued for use in enemy territories by the conquerors.

offices abroad: Postal agency of one country in another, usually because of the poor local postal network. Special stamps were usually overprinted for these offices, mainly from the country maintaining the office.

official reprint: Stamps reprinted at a later date by the original issuing entity from the original plates.

omnibus issue: A common theme used on the stamps of several different countries.

on cover: Stamps that are on the original envelope and may also be "tied" (postmark on stamp and cover tying the two together) to cover.

optical character reader (OCR): Mail-processing machine that reads an address and translates it into a sprayed-on bar code.

original: A stamp from the first issue and not a reprint or later issue.

original gum: Gum in the original state as applied by the printer and appears untouched by a hinge.

over (or under) inking: Stamps that have been received with more or less of one or more of the colors to complete the design.

overprint: An additional printing on a stamp that was not part of the original design. For example, the Molly Pitcher U.S. stamp of 1928 (see Chapter 16).

owls: Mail carriers in the magical world of Harry Potter.

oxidized: Term applied to a stamp that has been darkened from sulphurization or oxidation with age.

par avion: (Fr.) meaning *by air;* words stamped on material to be carried by air.

pen cancellation: A cancellation marking on a stamp that has been applied with a pen and ink.

Penny Black: The world's first adhesive postage stamp issued in Great Britain on May 6, 1840.

perf: Abbreviation for perforated or perforations.

perforation gauge: An instrument designed to measure the number of perf holes or teeth within a two-centimeter space.

perforations: Lines of small holes placed around stamps to provide an easier means of separation.

philately: Taken from the Greek *philos,* loving + *ateleia,* exemption from (further) tax, taken as the equivalent of postage paid; the collection and study of postage stamps, postmarks, stamped envelopes, and so on.

phosphor: A chemical printed on stamps. When placed under ultraviolet light, phosphor causes automated mail-processing machines to react. Started in Great Britain in 1959, phospor is used in many countries now for tagging on their stamps.

phosphorescence: The property of a luminescent material: Exposure to ultraviolet light activates the material, which continues to glow for a period of time after the UV light has been extinguished.

Photogravure: A process where Intaglio prints are made from flat plates having an irregular grain. Also known as *Gravure,* it's most often used for multicolor stamps. Photogravure uses images broken into small dots.

pictorial cancel: Cancellation with unique design elements.

Pl # Blk: *See* plate number block.

plate: A flat piece of metal (usually copper, zinc, or steel) on which an image has been photoengraved, hand engraved, or etched. The stamps are then printed from this object.

plate number: The file number engraved on a plate, which usually appears in a corner of a sheet of stamps. This number is used to keep the plates from getting mixed up at the printing plant.

plate number block: A block of stamps with the sheet margin attached showing the plate number used in printing that sheet. Also known as Plate Block.

plate number coil: U.S. coil stamps produced since 1981 with a plate number appearing at the bottom of the stamp at certain intervals.

plebiscite stamps: While a vote of the people is determining their national or political future, the town or district issues these temporary stamps.

pony express: A system to carry mail by horseback.

postage: Charge for transporting mail.

postage due: A stamp issued to collect unpaid postage.

postcard: A privately produced small card without an imprinted stamp, often with a picture on one side and a space for a written message on the reverse. Maximum dimensions permitted are 4¼-inches high and 6-inches long.

postal card: Cards with special printed stamps that don't exist as adhesive postage stamps.

postal history: Philatelic study of postal markings, rates, and routes.

postal stationery: Envelopes, air letter sheets, postal cards, and so on that have imprinted or embossed stamps.

precancel: Special cancel applied to stamps before being affixed to mail matter. In the United States, there are two categories of precancels: 1. *Bureau,* the BEP applies the precancel; 2. *Local,* the local city or town post office applies the precancel.

pseudo watermark: A device applied to simulate a true watermark.

quadrille: An album page ruled in faint squares as guides for making a variety of layout arrangements with stamps or covers.

railroad cancel: Postmark applied to mail in a railway mail car.

receiving mark: A postal marking applied by the receiving post office.

regionals: Definitive stamps issued by Great Britain since 1958 for the regions of Guernsey, Jersey, Isle of Man, Northern Ireland, Scotland, and Wales. The regionals are usually sold only in the assigned region, but are valid for postage throughout the country.

regummed: Stamp with artificial gum applied.

reissue: An official reprinting of a stamp that was discontinued.

rejoined perforations: Separated perforations that have been reattached by means of a hinge, gum, or other chemical means.

repaired: Stamps or covers that have been altered or repaired to reinforce or to resemble an undamaged item. This can be the repair of a tear, changing of perforations, and so forth.

reperforated: Stamp that has been perforated anew to defraud the collector.

reply postcards: Two postcards joined together, one for the original message and the other for reply.

rocket mail: Experimental rockets with mail enclosed as a method of transport. Many of these covers also have special labels affixed for the occasion.

rouletting: The cutting of paper between stamps in order to make the separation of the stamps easier. In perforations, paper is actually removed from the sheet in the punched holes, but rouletting creates the appearance of a series of dashes.

Rural Free Delivery (RFD): Begun in 1896, brought daily mail delivery to residents living outside urban areas.

safety paper: A type of paper that has been prepared to make stamps hard to forge. A common form of safety paper has silk threads in it.

SASE: Acronym for Self-Addressed Stamped Envelope, which is an unused envelope addressed to the sender with return postage affixed. Many stamp correspondents will not reply unless you include a SASE.

Scott Catalogue number: Number assigned to a philatelic item by *Scott Standard Postage Stamp Catalogue* editors according to that publisher's criteria for such assignment.

security watermark: Used to guard against postal misuse.

selvage: The unprinted paper on the edge or margin of a sheet of stamps.

semipostal: An additional monetary value devoted to a specific nonpostal purpose, such as the Red Cross. The surcharge has no postal validity and is usually separated from the official postal value with a plus (+) sign.

separations: The method employed in which stamps are separated from one another. Perforations are a form of separations.

service indicator: Inscription included in the design of a stamp to indicate category of postal service to be rendered, such as Bulk-Mail Rate.

set: A series of stamps with similarity in design or purpose, often all issued at the same time.

se-tenant: Two or more unseparated stamps having different colors, denominations, or designs. Se-tenant is French for *joined together.*

shade: Minor differences in the color of a stamp.

sheet: One full impression of stamps taken from a printing plate. A typical sheet of commemorative stamps is four panes of 50 stamps each. This is then cut into four panes of stamps for sale at the post office.

sheet watermark: A large watermark with only a portion showing on a stamp.

sheetlet: A small sheet of stamps; less than what is normally considered a usual sheet. In the United States, a normal sheet consists of 50 stamps, and a sheetlet would be sheets of less than that quantity.

ship cancellation: A postmark applied to mail on board a ship.

silk paper: Stamp paper containing small pieces of colored silk in the paper mixture.

silk thread: Paper used for stamps containing a silk thread as a means of preventing forgery. It is most easily seen on the back of the stamp.

slabbing: Encasing collectibles in a container after authentication and grading that shows evidence of any tampering.

soaking: The process where stamps are removed from the paper on which they were affixed.

socked-on-the-nose: A stamp with the postmark in the center of the stamp.

souvenir sheet: Sheets of a stamp or stamps, surrounded with a paper margin and issued for a specific event or purpose.

space cover: A cover commemorating an event that is related to a space or astro event.

space filler: A poor copy of a stamp used to fill the space in an album until a better example is found.

specialist: A stamp collector who has made a study of a limited field of collecting, such as a topic or a country.

staining: A discoloration in the paper of a stamp.

stamp: In stamp collecting, a term for an adhesive label for postal purposes.

straight edge (SE): A stamp that naturally lacks perforations on one edge

strike: A machine or handstamp cancel on a stamp or cover.

strip: Three or more stamps that have not been separated.

surcharge: An overprint that revalues a stamp up or down.

surtax: The additional denomination on a semipostal stamp over and above the amount that covers postage.

sweatbox: A closed box using humidity to soften the gum on stamps that are stuck together, making separation from each other easier.

tagging: The phosphor coating on a stamp used by automated mail-handling equipment.

tête-bêche: A pair of stamps connected together with one stamp right side up, the other upside down.

thematic collection: Some define this term as a collection of stamps, covers, cancellations, and other items related to one specific topic that relates a story.

tied: A stamp is considered *tied* when the cancellation is beyond the stamp onto the envelope. If the stamp is placed in its original position on the envelope, the cancellation lines fit like puzzle parts, proving the stamp originated on that cover.

tinted paper: Paper that has received a background tint before the paper is printed.

tongs: A tool used to handle stamps that looks like a tweezer but has a round or spade tip and no serrations on the insides of the pincers.

toning: Discoloration on envelopes or stamps caused by exposure to light, heat, humidity, air, or a combination of factors.

topical collection: Some define this term as a collection of stamps, covers, cancellations and other items related to one specific topic.

trimmed perforations: A stamp with perforations cut away after issuance.

triptych: Three stamps in a row with an interconnected and related design.

tropical gum: Gum discolored from its original issue by conditions that allowed for fungal growth.

typography: The art of typography involves choosing the typefaces that will display to the best advantage the art to the finished plate. Also known as *Letterpress* in commercial printing, typography does not use small dots; its color is continuous.

ultraviolet (UV): Lamp that gives off two different wave lengths — Shortwave and Longwave. Shortwave UV light highlights phosphor tagging in the printing ink or the coating on a stamp. Longwave UV light spots fluorescence in the paper of a stamp or cover.

unaddr: Unaddressed

ungummed: Stamps without any gum as issued.

unhinged: Stamps without any traces of hinge marks.

unissued: A stamp that has been prepared for use but not issued.

unit watermark: An arrangement so that a complete design appears on every sheet of paper.

Universal Postal Union (UPU): Organized in Berne, Switzerland, in 1874 to regulate and standardize international postal usages and rates.

unofficial first-day cancel: Cancels applied on the first day but not in the first-day-of-issue city.

unofficial reprints: Stamps reprinted at a later date from the original plates but not by the original issuing entity.

unused: A stamp in mint condition as purchased from the post office. Also can mean a stamp that has no gum or is regummed.

unwatermarked: Stamps printed on paper that has no watermark.

used: A stamp that has been used to pay postage, bearing a cancellation or defacing mark.

used abroad: Stamps of another country used in a nation or colony that already has its own stamps.

variety: A difference from the standard form of the stamp, such as a color variation or minor flaws, and so on.

vignette: Term for the picture or other main area of a stamp.

v-mail: Special forms and envelopes used by U.S. forces during WWII.

want list: A listing, given to a stamp dealer, of stamps that are needed or wanted by the collector.

watermark: A design, letter, or word impressed in the paper during the manufacture of the paper. This mark found on a stamp is helpful for identification purposes.

watermark detector: A black tray of glass or enameled metal in which a special fluid is placed on top of the stamp to reveal the watermark.

water soluble ink: Ink on a stamp that dissolves when immersed in water.

Wells Fargo: A company that operated stage routes carrying mail, freight, and passengers to and from the West from 1849. The firm issued stamps and applied cancels to envelopes, which are considered very desirable.

Western Express Mail: Served the mining regions of California and Nevada in the nineteenth century, where government postal service was inadequate.

wiremark: Original term for a watermark.

wove paper: Smooth, even finished paper, without watermarks, suitable for all types of stamp printing.

wrapper: A postal stationery item used in the mailing of newspapers, which is usually wrapped around the newspaper.

wreck cover: Item of mail that has been salvaged from a shipwreck.

Zeppelin Stamps: Stamps issued for use in conjunction with the flights of the Graf Zeppelin and other rigid airships. Covers carried on these ships are *Zeppelin Covers*.

ZIP insignia: A postmanlike cartoon character printed on the margins of U.S. stamp blocks and booklet panes since 1963. Referred to as "Mr. Zip," the cartoon is used to encourage people to use the Zone Improvement Plan Code.

Index

• *I* •

• Z •

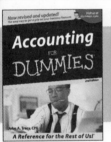

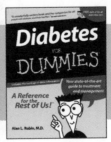

FOR DUMMIES®

A world of resources to help you grow

HOME, GARDEN & HOBBIES

Feng Shui FOR DUMMIES
A Reference for the Rest of Us!

0-7645-5295-3

Gardening FOR DUMMIES
A Reference for the Rest of Us!

0-7645-5130-2

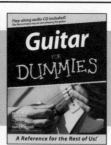

Guitar FOR DUMMIES
A Reference for the Rest of Us!

0-7645-5106-X

Also available:

Auto Repair For Dummies
(0-7645-5089-6)

Chess For Dummies
(0-7645-5003-9)

Home Maintenance For Dummies
(0-7645-5215-5)

Organizing For Dummies
(0-7645-5300-3)

Piano For Dummies
(0-7645-5105-1)

Poker For Dummies
(0-7645-5232-5)

Quilting For Dummies
(0-7645-5118-3)

Rock Guitar For Dummies
(0-7645-5356-9)

Roses For Dummies
(0-7645-5202-3)

Sewing For Dummies
(0-7645-5137-X)

FOOD & WINE

Cooking FOR DUMMIES
A Reference for the Rest of Us!

0-7645-5250-3

Cookies FOR DUMMIES
A Reference for the Rest of Us!

0-7645-5390-9

Wine FOR DUMMIES
A Reference for the Rest of Us!

0-7645-5114-0

Also available:

Bartending For Dummies
(0-7645-5051-9)

Chinese Cooking For Dummies
(0-7645-5247-3)

Christmas Cooking For Dummies
(0-7645-5407-7)

Diabetes Cookbook For Dummies
(0-7645-5230-9)

Grilling For Dummies
(0-7645-5076-4)

Low-Fat Cooking For Dummies
(0-7645-5035-7)

Slow Cookers For Dummies
(0-7645-5240-6)

TRAVEL

Italy FOR DUMMIES
A Travel Guide for the Rest of Us!

0-7645-5453-0

Hawaii FOR DUMMIES
A Travel Guide for the Rest of Us!

0-7645-5438-7

Las Vegas FOR DUMMIES
A Travel Guide for the Rest of Us!

0-7645-5448-4

Also available:

America's National Parks For Dummies
(0-7645-6204-5)

Caribbean For Dummies
(0-7645-5445-X)

Cruise Vacations For Dummies 2003
(0-7645-5459-X)

Europe For Dummies
(0-7645-5456-5)

Ireland For Dummies
(0-7645-6199-5)

France For Dummies
(0-7645-6292-4)

London For Dummies
(0-7645-5416-6)

Mexico's Beach Resorts For Dummies
(0-7645-6262-2)

Paris For Dummies
(0-7645-5494-8)

RV Vacations For Dummies
(0-7645-5443-3)

Walt Disney World & Orlando For Dummies
(0-7645-5444-1)

Available wherever books are sold. Go to www.dummies.com or call 1-877-762-2974 to order direct.